OFFICE-HOLDERS IN MODERN BRITAIN

II
Officials of the Secretaries of State
1660–1782

OFFICE-HOLDERS
IN MODERN BRITAIN

II

Officials of the Secretaries of State 1660–1782

compiled by

J. C. SAINTY

UNIVERSITY OF LONDON
INSTITUTE OF HISTORICAL RESEARCH
THE ATHLONE PRESS
1973

Published by
THE ATHLONE PRESS
UNIVERSITY OF LONDON
at 4 *Gower Street, London* WC1

Distributed by
Tiptree Book Services Ltd
Tiptree, Essex

U.S.A. & Canada
Humanities Press Inc
New York

© *University of London* 1973

0 485 17142 2

Printed in Great Britain by
WESTERN PRINTING SERVICES LTD
BRISTOL

Acknowledgements

I acknowledge with gratitude the help that I have received from many librarians and archivists who, by identifying and making available material in their custody, have contributed so much to the preparation of this work. I would like to thank the following for their kindness in allowing me to consult papers in their ownership: the Duke of Bedford (Bedford Official Papers, Bedford Settled Estates Office), the Duke of Marlborough (Sunderland Papers, Blenheim Palace), the Marquess of Bath (Coventry Papers, Longleat House), the Marquess of Downshire (Trumbull Papers, on deposit at the Berkshire Record Office) and the Earl of Dartmouth (Dartmouth Papers, on deposit at the Staffordshire Record Office).

J. C. S.

Contents

Abbreviations

Add. Additional
app. appointed, appointment
Bart. Baronet
BM British Museum
c. circa
cr. created
d. death, died
dis. dismissed
ed. edited, edition
f., ff. folio, folios
HC House of Commons
Hist. MSS Comm. Historical
Manuscripts Commission
Hon. Honourable
Kal. Kalendar

kt., ktd. knight, knighted
MI Monumental inscription
MS, MSS manuscript, manuscripts
occ. occurrence, occurs
pd. paid
pt. part
reapp. reappointed, reappointment
Rept. Report
res. resigned
ret. retired
succ. succeeded
TM Treasury minute
v. vice
vac. vacated office, vacation of office

References

IN MANUSCRIPT

All Souls Library, *Oxford*
All Souls MSS.

Bedford Settled Estates Office, *London*
Bedford Papers.

Berkshire Record Office, *Reading*
Trumbull Papers.

Blenheim Palace, *Oxfordshire*
Sunderland Papers.

Bodleian Library, *Oxford*
Rawlinson MSS.

British Museum, *London*

Add. 25118	Coventry Papers.
Add. 28875–28956	Ellis Papers.
Add. 32686–33057	Newcastle Papers.
Add. 34095, 34096	Dutton Colt Papers.
Add. 35104, 35107	Southwell Papers.
Add. 37983, 37990	Blathwayt Papers.
Add. 38339, 38357, 38358	Liverpool Papers.
Add. 40783–40786	Vernon Papers.
Add. 41806	Middleton Papers.
Add. 45519, 45520	Willes Papers.
Add. 45731	Poley Papers.
Add. 51463, 51464	Holland House Papers.
Add. 56240	Blathwayt Papers.
Loan 29/45A, 162–3, 263, 356	Harley Papers.

Folger Shakespeare Library, *Washington*
Folger MSS.

Kent Record Office, *Maidstone*
Stanhope Papers.

Leicestershire Record Office, *Leicester*
Finch Papers (Box V on temporary deposit at the National Register of Archives, London).

Longleat House, Warminster, Wiltshire
Coventry Papers.

National Library of Scotland, Edinburgh
Tweeddale Papers.

Northamptonshire Record Office, Northampton
Isham Papers.

Public Record Office, London

AO 1/420/119, AO 1/426/219	Declared Accounts: Treasurer of Chamber 1761–2, 1781–2.
AO 1/2324/62	Declared Accounts: Treasury Solicitor 1747–8.
AO 3/789	Declared Accounts: Paymaster of Pensions 1731–47.
AO 3/1102	Declared Accounts: Treasury Solicitor 1750–86.
C 66	Patent Rolls.
CO 389/36	Petitions, Orders in Council, etc., Board of Trade Accounts 1696–1710.
CO 701/1–3	Colonial Office Contingent Accounts 1795–1844.
FO 95/591/1	Foreign Office Establishment 1769–99.
FO 366/413	Papers relating to *London Gazette*.
FO 366/669, 671	Foreign Office Letter Books: Out Letters and internal memoranda 1779–89, 1797–1809.
HO 36/4	Home Office: Treasury Entry Book 1783–5.
HO 38	Home Office Warrant Books.
HO 39/6, 12	Papers relating to Signet Office 1800–50.
HO 42	Home Office: Domestic Letters and Papers.
HO 82/3	Home Office Contingent Accounts 1788–1837.
Ind. 6761–6770	Privy Seal Docquets 1724–1812.
LC 3/63–65	Lord Chamberlain's Appointment Books 1714–93.
LS 13/231	Poll Tax Assessment July 1689.
PC 2	Privy Council Registers.
PRO 30/8/83, 232	Chatham Papers.
PRO 30/47/31/1–7	Official Accounts of Earl of Egremont 1761–3.
Prob 8	Prerogative Court of Canterbury: Probate Act Books.
Prob 11	Prerogative Court of Canterbury: Registered copies of wills.
SO 5/1–4, 20–1	Signet Office Accounts 1711–1835.
SO 5/43	Signet Office Apportionment Book 1835–51.
SP 29/365	Secretary's Fee Book 1674–9.
SP 34	State Papers: Anne.
SP 35	State Papers: George I.
SP 36	State Papers: George II.
SP 44	Domestic Entry Books.
SP 45/8	Precedent Book 1706–80.
SP 45/26–35	Secretaries' Fee Books 1727–82.
SP 45/75	State Paper Office: Establishment Book 1800–54.
SP 55	Letter Books, Scotland.

SP 104/242   Under Secretaries' Foreign Entry Book 1763–8.
T 1/579 Schedule 2   Return relating to office of third Secretary of State 1782.
T 29   Treasury minutes.
T 52   King's warrants.
T 53   Warrants relating to money.
T 54   Warrants not relating to money.

Staffordshire Record Office, Stafford
Dartmouth Papers.

William L. Clements Library, Ann Arbor, Michigan
Shelburne Papers.

IN PRINT

Boyer, *Political State*   A. Boyer, *The Political State of Great Britain*, 38 vols. London 1711–29.

Chamberlayne, *Present State*   E. and J. Chamberlayne, *Angliae (Magnae Britanniae) Notitia; or the Present State of England (Great Britain)*.

CHOP   *Calendar of Home Office Papers*. 4 vols., 1760–75. London 1878–99.

Compleat History   *A Compleat History of Europe: or a view of the affairs thereof, civil and military*. 7 vols. London 1701–9.

Court and City Reg.   *Court and City Register*.

CSPD   *Calendar of State Papers Domestic*. 94 vols., 1547–1704. London 1856–1964.

CTB   *Calendar of Treasury Books*. 32 vols., 1660–1718. London 1904–69.

CTBP   *Calendar of Treasury Books and Papers*. 5 vols., 1729–45. London 1897–1903.

Dip. Rep.   *British Diplomatic Representatives 1689–1789*, ed. D. B. Horn. Camden 3rd ser., xiii, 1932.

Ellis, *Post Office*   K. Ellis, *The Post Office in the Eighteenth Century: A Study in Administrative History*. London 1958.

Ellis Corr.   *The Ellis Correspondence 1686–8*, ed. G. Agar Ellis. 2 vols. London 1829.

Evans, *Principal Secretary*   F. M. G. Evans (Mrs C. S. S. Higham), *The Principal Secretary of State: A Survey of the Office from 1558 to 1680*. Manchester 1923.

1st Rept. on Fees   *First Report from Commissioners for Enquiring into Fees in Public Offices 1786* (HC 1806, vii).

Gent. Mag.   *Gentleman's Magazine*.

Hist. Reg. Chron.   *Historical Register ... Chronological Diary*.

Lond. Mag.   *London Magazine and Monthly Chronologer*.

Luttrell, *Hist. Relation*   N. Luttrell, *A Brief Historical Relation of State Affairs from September 1678 to April 1714*. 6 vols. Oxford 1857.

Miège, *New (Present) State*   G. Miège, *The New (Present) State of England (Great Britain)*.

Nelson, *Home Office*　　R. R. Nelson, *The Home Office 1782–1801*. Durham, N.C. 1969.

16th Rept. on Finance　　*Sixteenth Report of Select Committee on Finance 1797*. Reports of Committees of House of Commons 1797–1803, xii.

Spector, *American Department*　　M. M. Spector, *The American Department of British Government 1768–1782*. New York 1940.

Thomson, *Secretaries of State*　　M. A. Thomson, *The Secretaries of State 1681–1782*. Oxford 1932.

Note on Editorial Method

This volume is designed to make available lists of the officials who served in the offices of the Secretaries of State between the Restoration in May 1660 and the reorganisation of the secretariat which took place in March 1782. Also included are the holders of those offices which were common to the secretariat as a whole. For these the year 1782 had no special significance and, in their case, the lists have been continued down to the abolition of their offices in the nineteenth century. The material is presented in four parts: an introduction, lists of appointments, periodic lists of officials and an alphabetical list of officials. The purpose of the introduction is to provide a short account of the institutional development of the Secretaries' offices during the period in order that the various offices and grades may be related to their general context. The lists of appointments give the dates of appointment to these offices and grades. They are preceded by introductory notes which bring together information concerning such matters as the methods of appointment and remuneration. The periodic lists enable the complete establishment of the secretariat to be seen at selected dates.

The alphabetical list is not intended to be a biographical index. Its purpose is confined simply to providing summarised accounts of the offices held by each individual within the secretariat. No information has been included unless it is directly relevant to this purpose. Thus dates of death are included only if the individual was in office at his death. Appointments to offices elsewhere have been ignored unless they occasioned, or can reasonably be held to have occasioned, the departure of the official from the secretariat. Except in the case of the offices common to the secretariat as a whole, the accounts of the careers of those who were in office in March 1782 have not been continued beyond this date.

All references have been concentrated in the alphabetical list. Where printed calendars of manuscript material exist they have been used as authorities provided that the calendaring is sufficiently full. Peers and holders of courtesy titles have been indexed under their titles. In the case of changes of name or status, appropriate cross-references have been inserted. Unless otherwise noted, information concerning peers and baronets has been taken from the *Complete Peerage* (ed. G.E.C. 2nd ed. 13 vols. London 1910–59), the *Complete Baronetage* (ed. G.E.C. 5 vols. Exeter 1900–6) and Burke's *Peerage*.

Certain conventions have been adopted for dating appointments. The year is taken to have begun on 1 January throughout the period. In the case of those offices which were conferred by an instrument, whether this took the form of letters patent under the great seal or of royal warrant, the date is that of the instrument. However, the appointments of Secretaries of State have been dated by reference to the date of the reception of the seals or, failing this, that of the taking of the oath in the Privy Council. So far as possible the appointments of Under Secretaries and Clerks have been dated by reference to the notifications sent to the Post Office in connection with the privilege of franking. Officials are taken to have remained in office until the appointment of their successors unless there is clear evidence to support the selection of an earlier date.

Where there is no indication of the date of appointment of an individual, his period of service has been dated by reference to the time during which he received a salary or other remuneration or, failing this, by reference to the earliest and latest date at which he is found occupying a particular office.

The task of presenting the material relating to the careers of those officials who were common to the secretariat as a whole creates few problems since, in most cases, the sources are reasonably satisfactory and the establishment of the succession of those holding the offices is all that is required. It is otherwise in the case of the Secretaries' immediate officials—the Under Secretaries, Clerks, Office Keepers and Necessary Women. Here difficulties arise for two principal reasons. On the one hand the structure of the Secretaries' offices was relatively fluid. The staff tended to become attached to a succession of Secretaries rather than to the departments of which they had charge. In consequence their careers are, in most cases, better understood in terms of their relationship to particular Secretaries. The arrangement of the entries in the alphabetical list reflects this consideration. The office held by each of the Secretaries' officials is followed by the names, in brackets, of the Secretaries whom they served and the dates of their service. In order to identify the departments in which officials were serving at particular times, reference should be made to the accounts of the careers of the Secretaries of State in question where details of their tenure of the various departments are given.

The second problem of presentation affecting the Secretaries' immediate officials arises from the unsatisfactory nature of the source material for their careers. This has necessitated, in many cases, reliance on a variety of incidental references and resort to conjecture for periods when information is wholly lacking. To have associated this supporting material with each stage of the officials' careers would have had the effect of seriously obscuring their general direction. In order to overcome this problem all references and conjectures have been removed to separate paragraphs so that the course, or probable course, of each official's career may be more readily understood.

Introduction

ORGANISATION OF THE SECRETARIAT

At the Restoration the practice of appointing two Secretaries of State, which was well established before the Civil War, was resumed. Apart from the modifications which were made necessary by the occasional existence of a third secretaryship, the organisation of the secretariat underwent no fundamental change from that time until the reforms of 1782 which resulted in the emergence of the Home and Foreign departments.[1] The powers of the Secretaries were in theory identical. They could undertake any of the business and were obliged to do so in cases where one of the offices was vacant or its occupant absent. However, while there were no binding rules, certain conventions governing the distribution of functions came to be generally understood and accepted. English domestic affairs remained the responsibility of both Secretaries throughout the period. In the field of foreign affairs there was a division into a Northern and a Southern Department, each of which was the responsibility of one Secretary. The distinction between the two departments emerged only gradually. It was not until after 1689 that their names passed into general currency. Nevertheless the division of foreign business itself can, in its broad outlines, be detected in the early years of the reign of Charles II.[2] Until 1674 the incoming Secretary took over the responsibilities of the Secretary whom he replaced. Between 1674 and 1706 it was usual for a newly appointed Secretary to take charge of the Northern Department and to move to the Southern Department, to which higher remuneration was attached, when a vacancy occurred and he came to occupy the senior position. There was, however, an exception to this convention. During Vernon's tenure of office (1697–1702) Jersey and Manchester took charge of the Southern Department immediately on appointment although both were junior to him in length of service. From 1706 it was usual for a Secretary to remain throughout his period of service in the Department to which he had been first appointed.[3] When the process of equalising the remuneration of the Secretaries was finally completed in 1709, the distinction which had previously existed between the senior and junior offices ceased to have any practical significance.

In 1709 a third Secretary was appointed and given responsibility for Scottish affairs which had formerly fallen to the Secretary in charge of the Northern Department.[4] Queensberry, the first holder of this office, was able to obtain a share in the conduct of foreign business but his successors were confined to Scottish affairs. The office was left vacant from 1726. It was revived in 1742 and was finally discontinued

---

[1] For the secretariat generally during this period, see Evans, *Principal Secretary*; Thomson, *Secretaries of State*; Spector, *American Department*.

[2] For the emergence of the two departments and the responsibilities assigned to each, see Evans, *Principal Secretary*, 102–5, 131–6; Thomson, *Secretaries of State*, 2–3, 90–4.

[3] Evans, *Principal Secretary*, 132–3; Thomson, *Secretaries of State*, 3–4; *The Letters of Joseph Addison*, ed. W. Graham (Oxford 1941), 64–5.

[4] For the Scottish Department, see Thomson, *Secretaries of State*, 29–37, 164–6.

in 1746. A third Secretary was again appointed in 1768 and given charge of colonial business which was transferred from the Southern Department.[5] In 1782 the secretariat was reorganised. The Colonial Department was abolished. All domestic and colonial business was transferred to the former Southern Department which came to be known as the Home Office while the sole responsibility for foreign business was allocated to the former Northern Department which came to be known as the Foreign Office.[6]

Special arrangements were made for the performance of secretarial functions when the King went abroad. It was generally accepted that he should be accompanied by a Secretary of State on such occasions. However, William III, although he took first Nottingham and then Sydney with him to the Low Countries in 1691, left both Secretaries in England at other times. During the expedition to Ireland in 1690 Sir Robert Southwell accompanied the King and undertook the necessary secretarial duties; and William Blathwayt acted similarly during the annual expeditions to Holland and Flanders between 1692 and 1701. Neither Southwell nor Blathwayt was ever actually appointed a Secretary of State.[7] George I and George II followed a more orthodox course when they visited their German possessions and were, as a general rule, accompanied by one of the Secretaries while the other remained in England. However, this practice was varied in 1723 when both Secretaries went with the King to Hanover and in 1736 when both remained in England, the King being accompanied abroad by Horatio Walpole.[8] On two occasions the royal absences abroad gave rise to the appointment of temporary Secretaries. In June 1716 Methuen was appointed to take charge of the Southern Department in the absence of Stanhope and in 1723 Walpole was appointed to conduct the secretarial business of the Northern and Southern Departments in England in the absence of Townshend and Carteret.

SOURCE MATERIALS

Before an attempt is made to give an account of the officials of the Secretaries of State, something must be said about the nature of the relevant evidence. It is in several respects less satisfactory than that available for other major departments. In consequence many details must remain tentative and imprecise. Precision is usually attainable in the case of the periods of service of the Secretaries of State themselves and of those officials who were appointed by instruments or who received their salaries from some public source. Included in these two groups are the Clerks of the Signet, the Secretaries for the Latin and French Tongues, the Writer of the Gazette (after 1719) and the Keeper, Collector and Methodisers of State Papers. It is otherwise in the case of the Secretaries' immediate officials—the Under Secretaries, the Clerks, the Office Keepers and the Necessary Women. These were appointed directly by the

[5] For the responsibilities of the Colonial Department, see Thomson, *Secretaries of State*, 52–64, 167–174; Spector, *American Department*, 11–32; A. H. Basye, *The Lords Commissioners of Trade and Plantations 1748–82* (New Haven 1925), 176–201.

[6] For the origins of the Home and Foreign Offices, see Nelson, *Home Office*, 3–10; *Public Record Office Handbook No. 13 : The Records of the Foreign Office 1782–1939* (London 1969), 1–3.

[7] For the arrangement of secretarial duties during the reign of William III, see G. A. Jacobsen, *William Blathwayt : A late 17th Century English Administrator* (New Haven 1932), 240–87, 484; R. A. Preston, 'William Blathwayt and the Evolution of a Royal Personal Secretariat', *History*, new ser., xxxiv (1949), 28–43. Southwell held the distinct office of Secretary of State for Ireland; Blathwayt that of Secretary at War.

[8] For the administrative arrangements made in connection with these journeys, see p. 5 n. 22.

Secretaries and until the end of the period remained in theory their personal servants. While conventions grew up in the course of time which were usually respected by successive Secretaries, these never found formal or binding expression. A few memoranda relating to office organisation have survived but they were evidently drawn up in response to particular contingencies and there is nothing to suggest that they formed part of a continuous collection of comparable material.[9]

The officials in this last category received no instruments of appointment and took no oaths of office. There was, therefore, no occasion for any systematic record of their appointments to be kept. However, there is one reasonably satisfactory source which in some measure supplies this deficiency. This is the series of letters written in connection with the privilege of franking which was enjoyed by the Under Secretaries, Clerks and certain other officials designated by the Secretaries of State. Following the appointment of a Secretary it was the usual practice for a letter to be sent to the Post Office giving details of the composition of his office. Further letters were sent in the event of subsequent changes. While the privilege itself was well established by 1685, the first letter of this kind to survive is of 1708.[10] There are considerable gaps but the series is reasonably complete from this date until the end of the period. These letters are of great value in determining the identity of Under Secretaries and Clerks. However, they must be used with caution since there are a number of cases in which it can be shown from other sources that they were written a considerable time after the appointments which they record.[11]

Also of value in determining the periods of service of the Secretaries' officials are the documents relating to their remuneration. These fall broadly into two categories— the accounts of the office fees and the accounts of the receipts and disbursements of the Secretaries of State. The practice of exacting fees of fixed amounts on certain types of business transacted by the Secretaries was already well established in the reign of Charles II. In 1684 the recipients in one of the offices were the Secretary himself, the senior 'Clerk', the 'Writing' Clerk and the Chamber Keeper. This was probably the case for the other office as well. As will be seen the pattern of distribution at this date was the basis of the eighteenth-century convention whereby the right to official fees in each office was enjoyed by the Secretary, the two Under Secretaries, the First or Chief Clerk and the two Office Keepers.[12] Originally there was considerable competition

---

[9] The most important memoranda for the earlier part of the period are those of 1673 and 1684 described below. The list of Secretaries' officials in the poll tax assessment of July 1689 is also of value (LS 13/231 pp. 13–14). A number of documents of 1766–8 survive amongst the Shelburne papers (Shelburne MS 134 pp. 101–61). A certain amount of material covering the years 1769–82 exists amongst the records of the Foreign Office (FO 95/591/1 ff. 1–8; FO 366/669 pp. 9–15). The first comprehensive account of the Secretaries' offices dates from 1785–6, after the separation of the secretariat into the Home and Foreign Departments, and is to be found in *1st Rept. on Fees*.

[10] *CTB*, viii, 461–2; SP 44/107 p. 280. Copies of the relevant letters are to be found in the Secretaries' and Under Secretaries' Domestic Letter Books. A search in the General Post Office for the originals proved unsuccessful. The privilege of franking was, so far as the Clerks were concerned, severely curtailed in 1764. See p. 34.

[11] For example, Brietzcke's appointment made on 29 April 1756 was not notified until 9 May 1757.

[12] Lists of fees payable exist as follows: c. 1684 (Evans, *Principal Secretary*, 192–3); c. 1714 (SP 44/326); c. 1719 (SP 35/19 ff. 190–1); 1786 (*1st Rept. on Fees*, 45–6). These lists indicate that for each royal 'signature' the fees of the Secretary of State, the Under Secretaries and the Office Keepers remained constant at £5, £1 and 2s 6d respectively. At some point between 1684 and 1699 the fee of the Writing or Entering Clerk rose from 2s 6d to 5s (BM Add. MS 40784). For summarised totals of fees at various dates during the 18th century, see Thomson, *Secretaries of State*, 115–16; Spector, *American Department*, 63 n. 26.

between the offices for those types of business which gave rise to the payment of fees. This was brought to an end in 1699 when an agreement was made according to which the fees received in each office were periodically brought to account and then divided equally between them.[13] By the eighteenth century the function of keeping the accounts of the office fees had devolved upon the Chief Clerks who were also responsible for collecting the fees and paying them to the officials who were entitled to them. Where signed receipts occur in the account books they enable these officials to be identified. The earliest accounts of fees to survive cover part of Coventry's period of office 1672–3 and the whole of Williamson's 1674–9 and Conway's 1681–3 but they contain nothing of value for the identification of their officials.[14] The first accounts to be of any use in this connection are for Vernon's secretaryship 1697–1702.[15] Apart from Harley's accounts nothing further survives until 1727 when the series in the Public Record Office begins. This series is far from complete.[16]

At least two other types of accounts were kept in connection with the Secretaries' official activities. The accounts of the *London Gazette*, the profits of which the Secretaries shared, were kept by the printer. A few of these accounts have survived and from these it is evident that, in the earlier part of the period, some Secretaries made provision for the remuneration of their officials out of their receipts from this source. Coventry assigned his share of the profits to his Under Secretary, Cooke. The elder Sunderland divided his share between one of his Under Secretaries and two of his Clerks.[17] Trumbull, Harley and, during his first period of office, the younger Sunderland paid salaries to their Clerks and inferior staff from the same source.[18] The more common practice, however, was for these salaries to be paid by the Chief Clerks who came to be responsible for receiving the Secretaries' various salaries and allowances and accounting for the disbursements made from them. The earliest accounts of this kind are for Vernon's term of office.[19] Others survive for part of Carteret's and Newcastle's terms of office between 1724 and 1739.[20] Receipts for the salaries of

---

[13] Thomson, *Secretaries of State*, 147; *Vernon Correspondence*, ed. G. P. R. James (London 1841), ii, 282–3; BM Add. MS 40785 f. 37. Except during Queensberry's period of office this arrangement was not extended to the third secretaryship (Thomson, *Secretaries of State*, 147–8; Spector, *American Department*, 52–5).

[14] Coventry MS 12 ff. 74–90; SP 29/365; Folger MS V.b.302.   [15] BM Add. MSS 40783, 40784.

[16] Monthly accounts survive for Harley's period of office 1704–8 (BM Loan 29/163, 356). The collection of account books in the Public Record Office is best understood when related to the Chief Clerks who kept them: SP 45/26 kept Jan. 1727–Dec. 1733 by Wace for Townshend and Harrington; SP 45/28 kept Jan. 1749–Dec. 1754 by Richardson for Bedford, Holdernesse and Robinson; SP 45/29 kept Aug. 1758–June 1761 by Richardson for Pitt; SP 45/27 kept Jan. 1746–Nov. 1756 by Prevereau and Larpent for Newcastle and Holdernesse; SP 45/31 kept Jan. 1764–Jan. 1768 by Larpent for Halifax and Seymour Conway; SP 45/33–5 kept Jan. 1772–May 1782 by Larpent and Shadwell for Suffolk, Weymouth, Hillsborough and Shelburne (Home Secretary); SP 45/32 kept Jan. 1768–March 1782 by Pollock for successive Secretaries for the Colonial Department. SP 45/30 is not a fee book but contains summarised accounts of Egremont and Sandwich 1761–5 which are of no value for the identification of their officials. Copies of the accounts of fees received in both offices during Bedford's secretaryship (1748–51) survive amongst his official papers.

[17] Evans, *Principal Secretary*, 292, 296; All Souls MS 204 f. 81c.

[18] Trumbull Add. MS 113; BM Loan 29/162; SP 34/12 f. 165. For details of payments to Harley's Clerks, see A. J. D. M. McInnes, 'Robert Harley, Secretary of State' (Unpublished M.A. thesis, University College of Wales, Aberystwyth, 1961), 185–90.   [19] BM Add. MSS 40785, 40786.

[20] MSS Rawlinson C 367, 123. An account book kept by Armstrong, Nottingham's Clerk and man of business, from 1687 to 1706 records the receipt of his salaries and allowances as Secretary 1689–93 and 1702–4 but no payments to Clerks or other officials (Finch MS DG 7/1/19a). Possibly the salaries of the latter were paid out of the *Gazette* account.

Clerks and others exist for the secretaryships of the younger Sunderland 1717–18, Stanhope 1718–21, Tweeddale 1742–6 and Egremont 1761–3.[21]

The rather meagre amount of information obtainable from these sources may be supplemented by that contained in the warrants for the payment of travelling allowances and board wages in connection with the journeys of the court either abroad or to one of the royal residences outside London. In the case of journeys abroad the Secretary of State who accompanied the King took some of his officials with him. In 1736 when both Secretaries remained in England, Horatio Walpole went to Hanover with a collection of officials drawn from both offices. Occasionally persons who were not Secretaries' officials were temporarily attached to the staff in these circumstances. Thus Luke Schaub acted as Under Secretary to Stanhope in 1719 and Caspar Wetstein to Carteret in 1743.[22] In the case of domestic journeys, which were either to Windsor or Hampton Court, it was the practice for both Secretaries to accompany the court.[23] Also of some value for an understanding of the Secretaries' offices is the diary of Brietzcke, who held office as a Clerk in the Northern and Southern departments from 1756 to 1782 and subsequently in the Home Office. The surviving portions of the diary which extend from 1759 to 1764 throw considerable light on working conditions and on the principles that governed the organisation of the offices at this period.[24]

Since so few of the documents most closely associated with establishment matters have survived, considerable reliance must be placed on incidental references to Secretaries' officials in tracing their careers. The appointments of Under Secretaries are often the subject of comment in newsletters, Luttrell's *Historical Relation* and, later, in the *Historical Register* and the *Gentleman's Magazine*. Their periods of service can be established reasonably accurately from references to them in the official letter books where these survive. The careers of the Clerks and inferior officials present greater problems since they attracted less attention in view of their relatively small importance. Contemporary published lists are, however, of some value in this connection. 'Chief Secretaries' to the Secretaries of State first appear in the edition of Chamberlayne's *Present State* for 1682.[25] The first reasonably full account of the

---

[21] Stanhope MS 76; Sunderland MS D 1/36; Tweeddale MSS Acc. 4862, Boxes 57/16, 160/1; PRO 30/31/1–7.

[22] The warrants for payments in connection with journeys abroad are as follows: 1716–17 (*CTB*, xxx, 312; ibid. xxxi, 138–9); 1719 (T 52/29 p. 403; T 52/30 p. 16); 1720 (T 52/30 p. 97; T 52/31 p. 10); 1723 (T 52/32 p. 361; T 52/33 pp. 23, 51, 79, 275); 1725–6 (T 52/33 p. 366; T 52/34 pp. 14, 82); 1727 (T 52/35 p. 2); 1729 (T 52/36 pp. 330–1, 403); 1732 (T 52/37 pp. 391, 469); 1735 (T 52/38 p. 474; T 52/39 p. 89); 1736–7 (T 52/39 pp. 164, 253, 326); 1740 (T 52/41 pp. 24, 151); 1741 (ibid. pp. 236–7, 350); 1742 (T 52/42 p. 82); 1743 (ibid. pp. 205, 324); 1745 (T 52/43 pp. 134, 213); 1748 (T 52/44 pp. 372, 386, 502); 1750 (T 52/45 pp. 162, 324); 1752 (T 52/46 pp. 44, 147); 1755 (T 52/47 pp. 101–2, 188). The officials received travelling allowances but no board wages for the journey in 1727 which was cut short by the King's death. Travelling allowances were paid in September 1742 in connection with a journey which never actually took place. From 1725 it was the general rule for the Secretary of State who accompanied the King to receive an allowance of £3000 for expenses (T 52/34 p. 77; T 52/47 p. 11).

[23] The warrants for payments in connection with domestic journeys are as follows: 1724 (T 52/33 p. 275); 1728 (T 52/36 pp. 335–6); 1730 (T 52/37 p. 122); 1731 (ibid. p. 319); 1733 (T 52/38 pp. 190–1); 1737 (T 52/40 p. 7). Board wages but not travelling allowances were paid on these occasions.

[24] The surviving portions of Brietzcke's diary have been printed in *Notes and Queries* as follows: cxcvi (1951), 185–8, 357–61; cxcvii (1952), 68–74, 141–2, 209–11, 543–4; cxcviii (1953), 29–31, 203–5, 346–9; cxcix (1954), 60–3, 165–9, 205–8, 259–62, 297–9, 340–3; cc (1955), 30–3, 70–6, 115–18, 161–4, 245–9, 310–11, 443–5, 486–8; cci (1956), 172–4, 311–14; cciii (1958), 66–70, 120–1, 153–61; cciv (1959), 94–7, 136–7, 178–81, 228–31, 281–4, 311–13, 373–5, 412–13; ccv (1960), 229–31, 301–2, 343–6, 389–95, 451–6; ccvi (1961), 9–14, 61–3, 83–6, 144–7, 191–3, 210–14, 258–62, 302–6, 335–8, 391–5, 433–4, 452–461.   [25] Chamberlayne, *Present State* (1682), pt. i, 193.

offices occurs in that for 1694. Most subsequent editions of this and other comparable works contain such lists although it is not until the second quarter of the eighteenth century that their accuracy can be relied upon.

It will be clear from the nature of the sources that any description of the principles which governed the organisation of the Secretaries' offices must in many respects be tentative. However, by the end of the reign of William III, a pattern had emerged which, with some minor modifications, was to endure until the end of the period. The arrangements in the offices of the two older Secretaries will first be described. Those in the Scottish and Colonial Departments will be considered later.

STRUCTURE OF THE OFFICES IN 1702

By 1702 it was the established practice for each office to be staffed by two Under Secretaries, a First or Chief Clerk, a varying number of other Clerks, two Chamber or Office Keepers and a Cleaner or Necessary Woman. Lack of evidence makes it impossible to trace the origin of these arrangements with any certainty. The practice of maintaining in unbroken succession two Secretaries of State dated from the latter part of the reign of James I. There was, therefore, a period of about a quarter of a century before the outbreak of the Civil War during which there was an opportunity for conventions governing the organisation of their offices to become established. A letter of 1628 describing the conditions in Secretary Coke's office implies that certain principles had already gained acceptance at that date.[26] The writer in this case was seeking appointment to the position of 'English and ancientest Secretary' to Coke. It is clear that the holder of this office was the Secretary of State's principal subordinate, ranking above a number of other Clerks or 'Secretaries' who received small salaries.

While there is no direct evidence on the point it is reasonable to suppose that in 1660 the Secretaries of State reconstructed their offices on the principles which had been current before the Interregnum. The first document to give a clear picture of the situation dates in its final form from 1684. It is a memorandum describing the situation in Middleton's office shortly after his appointment in that year.[27] It must be emphasised that this memorandum deals with only one of the Secretaries' offices. Nevertheless it embodies features which have enough in common with what is known about the situation both before and after the time when it was drawn up to make it a suitable point of departure for a discussion of the principles governing the organisation of the offices during the period covered by these lists. The memorandum names Middleton's Clerks in order of seniority and gives details of their functions and remuneration. The first Clerk in the list is Cooke who had important general responsibilities and undertook the direction of the office as a whole. He received no salary but was entitled to fees on official business. Next is Wynne who also had general responsibilities and was rewarded by the relatively large salary of £200 paid by the Secretary of State. Then follow three Clerks, de Paz, Chute and Carne, who received salaries ranging from £40 to £60. Finally there is a Writing Clerk, Widdows, who was particularly attached to the service of Cooke, the senior Clerk, from whom he received a salary. The memorandum indicates that the Writing Clerk and the Office Keeper, like the senior Clerk, were entitled to fees on official business which were distinct from

[26] Printed in Evans, *Principal Secretary*, 154–5.
[27] Printed ibid. 192–3 from All Souls MS 204 f. 119. Another version exists in BM Add. MS 41806 ff. 64–7.

those enjoyed by the Secretary of State himself. This suggests that they formed the original nucleus from which the Secretaries' offices developed.

UNDER SECRETARIES

The first question to be considered in the light of the memorandum of 1684 is the origin of the office of Under Secretary. It should be emphasised in this connection that the term 'Under Secretary', although found in use as early as 1672,[28] passed only gradually into general currency. For a considerable period it was used concurrently with the designations 'Secretary', 'Clerk', and even 'Chief Secretary' and 'Chief Clerk'.[29] This confusion adds appreciably to the difficulty of tracing the development of the office in the earlier part of the period. However, it is clear that in 1684, although all Middleton's subordinates are described as 'Clerks', the two most senior, Cooke and Wynne, are, from the point of view of function and remuneration, in a different category from the rest and approximate to the condition of 'Under Secretaries'. It seems that Cooke's situation corresponded to that of the 'English or ancientest Secretary' in Coke's office in 1628 and of the 'inward men' of other early Stuart Secretaries of State. On the other hand, the fact that the fees to which Cooke was entitled as senior 'Clerk' in 1684 were the same as those received by the Under Secretaries in the eighteenth century places the basic identity of his office with theirs beyond doubt.[30] Cooke's position as the principal subordinate in one of the offices can be traced back to the Restoration. For how long he had had a colleague of comparable standing is unknown. Wynne was brought into the office by Secretary Jenkins in 1680 almost certainly to replace Thynne who had served Coventry in a similar capacity since 1672. There is thus reasonable justification for tracing the pattern of two 'Under Secretaries' in this office at least as far back as the latter year. Wynne received his renumeration in 1684 in the form not of fees but of a salary from the Secretary of State which suggests that the practice of appointing a second 'Under Secretary' may have been a relatively late development. As will be seen it was later the practice for the two Under Secretaries to share equally in the product of the fees accruing to the Secretary's principal subordinate, a development which had the effect of placing them more in a position of parity. Nevertheless, in spite of this distinction between Cooke and Wynne, it seems reasonable to describe them both as Under Secretaries. It is worth noting in this connection that in the edition of Chamberlayne's *Present State* for 1684 both are designated 'Chief Secretaries' to Jenkins.[31]

It is difficult to say how far the arrangements just described were reflected in the other office during the reign of Charles II. The only document to throw any light on this question is a memorandum drawn up by Williamson in 1673 which gives some information about the state of Arlington's office at that date.[32] Williamson had occupied a leading position in this office ever since the Restoration. He frequently received communications on official business from Cooke which suggests that the two men

---

[28] In a letter of 31 May 1672 Sir William Coventry passed on to his brother, Henry, an application from Francis Vernon 'desiring to be one of your under Secretaries' (Coventry MS 119 f. 2).

[29] For the use of the term 'Chief Secretaries' in 1682, see Chamberlayne, *Present State* (1682), pt. i, 193 and *Memoirs of Thomas, Earl of Ailesbury* (London 1890), i, 63; for the use of the term 'Chief Clerk' in 1698, see *Camden Miscellany*, xx (Camden 3rd ser., lxxxiii, 1953), 48. As late as 1759 Pitt's Under Secretaries were officially referred to as 'Secretaries' (SP 44/137 p. 64).

[30] See p. 3 n. 12.   [31] Chamberlayne, *Present State* (1684), pt. ii, 7–8.

[32] Printed in Evans, *Principal Secretary*, 191–2 and in *CSPD Addenda 1660–85*, 403.

INTRODUCTION

were of comparable standing.[33] The precise nature of Williamson's functions is nowhere defined and he appears not to have had any consistent designation. In his earlier years in the office he is occasionally called 'Secretary' to Nicholas and Arlington and seems to have occupied a position similar to that of Whittaker and Godolphin who are also so described. But in 1673 he differentiated his situation from that of Arlington's then Secretaries, Bridgeman and Richards. At that date the direction of the office was in Williamson's hands while Bridgeman and Richards were acting more as Private Secretaries than as the later Under Secretaries. However, Williamson's career was unusual. There is no parallel to the employment of a person of his prominence in a subordinate position in the Secretaries' offices and the customary pattern of organisation may have been adapted to meet his case. When he became Secretary himself in 1674 in succession to Arlington he does not appear to have appointed a single individual to fill the role which he had occupied in the office. He retained the services of Bridgeman as one of his 'Secretaries' and replaced Richards by Brisbane. Bridgeman appears to have been the more important of the two and to have carried out many of the functions that Williamson had performed[34] but, so far as the fragmentary nature of the evidence allows a judgment to be formed, it seems that from 1674 the pattern of organisation in this office conformed closely to that already observed in the other. Certainly the compiler of the edition of Chamberlayne's *Present State* for 1684 felt able to equate the position of Bridgeman and Mountsteven, 'Chief Secretaries' to Sunderland with that of Cooke and Wynne, 'Chief Secretaries' to Jenkins. After 1689 the position of the two Under Secretaries at the head of each office was securely established. From this date their identity and periods of service can in most cases be accurately determined although, as has already been noted, their actual designation continued to vary considerably.

The right of appointing and dismissing the Under Secretaries lay with the Secretaries of State. However, it is clear that from an early date they were obliged to take into account the interest of the crown in the matter. Thus Shrewsbury dismissed Wynne in 1689 because the King disapproved of him. Newcastle was careful to consult the Queen, in the King's absence, before appointing Couraud in 1729.[35] There were probably many other similar instances of which no record has survived. Later in the eighteenth century the crown's interest was formally acknowledged. This is indicated by the fact that after 1766 the Secretary of State, when notifying the Post Office of the appointment of a new Under Secretary, on several occasions stated that it had been made with the King's approbation.[36] So long as this condition was satisfied, an incoming Secretary was free to appoint whom he wished. He was under no obligation to retain the Under Secretaries who had served his predecessor. It was, however, almost invariable for a Secretary to ensure that at least one of his Under Secretaries had had previous experience of the office.[37]

[33] These communications were frequent between 1662 and 1673 (*CSPD 1661-2*, 457; *CSPD 1672-3*, 399).
[34] Cooke began to communicate with Bridgeman shortly after Williamson's promotion (*CSPD 1673-5*, 573). [35] Thomson, *Secretaries of State*, 130.
[36] See the notifications of the appointments of Macleane and Morgann in 1766 (SP 44/141 p. 119), Eden and Willes in 1772 (ibid. p. 311; SP 44/142 p. 363), Oakes in 1778 (SP 44/141 p. 458) and Bell in 1781 (SP 44/143 p. 189). Porten was said to have been 'permitted to retire' by the King in 1782 (F. B. Wickwire, *British Subministers and Colonial America 1763-83* (Princeton 1966), 72-3).
[37] However, Conway appointed Gwyn and Blathwayt in 1681 and Boyle appointed Walpole and Tilson in 1708, none of whom had previously been Under Secretaries.

8

There was no firm convention corresponding to the modern distinction between the parliamentary and permanent under secretaryships. Under Secretaries were specifically exempted from the provisions of the Place Act of 1742[38] and between 1660 and 1782 twenty-seven individuals sat in the House of Commons while holding the office of Under Secretary in the two older departments.[39] However, their membership appears to have been determined largely by factors unconnected with their official position and there is nothing to suggest that any steps were taken to ensure that there was a regular succession of Under Secretaries with seats in Parliament. On the other hand a broad distinction can be made between men of business who made a career as Under Secretaries and those individuals whose presence in the office was determined largely by their attachment to a particular patron. Of the seventy-three men who held the office in the Northern and Southern departments during the period, thirty-seven served only once.[40] Of the careers of the remainder[41] the most remarkable was that of Tilson who was appointed in 1708 and remained in office until his death in 1738 after having served during eight separate secretaryships. Also noteworthy was that of Cooke who served under six Secretaries from 1660 to 1688. The periods of service of this type of Under Secretary were not always continuous. For example Bridgeman's career (c. 1667–81; 1683–8; 1690–4) was interrupted twice and Weston's (1729–46; 1761–4) once. While an analysis of the careers of Under Secretaries reveals certain trends,[42] the situation remained fluid and largely defies generalisation. Secretaries naturally tended to take care that at least one of their Under Secretaries was a man of business but it was not until the end of the period that the idea of a 'Permanent' Under Secretary began to take root. Fraser (1765–71; 1771–89) held what amounted to this situation in one office and Porten (1768–82) in the other while Bell considered that he had been appointed in 1781 on the understanding that he would succeed Porten as 'what is considered the fix'd and Resident' Under Secretary.[43]

For the greater part of the period covered by these lists the Under Secretaries derived their remuneration principally from official fees. As already noted these fees were in 1684 received in Middleton's office by his senior subordinate, Cooke, whose colleague, Wynne, was paid a salary by the Secretary of State. Later a new arrangement

[38] 15 Geo. II, c 22.

[39] Addison, Aldworth, Amyand, Bridgeman, Burke, Chamier, Chetwynd, Digby, Eden, Ellis, Finch, Godolphin, Hare, Hopkins, Jenkinson, Langlois, Leveson Gower, Lewis, Mountsteven, Stone, Townshend, Vernon, Walpole, Whately, Williamson, Wood and Yard. Macleane, an Assistant Under Secretary, may still have been in office on his election in 1768. Three Under Secretaries in the Colonial Department, de Grey, D'Oyly and Pownall, were members of the Commons while holding office. Delafaye was a member of the Irish parliament of George I.

[40] Aglionby, Aldworth, Balaguier, Bell (Under Secretary, Home Office March–April 1782), Blathwayt, Brisbane, Burke, Burnaby, Couraud, Digby, Eden, Finch, Godolphin, Graham, Gwyn, Hare, Holt, Hume, Jenkinson, Jones, Langlois, Leveson Gower, Oakes, Potenger, Prior, Ramsden, Richards, C. Stanhope, T. Stanhope, A. Stanyan, Stawell, Stone, Thynne, Townshend, Whately, Whittaker and Willes.

[41] Under Secretaries who served twice: Addison, Chamier, Isham, Mountsteven, Phelps (Under Secretary, Colonial Department 1768), Potter, Pringle, Pulteney, Sedgwick, Stonehewer, Sutton, Wallace, Walpole, Williamson; three times: Chetwynd, Hopkins, Lewis, L. Stanhope, Tickell, Vernon, Wood, Yard; four times: Amyand, Delafaye, Porten, Rivers, Tucker, Wynne; five times: Ellis; six times: Cooke, T. Stanyan, Warre; seven times: Bridgeman, Fraser (Under Secretary, Foreign Office 1782–9), Weston; eight times: Tilson.

[42] For a detailed study of the careers of some of the 18th century Under Secretaries, see L. Scott, 'Under Secretaries of State, 1755–75' (Unpublished M.A. thesis, Manchester University, 1950).

[43] Nelson, *Home Office*, 28; HO 42/2, Bell's memorial, 28 Feb. 1783.

was made whereby neither Under Secretary received a salary but both shared equally in the product of the fees to which Cooke had been solely entitled. The date of this arrangement cannot be established precisely. It was presumably not made before Cooke's retirement in 1688. On the other hand, the fact that all four Under Secretaries are shown in the poll tax assessment for July 1689 as receiving their remuneration in the form not of 'Wages' but of 'Perquisites' may indicate that the change had taken place by that date.[44] By 1697 it was certainly the practice in one of the offices for the product of the fees to be equally divided between the two Under Secretaries[45] and it is probable that the effect of the agreement of 1699 was to make the receipts of all four Under Secretaries equal. In 1674 and 1675 Cooke and Bridgeman respectively were granted annuities of £400 from the Exchequer in consideration of their services in the Secretaries' offices.[46] However, these grants were of a personal character and did not result in salaries from public funds being accorded to their successors. The creation of the Scottish secretaryship in 1709 brought about, at least temporarily, a reduction in the share of the office fees available to each Under Secretary which led to a demand that they should be accorded fixed allowances in recompense.[47] This demand proved unsuccessful and it was not until 1770, shortly after the creation of the Colonial Department, that salaries of £500 from public funds were established for each of the six Under Secretaries.[48]

In view of their relatively precarious tenure Under Secretaries sought to acquire additional offices, which were either sinecures or could be exercised by deputy, in order both to augment their incomes while actually serving and to provide for their retirement. Particularly favoured for this purpose were the patent offices in the colonies. In 1719 the Under Secretaries prepared a petition in which they asked to be accorded salaries or, failing that, for certain offices under the general authority of the Secretaries of State to be reserved to them. If this petition was ever presented no response has survived, but the Under Secretaries succeeded in establishing the substance of their case. In the course of the eighteenth century they came virtually to monopolise the offices of Secretary for the Latin Tongue, Writer of the Gazette, Keeper and Collector of State Papers and the clerkships of the Signet.[49] In some cases provision was made for them either from the secret service or in the form of a pension at the Exchequer.[50]

---

[44] LS 13/231 pp. 13–14.

[45] BM Add. MS 40783 ff. 1–13.

[46] Evans, *Principal Secretary*, 164–5.

[47] The memorial in which this request is made is calendared under the year 1702 (*CSPD 1702–3*, 516–17). Its reference to the third secretaryship, however, makes it clear that it cannot have been drawn up before 1709.

[48] Royal warrant 12 July 1770 (T 52/60 p. 463).

[49] The petition is printed in Thomson, *Secretaries of State*, 178–9. The word described as illegible by Thomson appears to be 'Court Post' (SP 35/14 ff. 19–20). The Secretaries of State successfully resisted a recommendation by the Commissioners on Fees of 1786 that the offices of Keeper and Collector of State Papers, Secretary for the Latin Tongue and Writer of the Gazette should be abolished, on the ground that 'the nomination to these offices . . . affords almost the only means which the Secretaries of State have of rewarding Officers for diligence and long services' (*1st Rept. on Fees*, 12; *16th Rept. on Finance*, 310–11). They did, however, suggest the abolition of the sinecure office of Translator of the German Language (*16th Rept. on Finance*, 310).

[50] Ellis, *Post Office*, 132. In 1769 Sutton was granted a pension at the Exchequer which became payable on his retirement in 1772 (*CHOP 1770–2*, 556). In 1771 L. Stanhope was granted a pension from the same source (C 66/3731).

While the conventions governing the under secretaryships were in general firmly fixed it was not unknown for individual Secretaries of State to vary them in detail. In addition to his Under Secretaries a Secretary might employ other individuals whose standing in the office approximated more closely to theirs than to that of the Clerks. On entering office in 1755 Fox removed Rivers from the position of Under Secretary to make way for Digby. However, he retained the services of the former who was given a salary of £200 with the title of Interpreter of Southern Languages and in fact acted as an additional Under Secretary until he regained his former position in the following year.[51] In 1759 Holdernesse took what was apparently an unprecedented step in replacing one of his Under Secretaries, Wallace, by Fraser and Morin, whose subordinate position relative to the remaining Under Secretary, Potenger, was marked by the fact that he retained a half share in the Under Secretaries' fees for the office while they were obliged to divide the other share between them.[52] For a decade thereafter it was usual for this pattern to be reproduced in one of the offices. No consistent designation was applied to the Under Secretaries in this subordinate position. They were most commonly described as 'Assistants to the Under Secretary' or 'Assistant Under Secretaries'.[53] For the sake of convenience the latter term has been used throughout these lists. The usual number of Assistant Under Secretaries was two but Shelburne employed three between 1766 and 1768. After 1768 no more were appointed and the earlier practice of having two Under Secretaries of equal standing in each office was observed until the end of the period.

While the Under Secretaries remained formally the personal servants of the Secretaries of State, they gradually acquired public functions in their own right. During the reign of Charles II it was the practice for one of the Under Secretaries in the office of the senior Secretary to be appointed by the Irish government its salaried agent in England.[54] From 1695 the Lords Justices selected their Secretaries from amongst the Under Secretaries.[55] In the early eighteenth century they were regularly included in the commissions of the peace for Middlesex in order that they might

[51] *Grenville Papers*, ed. W. J. Smith (London 1852–3), i, 180–1; T 53/45 p. 461.

[52] *Notes and Queries*, cxcix (1954), 208. Between 1762 and 1764 Weston evidently received all the Under Secretaries' fees in his office (ibid. cciv (1959), 284; SP 45/31). During this period the Assistant Under Secretaries were presumably paid salaries by the Secretaries of State. For the arrangements made in Seymour Conway's office in 1765, see Hist. MSS Comm. *10th Rept.*, 391–2.

[53] In 1749 Aspinwall, one of Newcastle's Clerks, was described as 'Assistant Secretary' (*Court and City Reg.* (1749), 106). The significance of this designation is obscure.

[54] The agency, to which a salary of £100 was attached, was exercised by Bridgeman to 1674, Thynne 1674–80 and again by Bridgeman from 1680 (*CSPD 1670*, 285; Coventry MS 17 ff. 147–9; Hist. MSS Comm. *Ormonde*, iv, 579; ibid. v, 271; ibid. vi, 40; Evans, *Principal Secretary*, 165). The subsequent history of the agency is obscure. It may have been replaced by the practice, first recorded in 1702, of paying allowances of £50 from the Irish concordatum fund to each of the four Under Secretaries (BM Add. MS 28889 ff. 158, 179, 183).

[55] The following Under Secretaries acted as Secretaries to the Lords Justices: Vernon 1695–7 (*CTB*, xiii, 406); Yard 1698–1701 (ibid. xiv, 222; ibid. xv, 187; ibid. xvi, 141, 391); Delafaye 1719–26 (T 52/30 pp. 59, 442; T 52/33 p. 73; T 29/25 p. 135); Couraud and Stone 1740–1 (*CTBP 1739–41*, 407, 606); Stone and Weston 1743 (*CTBP 1742–5*, 426); Stone and Ramsden 1743 (ibid. 824); Aldworth and Potter 1748 (T 52/44 p. 450); Aldworth and Leveson Gower 1750 (T 52/45 p. 248); Amyand and Potenger 1752 (T 52/46 p. 130); Amyand and Rivers 1755 (T 52/47 p. 170). Addison, a former Under Secretary, acted as Secretary in 1714 (*CTB*, xxix, 776). As Secretaries these individuals received £500 for each period during which the Lords Justices acted. From 1719 an allowance was also made available for distribution amongst the Clerks and other officials of the secretariat for their services to the Lords Justices. Originally £200, this allowance was raised to £300 in 1740 and to £400 in 1743 (T 53/28 p. 42; *CTBP 1739–41*, 407; *CTBP 1742–5*, 426).

conduct examinations of witnesses.[56] Their public standing was confirmed in the Place Act of 1742, the need for the approval by the crown of their appointments and the grant of a regular salary from public funds in 1770.

Lack of evidence makes it difficult to say how far there was a regular division of duties between the Under Secretaries. In the memorandum of 1684 specific duties were assigned to Cooke and Wynne. Cooke's functions were in some respects similar to those undertaken by the 'English and ancientest' Secretary in Coke's office in 1628. After about 1689 the distinction of rank that can be observed in the case of Cooke and Wynne seems to have disappeared and given way to the convention that the Under Secretaries were equal in standing if not in actual importance.[57] This may have resulted in greater flexibility in the distribution of duties. In 1737 Couraud, Under Secretary to Newcastle, was able to say that 'Domestic Business falls chiefly to my care: Foreign to my brother Stone'.[58] This distinction is a perfectly reasonable one but there is little to suggest that it hardened into a permanent convention. It would appear that each incoming Secretary was free to arrange the distribution of business as he thought fit.[59] The only occasions on which the fact that Under Secretaries were specialising in a particular field of business was publicly acknowledged occurred in 1763 when Sedgwick was appointed Under Secretary for American Affairs by Halifax and in 1766 when Shelburne gave two of his Assistant Under Secretaries, Macleane and Morgann, similar responsibilities.[60]

A detailed account of the recruitment of Under Secretaries is outside the scope of this introduction. Broadly speaking, the holders of these offices fall into a number of different but by no means necessarily exclusive categories.[61] Some were close relatives or dependants of the Secretaries who brought them into office. Others had diplomatic experience. Perhaps of greatest interest in the context of these lists are those who had had earlier careers in the Secretaries' offices. There is no evidence that Clerks could look forward to promotion to under secretaryships as a matter of right.[62] Examples of such promotion are not frequent and appear in every case to have resulted from the special qualities of the individuals in question. Some were appointed directly from the offices; others after a period of service elsewhere.[63]

[56] See the following letters requesting the appointment of Under Secretaries as Justices: 26 Jan. 1705 for Lewis (BM Loan 29/263 p. 56); 1 July 1710 for Warre and Lewis (SP 44/110 p. 8); 8 Oct. 1714 for C. Stanhope, Pringle, Tilson and Walpole (SP 44/117 p. 5; SP 44/147); 8 May 1717 for Delafaye (SP 44/120 p.157). See also SP 45/8 pp. 111–15.

[57] Occasional references to 'First' and 'Second' Under Secretaries imply a distinction of rank but this was not reflected in any permanent administrative arrangements. See, for example, *Gent. Mag.* (1754), xxiv, 143; Hist. MSS Comm. *10th Rept.*, 392–3.

[58] BM Add. MS 32690 f. 265. A plea for a regular division of duties between the Under Secretaries was made by Pulteney in 1691 (BM Add. MS 34095 f. 351).

[59] There is no suggestion in the evidence given by the Under Secretaries in 1785 that there was any permanent arrangement for the distribution of business at that date (*1st Rept. on Fees*, 19, 27). See also Jenkinson's memorandum on the Secretary's office 1761 (*The Jenkinson Papers 1760–6*, ed. N. S. Jucker (London 1949) 3–5).   [60] *CHOP 1760–5*, 303; *Court and City Reg.* (1767), 109.

[61] For a classification of the Under Secretaries in the latter part of the 18th century, see Scott, 'Under Secretaries of State, 1755–75'.

[62] Some information on this point is provided in a letter of 1705 from de Fonvive to Harley (Hist. MSS Comm. *Portland*, viii, 187–8).

[63] Under Secretaries and Assistant Under Secretaries appointed directly from the offices: Couraud, Fraser, Jones, Morin, Ramsden, Richards, Rivers, Roberts, T. Stanyan, Tucker, Wallace, Yard; those appointed after service elsewhere: Burnaby, Delafaye, Digby, Lewis, A. Stanyan, Tilson. Scott, an Under Secretary in the Scottish office, had earlier served as a Clerk in that department.

CHIEF CLERKS

By 1702 the place in the hierarchy of the two offices immediately after the Under Secretaries had come to be occupied by an official known as the First or Chief Clerk. The early history of this office, to which reference is first made in 1700, is obscure. In 1786 the Chief Clerk in the Home Department summarised his duties as follows: 'to prepare all warrants and commissions for the Royal Signature, to distribute the official business to the Clerks, to examine it when done, to take care that the public dispatches are properly entered in the books of the Office, and punctually transmitted, to receive the Secretary of State's salary, all the fees, and to pay all the Under Clerks salaries, and contingencies of Office'. He went on to state that he had no salary and that his official income arose principally under the following heads: 'a fixed proportion of the fees of office' and 'a moiety of gratuities received upon certain warrants signed by the King'.[64] While this description dates from after the division of the secretariat into the Home and Foreign Departments, there is no reason to suppose that it does not provide a generally accurate account of the functions and remuneration of the Chief Clerks throughout the eighteenth century. The evidence suggests, however, that the special position enjoyed by the Chief Clerks was achieved gradually and only as a result of the transfer to them of functions which had previously been carried out by distinct officials. The earliest document to throw any light on this question is the memorandum of 1684. In it one Clerk is singled out from the rest and described in the following terms: 'Mr. Widdows (who may be styled the writing clerk) transcribes all papers for the King's hand, and enters them when signed; is reckoned Mr. Cooke's clerk and to be paid by him at £50 a year, besides 2s 6d out of each signature that passeth and pays . . .'.[65] It will be clear that this Clerk has some features in common with the later Chief Clerks. Unlike the other junior Clerks in the office at this date he had a recognised right to fees. He was particularly concerned with royal documents. In connection with his duty of entering papers it should be noted that as early as 1610 there was a Clerk of the Entries in Salisbury's office and that as late as 1719 the fees of the Chief Clerks are described as arising in favour of the 'Entering Clerk'.[66] The fact that Widdows was 'reckoned' Cooke's clerk and was paid by him suggests that the functions which he performed had originally been part of the duties of the Secretary's senior subordinate who had found it convenient to delegate them. If this is correct it seems likely that the process of delegation continued since the task of judging 'of the style and forms of the office when anything occurs that is difficult or without precedent'[67] which fell to Cooke in 1684 was later one of the special responsibilities of the Chief Clerks.

While, therefore, there seems little doubt that the office of Chief Clerk evolved from that of Entering or Writing Clerk, the nature of the evidence makes it impossible to state with certainty when the former achieved its distinctive position at the head of the clerical staff. One factor that would appear to be relevant in this connection is the doubling of the fee due to the Entering Clerk on royal 'signatures' which occurred between 1684 and 1699.[68] It has already been suggested that it was about 1689 that a new arrangement was made for the division of the fees between the Under Secretaries. It is conceivable that this was part of a general reorganisation of the functions and

[64] *1st Rept. on Fees*, 20. [65] Evans, *Principal Secretary*, 193.
[66] Ibid. 161; SP 35/19 ff. 190–1. [67] Evans, *Principal Secretary*, 192. [68] See p. 3 n. 12.

remuneration of the Secretaries' officials. The opportunity may have been taken to discontinue the Entering Clerk's salary which had been a charge on the senior Under Secretary and to increase the fee due to him in compensation. At the same time the recipient of this increased fee may have been given enlarged responsibilities and authority over the more junior Clerks—a development which in the course of time gave rise to the adoption of the title 'First' or Chief Clerk.

One of the problems of drawing up lists of the early Chief Clerks arises from the fact that it was only from 1718 that the holders of these offices are regularly distinguished from their colleagues in lists of Secretaries' officials. Before this date identification must in many cases be tentative. However, some indication of their identity is to be found in an examination of the arrangements for keeping the accounts of the offices. It has already been noted that this was one of the principal functions of the Chief Clerks in the later eighteenth century. At that time they kept two separate sets of accounts: one of the office fees and the other of the receipts and disbursements of the Secretaries of State. According to the memorandum of 1684 the accounts of the fees were kept at that date by the Office Keeper in one office and by a Clerk in the other. No further information is available on this subject until the period of Vernon's secretaryship 1697–1702. The accounts of Vernon's receipts and expenditure as Secretary of State were kept throughout by Welby. It is clear that at this date this function was not necessarily combined with that of keeping accounts of the office fees. Welby was indeed responsible for keeping such accounts from 1697 to 1698 and again from 1699 to 1702 but between May 1698 and March 1699 this function was undertaken by A. Stanyan. In this connection it should be noted that in the earliest list which specifically mentions these officials Stanyan is designated Chief Clerk to Vernon.[69] This list was published in 1700 by which time Stanyan had left the office and it must, therefore, be used with caution. Nevertheless, it is unlikely that Stanyan would have been singled out in this way if he had not in fact occupied the office at some point. It is significant that the next list, published in 1701, names Welby as Vernon's Chief Clerk. In the other office Swinford appears as Chief Clerk both in 1700 (to Jersey) and in 1701 (to Hedges).[70] Swinford is known to have kept the accounts of the fees in Hedges' office. On the basis of this evidence it would appear that, by the time of the appointments of Vernon in 1697 and Jersey in 1699, the Chief Clerks had already acquired the distinctive function of keeping the accounts of the office fees.

Any attempt to distinguish earlier Chief Clerks must be highly speculative. One or two suggestions may, however, be made. In 1697 Bernard was receiving fees for Shrewsbury and it is possible that he was doing so as his Chief Clerk. Stanyan was in Trumbull's office in the same year. It is clear from the surviving accounts that he was not being paid a regular salary like Trumbull's other Clerks and the explanation for this may be that he was receiving his remuneration in the form of the fees due to the Chief Clerk. In 1694 Stanyan occurs first in a list of the Clerks in the office of Trenchard, Trumbull's predecessor as Secretary of State, which may mean that he served him as Chief Clerk as well. In the same list the Clerk occupying the corresponding

---

[69] Chamberlayne, *Present State* (1700), 502–3. Detailed references to the evidence for the careers of the Chief Clerks will be found in the Alphabetical List of Officials.

[70] Ibid.; Miège, *New State* (1701), pt. iii, 109. In 1701 Swinford's name is coupled with that of Charles (sic) Rowley. There is no other evidence that Rowley occupied this position or that the office of Chief Clerk was ever held jointly.

position in Nottingham's office is Yard.[71] Yard heads the list of Shrewsbury's Clerks in 1689 and may have entered Nottingham's service as Chief Clerk when the latter became sole Secretary in 1690, displacing Armstrong who is listed as Nottingham's most senior Clerk in the previous year.[72]

After 1700 the identity of the Chief Clerks can be established more securely. Although, as has been seen, it is not until 1718 that they are regularly distinguished from their colleagues, there seems no reason to doubt that the names which appear first on the lists of Clerks are those of the Chief Clerks. Where other evidence is available it supports this conclusion. Thus it seems clear that Armstrong served as Chief Clerk to Nottingham from 1702 to 1704. Harley appointed Jones, probably on succeeding Nottingham in the latter year. Jones served all succeeding Secretaries until his death in 1719. In the other office Swinford evidently served Hedges during both his secretaryships (1700–1; 1702–6), his tenure of office being interrupted while Manchester was Secretary in 1702. The latter apparently employed Lewis as Chief Clerk. Delafaye is named first in the list of Sunderland's Clerks in 1708 and may have been appointed Chief Clerk by him on his entry into office in 1706. Delafaye remained to serve the succeeding Secretary, Dartmouth, but left the office in 1713 on being appointed Private Secretary to the Lord Lieutenant of Ireland. The identity of the individual who served as Chief Clerk to Bromley, Dartmouth's successor, is unknown. The next Secretary, Stanhope, appointed Micklethwaite in 1714 and when Sunderland succeeded Stanhope in 1717 he replaced Micklethwaite by Wace who remained in office under all succeeding Secretaries until his death in 1745.

The details of the probable succession to the two chief clerkships have been given at some length in order to illustrate a significant change that occurred in the character of the offices during the early years of the eighteenth century. Of the first identifiable Chief Clerks several had a special personal relationship with the Secretaries whom they were serving and a tenure similar to that of the Under Secretaries. Thus Welby, who was Vernon's nephew, acted as Chief Clerk only during his uncle's secretaryship. Swinford, although apparently taken over by Hedges from Jersey, served only Hedges thereafter, leaving office with him both in 1701 and 1706. Armstrong, who was Nottingham's man of business, served only while his master was Secretary. Lewis had been in the service of Manchester while the latter had been Ambassador to France. A rather different case was that of A. Stanyan whose probable tenure of the office of Chief Clerk was punctuated by his appointment as Secretary to the Embassy to Venice (1697–8) and terminated by his appointment as Secretary to the Embassy to France (1699–1700). It is not difficult to see the disadvantages of this situation. With the two Under Secretaries on a precarious tenure the fact that the Chief Clerk was not normally a permanent official meant that there could be a serious loss of continuity on a change of Secretary. This was probably one of the considerations which led to the acceptance of the convention that the post should be filled from amongst the more senior of the Clerks serving in the offices and should be held on what amounted to a permanent tenure, unaffected by changes of Secretary. In one of the offices this convention was established during Jones's period of service (1704–19). In the other, the career of Delafaye, Chief Clerk 1706–13, appears to indicate the acceptance of the same convention. However, Stanhope, by selecting as his Chief Clerk Micklethwaite

[71] Chamberlayne, *Present State* (1694), 243. In fact this list must reflect the situation before Nottingham's resignation in Nov. 1693.
[72] Poll tax assessment July 1689 (LS 13/231 pp. 13–14).

who had been his Secretary when he was Ambassador to Spain, reverted to the older practice and it was only with the appointment of Wace, Chief Clerk 1717-45, that the new convention finally became established in this office.

CLERKS

By 1702 it had long been accepted that the Secretaries should employ a number of Clerks apart from the Under Secretaries and the Chief Clerks. In the absence of the relevant records it is impossible to give a complete account of these Clerks until the eighteenth century although a few documents do survive which enable some idea to be formed of their place in the structure of the offices in the earlier period. The memorandum on the state of Arlington's office in 1673 suggests that in this office at this date Arlington's two 'Secretaries', Bridgeman and Richards, were the only officials in his direct employment and that the Clerks, Yard, Ball and Swaddell, belonged rather to Williamson than to him. This inference is supported by the evidence of the rivalry which existed between the Secretaries and Clerks which is to be found in the letters written to Williamson whilst he was on a diplomatic mission to Cologne in 1673.[73] However, as already suggested, Williamson's position was unusual and it is doubtful whether the organisation of Arlington's office was typical. The memorandum on Middleton's office of 1684 is the next document to throw any light on the position of the Clerks. This memorandum has several characteristics in common with the description of Coke's office in 1628 which suggests that it is more representative of the normal state of affairs. In the list of Middleton's Clerks the names of Cooke and Wynne are followed by those of three Clerks, de Paz, Chute and Carne, who are stated to have received salaries 'at the rate of £40 or £50 per annum and Mr. Chute at £60'. In 1628 the Junior Clerks or 'Secretaries' in Coke's office had 'allowances the best 40 l., the others 20 l. or 30 l. per annum apiece at most'.[74] The distinguishing features of these Clerks were that they had no entitlement to official fees and that they received fixed salaries. It may be inferred from the document of 1684 that these salaries were paid directly by the Secretary of State. This was certainly the case for both offices in 1698[75] and continued to be so until the end of the period.

The right of appointing the Clerks belonged to the Secretaries as did that of dismissing them and fixing the level of their salaries. Before 1689 lack of evidence makes it difficult to say how far it was the practice for an incoming Secretary to take over his predecessor's Clerks. An examination of the careers of such Clerks as Benson, Tucker and Yard shows that this occasionally occurred earlier. The retention of Clerks was not, however, an automatic process at this period. In 1693 Trenchard dispensed with the services of Le Pin, who had spent eighteen years as a Clerk in the Secretaries' offices. In his petition for a retiring pension Le Pin makes it clear that his employment by Shrewsbury (1689) and Sydney (1690) had in each case involved the intervention of influential patrons.[76] However, within a few years of this there is an indication that the Clerks had succeeded in establishing themselves on a more or less permanent basis.

[73] Evans, *Principal Secretary*, 292.

[74] Ibid. 155. Miss Evans was of the view that the 'Secretaries' referred to in 1628 were the Secretaries for the Latin and French Tongues—officials appointed by the crown (ibid. 168). While there can be no certainty on the point, the context seems to make it more natural to suppose that the individuals in question were in the direct employment of the Secretary of State as 'Clerks'. Furthermore the salaries are smaller than those enjoyed by the Secretaries for the Latin and French Tongues.

[75] BM Add. MS 40785 f. 34.   [76] *CSPD 1693*, 255.

The accounts of Vernon's secretaryship cover two periods when the other office was left vacant for more than a quarter. On both occasions Vernon paid the salaries of some at least of the Clerks in that office as well as those in his own.[77]

From the beginning of Anne's reign it seems to have been accepted that an incoming Secretary would take over such of his predecessor's Clerks as wished to remain in the office. While dismissals were not unknown,[78] it is clear that, during the eighteenth century, the Secretaries' power was in practical terms limited to the making of new appointments.[79] In this respect the Secretaries' offices conformed to the general pattern which prevailed in the government service throughout the eighteenth century. There was a natural desire to retain the services of efficient Clerks in the interests of continuity. On the other hand the absence of any comprehensive system of retiring allowances made it a matter of humanity not to deprive the old or infirm of their means of livelihood. This approach to the problem is illustrated by Newcastle's statement 'There are some (Clerks) that are of very little use but being there I don't care to displace them'.[80]

Subject to these considerations the Secretaries were free to fix the number of their Clerks at whatever level they wished. In 1732 Newcastle summed up the situation by saying '. . . there is not any fixed Number of clerks in my office and as they are paid by me there are more or less as the business requires'.[81] During the period covered by these lists there were considerable variations in the number employed. As already noted there were three Clerks in Arlington's office in 1673 and in Middleton's in 1684. Trumbull (1695–7) employed four and Vernon (1697–1702) from four to five. During the first half of the eighteenth century the average number of Clerks in each office increased from five to six. Between 1750 and 1782 there were usually between seven and nine although there were occasionally more marked variations. The most significant of these occurred in the years immediately after 1766 when Shelburne's appointment of additional Clerks in connection with colonial business had the effect of increasing the number in one of the offices to thirteen. On the eve of the reorganisation of the secretariat in 1782 there were, apart from the Chief Clerks, seven Clerks in the Northern and nine in the Southern Department.

Little is known of the functions of the Clerks. The memoranda of 1673 and 1684 give some indication of their activities at these dates. There is, however, no evidence of any permanent arrangements for the distribution of work. Even as late as 1786 the Clerks in the Home and Foreign Offices had 'no particular branches of business assigned to them'.[82] Towards the end of the period the more senior Clerks came to be

[77] BM Add. MS 40785 ff. 34, 65–6.

[78] The following cases of dismissal are recorded: P. Roberts (1706), Shuckburgh (1761), Taylor (1774) and, possibly, Draper and the younger Payzant (1756). An earlier instance was that of Bernard (1697).

[79] There is no suggestion in Brietzcke's diary that a change of Secretary imperilled his position in the office. The diary records the entry into office of Bute in 1761, Grenville in 1762 and Halifax in 1764 (*Notes and Queries*, cc (1955), 162–3; ibid. cciv (1959), 283; ibid. ccv (1960), 391). See also Stormont's minute 6 Nov. 1779 (FO 95/591/1 f. 3).

[80] BM Add. MS 32687 f. 512. The elder Payzant, on his death in 1757 aged 100, was said to have served for 70 years in the Secretaries' offices (*Gent. Mag.* (1757), xxvii, 339).

[81] BM Add. MS 32687 f. 512.

[82] *1st Rept. on Fees*, 4. Some insight into the work of the Clerks in Harley's office may be obtained from the evidence given by Gregg in 1708 (*Lords Journals*, xviii, 516–19). Brietzcke's diary is valuable for the 1760s. For the regulations governing the attendance of Clerks in Richmond's office in 1766, see SP 104/242 pp. 28–9 and of those in Rochford's office in 1775, see BM Add. MS 45519 f. 43.

distinguished by the designation 'Senior Clerks'. In one office this was applied to two Clerks from 1763 and in the other to three from 1772. The origin of this distinction is unknown and there is no means of discovering whether it reflected any significant change in the organisation of business. Much of the Clerks' time was spent in copying letters and other documents although the more able were, in all probability, given greater responsibilities. In 1735 and 1736 one of the Clerks, the elder Payzant, was described as 'Translator'.[83] Obviously a knowledge of at least one foreign language was a useful accomplishment—a fact which no doubt explains the employment of a significant number of Clerks of Huguenot origin. However, the fact that special arrangements were made for the translation of German, Southern (Italian and Spanish) and Oriental languages suggests that the Clerks' knowledge rarely extended beyond French.[84]

There are indications that, in addition to the Clerks on the establishments of the offices, it was the practice to appoint supernumeraries. Delafaye began his career as an unsalaried 'Extraordinary' Clerk to Jersey and Vernon. In 1717 an application was made on behalf of a candidate that he might 'succeed Mr. Armestead or at least stand next . . . as a Clerk Extraordinary which I think has been of late practised'.[85] Similarly in 1732 the Earl of Carlisle asked Newcastle to admit a candidate 'as a Clerk in your office and if at present you have no room for him that you will allow him to attend as a supernumerary which I am told is frequently done'.[86] There are traces of this practice later in the century although in 1785 there were no supernumeraries in either the Home or Foreign Offices.[87] Occasionally Secretaries of State allowed certain individuals to spend some time in their offices on an unpaid basis in order to prepare themselves for a career in public life. This practice is illustrated by the career of Jenkinson who served in Holdernesse's office on this basis. In 1785 there was a person in the Home Office who 'has no salary, but attends the office merely to obtain a knowledge of the management of public business'.[88]

PRIVATE SECRETARIES

Something should be said at this point about Private Secretaries. In the establishments of the Home, Foreign and War Offices drawn up in 1795 provision was made for salaried Private Secretaries to the Secretaries of State.[89] Before 1782, however, the arrangements in this respect lacked definition and appear to have varied widely. In all probability most Secretaries of State employed some kind of Private Secretary in addition to their Under Secretaries. The nature of the evidence is such that these individuals can only rarely be identified and it is impossible to draw up satisfactory lists

---

[83] Chamberlayne, *Present State* (1735), pt. ii, 43; ibid. (1736), pt. ii, 47. On Payzant's death in 1757 he was succeeded by Jouvencel as 'Translator of modern languages in the secretary of state's office for the southern department' (*Gent. Mag.* (1757), xxvii, 482). No other trace of this office has been found.
[84] For the question of the teaching of modern languages as a preparation for the public service at this date, see D. B. Horn, *The British Diplomatic Service 1689–1789* (Oxford 1961), 131–2; C. H. Firth, *Modern Languages at Oxford 1724–1929* (Oxford 1929), 1–19; see also Burnaby's representations to Newcastle in 1734 (BM Add. MSS 32689 f. 288, 33057 ff. 49–50).
[85] SP 35/10 f. 16.   [86] BM Add. MS 32687 f. 497.
[87] *1st Rept. on Fees*, 21, 28. 'Extra' Clerks were employed on a temporary basis to deal with exceptional business such as that arising at the beginning of a new reign (*Notes and Queries*, cxcix (1954), 297–9). Pollock stated that he had been employed as an Extra Clerk 1757–8 (*1st Rept. on Fees*, 19).
[88] *1st Rept. on Fees*, 19.   [89] *16th Rept. on Finance*, 311.

for the period. Some Secretaries of State selected their Private Secretaries from amongst the Clerks already on the establishment of their offices.[90] Others brought their Private Secretaries from outside. As early as 1688 Preston brought Tempest with him to attend to his 'private affairs in the office'.[91] Balaguier's position in Carteret's office 1721–4 appears to have been that of Private Secretary. However, the only Private Secretaries whose appointments were publicly acknowledged in the sense that they were notified to the Post Office were Blair, Private Secretary to Harrington (1730 and 1742) and Cosby, Private Secretary to Halifax (1762).[92] The standing and importance of the Private Secretaries varied greatly. Balaguier acted as Carteret's Under Secretary when he accompanied the King to Hanover in 1723 and when Blair accompanied Harrington there during his periods of office he was always ranked between the Under Secretaries and the Chief Clerk. H. V. Jones was similarly ranked in 1748 and 1750 when he was acting in fact, if not in name, as Private Secretary to Newcastle.[93] These are isolated cases, however, and the Private Secretary's position appears usually to have been more humble.

SUBORDINATE OFFICIALS

In 1702 the personnel of each office was completed by two Chamber or Office Keepers and one Cleaner or Necessary Woman. The employment of some kind of Office Keeper was probably as old as the Secretaries' offices themselves. In 1684 'the Office Keeper' was amongst those entitled to official fees. Before the end of the seventeenth century the number of Office Keepers employed appears to have varied. By 1698 it was fixed at two for each office who received, in addition to their fees, salaries from the Secretaries of State. A Cleaner is first mentioned in Trumbull's office in 1695. From 1698 it was the rule for there to be one salaried Office Cleaner or, as she was more commonly designated in the later eighteenth century, 'Necessary Woman', in each office. Office Keepers sometimes executed their duties by deputy.

RELATIONSHIP OF OFFICIALS TO THE SECRETARIES OF STATE

Throughout the period the attachment of the staff at all levels was to the Secretaries of State rather than to the departments in which they were serving. It was the general rule for a newly appointed Secretary to take over the officials who had served his predecessor and to take his staff with him if he subsequently moved from one department to the other. But there were exceptions to this convention. When Vernon moved from the Northern to the Southern Department in 1700 he retained one of his Under Secretaries, Hopkins, and replaced the other, Ellis, by Yard who had served as Under Secretary to Jersey, the last Secretary in the Southern Department. Ellis was appointed an Under Secretary by Hedges, the incoming Secretary for the Northern Department. As far as the Clerks were concerned, Vernon took two, Jones and de Lacombe de Vrigny, with him, left three, Payzant, Vanbrugh and Roberts, in the

[90] Amongst Clerks who acted as Private Secretaries were Higden (to Rochford), Jones (to Newcastle), Jouvencel (to Grafton) and Kluft (to Bute).
[91] *Ellis Corr.*, ii, 287.
[92] SP 44/122 p. 457: SP 44/129 p. 369; *CHOP 1760–5*, 202.
[93] T 52/44 pp. 372, 386, 502; T 52/45 pp. 162, 324.

Northern Department, and took on three, Egar, Tilson and Weston, who had served Jersey in the Southern Department. Finally Vernon left to Hedges the Office Keepers, Smith and Ramsey, who had served him in the Northern Department and took on Shorter and Turner, who had previously been employed in the Southern Department. However, when Vernon returned to the Northern Department in 1702, he took his entire staff with him. For the next three instances in which a Secretary was transferred from one department to the other during his term of office information is scarce but it appears that, as a rule, the Secretary took his officials with him.[94] There were no further transfers until 1748 when Newcastle, on moving from the Southern to the Northern Department, took all his staff with him. With one exception, Wallace, the Clerks and subordinate staff who had served Chesterfield, the previous Secretary for the Northern Department, moved to the Southern Department. Wallace was, however, retained by Newcastle in his old department. Perhaps the greatest change to take place in the personnel of a Secretary's office occurred in 1754 when Holdernesse moved from the Southern to the Northern Department. Holdernesse brought one of his Under Secretaries, Potenger, with him to replace Amyand who was transferred to the Southern Department. He also brought with him two Clerks, F. Wace and Fraser, who had served him in the Southern Department. Otherwise the personnel of the two departments was unaffected by the transfer. Halifax took his whole staff with him on being transferred from the Northern to the Southern Department in 1763. In 1766, Seymour Conway, on being transferred from the Southern to the Northern Department took all his staff with him with the exception of two Assistant Under Secretaries, P. M. Morin and Roberts, and two Clerks, Brietzcke and J. Morin, who remained to serve Richmond, the incoming Southern Secretary. In addition Seymour Conway retained one Clerk, Jouvencel, who had served Grafton, the previous Secretary for the Northern Department. In 1768 Weymouth, on moving from the Northern to the Southern Department, took all his officials with him. In 1770 Rochford did the same in similar circumstances for all his staff except the Office Keepers and the Necessary Woman.

There are a few examples of officials changing departments in other circumstances. In 1724 Delafaye, Under Secretary to Townshend in the Northern Department, was transferred to the Southern Department as Under Secretary to Newcastle. In the following year one of Townshend's Clerks, Couraud, was also transferred to Newcastle's service. In 1746 Newcastle selected as his Chief Clerk the elder Larpent who was serving not in his own office but in that of his colleague, Harrington. In 1775, on the appointment of Weymouth as Secretary of State for the South, the two Chief Clerks, Sneyd and Shadwell, exchanged places as did the Office Keepers and Necessary Women.

OFFICIALS OF THE SCOTTISH AND COLONIAL DEPARTMENTS

The pattern of organisation which evolved for the two older offices naturally influenced the arrangements made when the Scottish and Colonial Departments were created in 1709 and 1768. Little is known of the officials of the Scottish Secretaries except for

---

[94] The transfers in question were those of Hedges (1704), Bolingbroke (1713) and Stanhope (1716). However, in 1704 Delafaye, instead of being taken on by Harley with the rest of Nottingham's Clerks, appears to have remained in the Southern Department to serve Hedges on his transfer there.

Tweeddale's period of office. Queensberry (1709–11) employed two Under Secretaries, a Chief Clerk, two other Clerks and an Office Keeper. Mar (1713–14) appears to have appointed only one Under Secretary, and in this seems to have been followed by his successors. Tweeddale (1742–6) employed one Under Secretary, a Chief Clerk, one other Clerk, an Office Keeper and a Necessary Woman. In the Colonial Department only one Under Secretary was at first appointed, presumably because the fees in the department were insufficient to provide remuneration for another. In 1770, however, when salaries were made available by the crown for two Under Secretaries in each department, a second was appointed. In other respects the structure of the department conformed closely to that of the Northern and Southern offices. Successive Secretaries employed two Under Secretaries, a Chief Clerk, two Senior Clerks, between four and five other Clerks, an Office Keeper and a Necessary Woman. In general there was little interchange of personnel between the office of the third Secretary and those of the two older Secretaries. There were, however, a few cases where this occurred.[95]

OTHER OFFICIALS OF THE SECRETARIAT

Throughout the period covered by these lists there were in existence a number of offices whose holders, while not under the immediate direction of the Secretaries of State, were in varying degrees subject to their general authority. Of these the Keeper of State Papers, the Clerks of the Signet, the Secretaries for the Latin and French Tongues and the Embellisher of Letters originated before the Restoration. The rest, comprising the Gazette Writer (1665), the Decipherers (1701), the Interpreter of Oriental Languages (1723), the Collector of State Papers (1725), the Translator of the German Language (1735), the Law Clerk (1743), the Translator of Southern Languages (1755) and the Methodisers of State Papers (1764) were instituted subsequently. All these officials were common to the secretariat as a whole. The offices of Secretary for the French Tongue, Law Clerk and Translator of Southern Languages had been discontinued by 1782. For the remainder the reorganisation of that year had no special significance and they continued to exist largely unchanged. Details of these offices will be found in the introductory notes to the lists of appointments. In the interests of continuity their holders have been included in the lists down to their abolition in the nineteenth century.[96]

[95] T. Stanyan, the first Chief Clerk in the Scottish Department, was transferred from one of the older offices to which he later returned as Under Secretary. Kineir, originally appointed to one of the older offices, later served in the Scottish Department. The staff of the Colonial Department included three individuals with previous experience in the older offices: Phelps (Under Secretary), Pollock (Chief Clerk) and the younger Larpent (Senior Clerk). On the suppression of the department in 1782 three of its Clerks, Pollock, Wilmot and Palman and its Deputy Office Keeper, Crowder, were absorbed into the Home Office. Another former Clerk, Peace, eventually became its Librarian.

[96] The Messengers of the Chamber or King's Messengers are not included in these lists. Technically they formed part of the Royal Household under the authority of the Lord Chamberlain. During the 18th century, and especially after 1772, they passed increasingly under the control of the Secretaries of State. For some account of these officials, see A. V. Wheeler-Holohan, *The History of the King's Messengers* (London 1935); *1st Rept. on Fees*, 8–9, 35–7.

Secretaries of State 1660-1782

The Secretaries of State were appointed by the crown. They entered office on receiving the seals from the Sovereign and, as soon as was convenient, took the required oath at a meeting of the Privy Council. In due course their appointments were embodied in letters patent under the great seal which granted the offices during pleasure. The patents conferred the offices in similar terms on all their holders. The assignment of particular areas of responsibility and any subsequent transfer from one department to another were matters for informal communication from the crown.[1] The authority of the Secretaries lasted until such time as they delivered up the seals.

The remuneration attached to the offices was derived from a number of different sources.[2] From 1660 each Secretary enjoyed a patent salary of £100 payable at the Exchequer. This salary was granted for life until the appointment of Trevor in 1668 and thereafter, like the offices themselves, during pleasure. From 1660 each Secretary also received an additional salary of £1850.[3] There were two further types of allowance which at first varied with the responsibilities of particular Secretaries. One of these was a payment at the Exchequer for secret service. The amounts were fixed from 1675 at £3000 for the Secretary who had charge of the Southern Department, who was normally the senior Secretary in length of service, and £2000 for the Secretary responsible for the Northern Department.[4] This remained the case until the appointment of Sunderland in 1706 after which the secret service allowance was £3000 for all Secretaries.[5] The other type of allowance was the board wages payable by the Cofferer of the Household. From 1689 the allowance was fixed at £730 for the Secretary for the Southern Department and £292 for the Secretary for the Northern Department. This remained the case until the establishment of the third office in 1709 when the board wages of all Secretaries were fixed at £730.[6] Thus from 1709 until the end of the period the total fixed allowances for all Secretaries amounted to £5680 a year. Secretaries were also entitled to 1000 ounces of white plate from the Jewel Office on entering office.

In addition to their fixed allowances the Secretaries enjoyed certain perquisites which yielded variable amounts. These included the profits of the *London Gazette* which were divided equally from 1672, fees from the Signet Office and fees arising on instruments passing through their own offices. From 1699 the product of the latter

[1] For the principles governing the distribution of functions between the Secretaries, see pp. 1-2.

[2] For the remuneration of the Secretaries generally, see F. M. G. Evans (Mrs C. S. S. Higham), 'The Emoluments of the Principal Secretaries of State in the 17th Century', *Eng. Hist. Rev.*, xxxv (1920), 513-28; Thomson, *Secretaries of State*, 145-7.

[3] This additional salary was a charge on the farm of the Post Office 1660-8, on the farm of the customs on unwrought wood 1668-74, on the customs in general 1674-99 and on the Exchequer from 1699 (Evans, *Principal Secretary*, 212-13; *CTB*, xiv, 412).

[4] Both Jersey (1699-1700) and Manchester (1702) received the larger allowance as Secretaries for the Southern Department although they were junior to Vernon (1697-1702) in length of service.

[5] *CTB*, xxi, 132, 169.

[6] Warrants to Cofferer 3 and 12 Feb. 1709 (BM Loan 29/45A f. 4/121).

was equally divided between the two Secretaries. The question how far the third Secretary was entitled to a share in these fees was the subject of considerable dispute. Queensberry seems to have been successful in establishing that all the fees should be placed in a common pool and divided equally between the three Secretaries. Subsequent holders of the third office, whether their responsibilities covered Scotland or the Colonies, received only those fees which arose in connection with the work of their own department.[7]

In the following lists the appointments of Secretaries for the Northern and Southern Departments have been grouped together into a single chronological list; those of Secretaries for Scotland and the Colonies have been grouped in separate lists. In the case of Secretaries for the Northern and Southern Departments the letters (N) or (S) have been placed after their names to indicate the department with which they were first entrusted. Subsequent transfers to another department and instances in which a Secretary acted alone for more than a month have been noted.[8] The date of appointment given is, where possible, that on which the seals were received. Before 1700 this date cannot be established precisely except in a few cases. Thereafter it can usually be ascertained from the salary warrants. Where evidence about the reception of the seals is either lacking or unsatisfactory, the date on which the oath was taken in the Privy Council has been adopted.

LISTS OF APPOINTMENTS

Northern and Southern Departments

1659	27 Feb.	Nicholas, Sir E. (S)	1681	2 Feb.	Conway, Earl of (N)
1660	27 May	Morrice, Sir W. (N)	1683	28 Jan.	Sunderland, 2nd Earl of (N)[12]
1662	15 Oct.	Bennet, Sir H. (S)	1684	17 April	Godolphin, S. (N)
1668	29 Sept.	Trevor, Sir J. (N)	1684	24 Aug.	Middleton, Earl of (N)[13]
1672	3 July	Coventry, Hon. H. (N)[9]	1688	29 Oct.	Preston, Viscount (N)
1674	11 Sept.	Williamson, Sir J. (N)	1689	19 Feb.	Shrewsbury, Earl of (S)
1679	10 Feb.	Sunderland, 2nd Earl of (N)[10]	1689	5 March	Nottingham, Earl of (N)[14]
1680	26 April	Jenkins, Sir L. (N)[11]			

[7] Thomson, *Secretaries of State*, 31–2, 164–6; Spector, *American Department*, 52–5.

[8] For the purpose of the lists the authorities used for the allocation of duties between the Secretaries are Evans, *Principal Secretary*, 349–51; Thomson, *Secretaries of State*, 180–5; *Handbook of British Chronology*, 2nd ed., ed. F. M. Powicke and E. B. Fryde (London 1961), 110–15. The proposed appointment of Granville in Feb. 1746 has been ignored since the formalities attending his entry into office were not completed.

[9] Transferred to Southern Department Sept. 1674.

[10] Transferred to Southern Department April 1680.

[11] Transferred to Southern Department Feb. 1681.

[12] Transferred to Southern Department April 1684.

[13] Transferred to Southern Department Oct. 1688.

[14] Sole Secretary June–Dec. 1690; Secretary for Southern Department Dec. 1690–March 1692; Sole Secretary March 1692–March 1693; Secretary for Southern Department March–Nov. 1693.

1690	26 Dec.	Sydney, Viscount (N)		1721	6 Feb.	Townshend, Viscount (N)
1693	23 March	Trenchard, Sir J. (N)[15]		1721	4 March	Carteret, Lord (S)
				1723	29 May	Walpole, R.[22]
1694	2 March	Shrewsbury, Earl of (N)[16]		1724	4 April	Newcastle, Duke of (S)[23]
1695	3 May	Trumbull, Sir W. (N)		1730	16 May	Harrington, Lord (N)
1697	2 Dec.	Vernon, J. (N)[17]		1742	12 Feb.	Carteret, Lord (N)
1699	13 May	Jersey, Earl of (S)		1744	24 Nov.	Harrington, Earl of (N)
1700	5 Nov.	Hedges, Sir C. (N)				
1702	3 Jan.	Manchester, Earl of (S)		1746	19 Oct.	Chesterfield, Earl of (N)
1702	2 May	Nottingham, Earl of (S)		1748	13 Feb.	Bedford, Duke of (S)
1702	2 May	Hedges, Sir C. (N)[18]		1751	21 June	Holdernesse, Earl of (S)[24]
1704	16 May	Harley, R. (N)				
1706	3 Dec.	Sunderland, 3rd Earl of (S)		1754	24 March	Robinson, Sir T. (S)
				1755	14 Nov.	Fox, H. (S)
1708	13 Feb.	Boyle, Hon. H. (N)		1756	6 Dec.	Pitt, W. (S)
1710	14 June	Dartmouth, Lord (S)		1761	25 March	Bute, Earl of (N)
				1761	9 Oct.	Egremont, Earl of (S)
1710	21 Sept.	St. John, Hon. H. (N)[19]		1762	5 June	Grenville, Hon. G. (N)
1713	17 Aug.	Bromley, W. (N)				
1714	17 Sept.	Townshend, Viscount (N)		1762	14 Oct.	Halifax, Earl of (N)[25]
1714	22 Sept.	Stanhope, J. (S)[20]		1763	9 Sept.	Sandwich, Earl of (N)
1716	21 June	Methuen, P. (S)[21]				
1717	12 April	Sunderland, 3rd Earl of (N)		1765	10 July	Seymour Conway, Hon. H. (S)[26]
1717	12 April	Addison, J. (S)		1765	11 July	Grafton, Duke of (N)
1718	15 March	Craggs, J. (S)				
1718	19 March	Stanhope, Viscount (N)		1766	23 May	Richmond, Duke of (S)

[15] Sole Secretary Nov. 1693–March 1694; Secretary for Southern Department March 1694.

[16] Transferred to Southern Department April 1695.

[17] Sole Secretary Dec. 1698–May 1699; Secretary for Northern Department May 1699–June 1700; Sole Secretary June–Nov. 1700; Secretary for Southern Department Nov. 1700–Dec. 1701; transferred to Northern Department Jan. 1702.

[18] Transferred to Southern Department May 1704.

[19] Transferred to Southern Department Aug. 1713.

[20] Transferred to Northern Department Dec. 1716.

[21] App. temporary Secretary for Southern Department in absence of Stanhope; assumed full responsibility for Southern Department Dec. 1716 on Stanhope's transfer to Northern Department.

[22] Temporary Secretary for both departments in absence of Townshend and Carteret.

[23] Transferred to Northern Department Feb. 1748.

[24] Transferred to Northern Department March 1754.

[25] Transferred to Southern Department Aug. 1763.

[26] Transferred to Northern Department May 1766.

1766	30 July	Shelburne, Earl of (S)	1771	22 Jan.	Halifax, Earl of (N)
1768	20 Jan.	Weymouth, Viscount (N)[27]	1771	12 June	Suffolk, Earl of (N)
			1775	10 Nov.	Weymouth, Viscount (S)[29]
1768	21 Oct.	Rochford, Earl of (N)[28]	1779	27 Oct.	Stormont, Viscount (N)
1770	19 Dec.	Sandwich, Earl of (N)	1779	25 Nov.	Hillsborough, Earl of (S)

Scottish Department

1709	3 Feb.	Queensberry, Duke of	1716	13 Dec.	Roxburghe, Duke of
1713	9 Sept.	Mar, Earl of	1742	25 Feb.	Tweeddale, Marquess of
1714	24 Sept.	Montrose, Duke of			

Colonial Department

1768	21 Jan.	Hillsborough, Earl of	1775	10 Nov.	Germain, Lord G.
1772	15 Aug.	Dartmouth, Earl of	1782	11 Feb.	Ellis, W.

[27] Transferred to Southern Department Oct. 1768.
[28] Transferred to Southern Department Dec. 1770.
[29] Sole Secretary March–Oct. 1779.

Under Secretaries and
Assistant Under Secretaries 1660-1782

Although it occurs as early as 1672 and passed increasingly into current use thereafter, it was only towards the end of the period covered by these lists that the title 'Under Secretary' finally superseded other designations.[1] The offices which it denoted were those filled by the principal subordinates of the Secretaries of State. At the Restoration each Secretary appears to have followed earlier practice in appointing a single individual, ranking above his other officials, to whom he entrusted the running of his department. However, before the end of the reign of Charles II, it had become customary for this principal subordinate to have a colleague of comparable standing and from at least 1689 it was the convention for there to be two Under Secretaries of equal standing in each of the older offices. This convention was only varied between 1759 and 1768 when it was the practice in one of these offices for the Secretary of State to appoint one Under Secretary and two or three Assistant Under Secretaries instead of two Under Secretaries. With the exception of Bute (1761–2) who appointed two Under Secretaries, this practice was observed between 1759 and 1763 by the successive Secretaries for the Northern Department, Holdernesse, Grenville and Halifax. After 1763, when Halifax was transferred to the Southern Department, Secretaries for the Northern Department reverted to the older convention of appointing two Under Secretaries. As Secretary for the Southern Department Halifax retained the Under Secretary and two Assistant Under Secretaries who had served him in the Northern and appointed another full Under Secretary with specific responsibility for American affairs. Halifax's successors in the Southern Department, Seymour Conway and Richmond, each appointed an Under Secretary and two Assistant Under Secretaries. Shelburne, shortly after succeeding Richmond in 1766, replaced one of his Assistant Under Secretaries by two Assistant Under Secretaries with specific responsibilities for American affairs. Until 1768 he was thus served by one Under Secretary and three Assistant Under Secretaries. In July of that year he reverted to the older convention of appointing two Under Secretaries and was followed in this by succeeding Secretaries for the Southern Department.

Queensberry, the first Secretary of State for the Scottish Department, appointed two Under Secretaries in 1709; his successors, however, employed only one. In the Colonial Department one Under Secretary was at first appointed in 1768; a second was added in 1770.

The remuneration attached to these offices was derived mainly from official fees. Until 1689 these fees appear to have been enjoyed by the Secretary of State's principal subordinate alone while his colleague received a fixed salary. From about this year it was the practice for the two Under Secretaries in each office to divide the product of the fees equally between them. The effect of the agreement of 1699 to divide the fees between the two offices appears to have been to make the receipts of all four Under Secretaries equal. From at least 1702 each of the Under Secretaries in the older offices

---

[1] For a discussion of the origin and development of these offices, see pp. 7–12.

received £50 a year from the Irish concordatum fund.[2] In 1770 salaries of £500 were made available by the crown for two Under Secretaries in each of the three offices.[3] The Assistant Under Secretaries received their remuneration either in the form of equal shares in the product of one of the Under Secretaries' fees or of a salary from the Secretary of State.[4]

While there is no evidence on the point, it is likely that the Under Secretaries in the Scottish Department received fees like their colleagues in the older departments. In the Colonial Department Phelps (1768) and his successor, Pownall (1768–76), received all the Under Secretaries' fees, the Secretary of State making up the deficiency in the event of the product amounting to less than £452 11s. Knox, appointed in 1770, at first received only his salary of £500 from the crown. When Pownall left office in 1776 a new arrangement was made according to which the two Under Secretaries, in addition to their salaries from the crown, shared equally in the fees, the Secretary of State making up the deficiency in the event of the product amounting to less than £250 each.[5]

LISTS OF APPOINTMENTS

NORTHERN AND SOUTHERN DEPARTMENTS

Nicholas	1660–2	1660	May	Whittaker, C.
		1660	July	Williamson, J.
Morrice	1660–8	1660	May	Cooke, J.
Bennet/	1662–74	1662	Oct.	Williamson, J.
Arlington		1662	Oct.	Godolphin, W.
		c. 1667		Bridgeman, W.[6]
				(? v. Godolphin)
		By 1673		Richards, J.[6]
Trevor	1668–72	1668	Sept.	Cooke, J.
Coventry	1672–80	1672	July	Cooke, J.
		1672	July	Thynne, H. F.
Williamson	1674–9	1674	Sept.	Bridgeman, W.
		1674	Sept.	Brisbane, J.
		(?) 1676	Sept.	Warre, R.
				(v. Brisbane)
Sunderland	1679–81	1679	Feb.	Bridgeman, W.
		1679	Feb.	Mountsteven, J.
Jenkins	1680–4	1680	April	Cooke, J.
		1680	April	Wynne, O.
Conway	1681–3	1681	Feb.	Gwyn, F.
		1681	Feb.	Blathwayt, W.

[2] BM Add. MS 28889 ff. 158, 179, 183; *1st Rept. on Fees*, 19, 27. These payments were probably related to the allowance of £100 formerly paid to the Under Secretary who acted as Agent for the Irish government (Hist. MSS Comm. *Ormonde*, vi, 40).

[3] Royal warrant 12 July 1770 (T 52/60 p. 463) effective from 1 Jan. 1770. These salaries were paid by the Treasurer of the Chamber until 1782; in that year they were transferred to the Exchequer (T 52/64 pp. 452–3).

[4] *Notes and Queries*, cxcix (1954), 208; ibid. cciv (1959), 284, 413; SP 45/31.

[5] SP 45/32; Spector, *American Department*, 50–1.

[6] The standing of Bridgeman and Richards relative to that of Williamson in Arlington's office is obscure.

Sunderland	1683–8	1683	Jan.	Bridgeman, W.
		1683	Jan.	Mountsteven, J.
Godolphin	1684	1684	April	Cooke, J.
		1684	April	Wynne, O.
Middleton	1684–8	1684	Aug.	Cooke, J.
		1684	Aug.	Wynne, O.
		1688	Nov.	Bridgeman, W. (v. Cooke)
Preston	1688	1688	Nov.	Graham, F.
		1688	Nov.	Warre, R.
Shrewsbury	1689–90	1689	Feb.	Wynne, O.
		1689	Feb.	Vernon, J.
		1689	Sept.	Pulteney, J. (v. Wynne)
Nottingham	1689–93	1689	March	Finch, Hon. E.
		1689	March	Warre, R.
		1693	April	Isham, J. (v. Finch)
Sydney	1690–2	1690	Dec.	Bridgeman, W.
		1690	Dec.	Pulteney, J.
Trenchard	1693–5	1693	March	Bridgeman, W.
		1693	March	Vernon, J.
		1694	April	Hopkins, T. (v. Vernon)
		1694	July	Tucker, J. (v. Bridgeman)
Shrewsbury	1694–8	1694	March	Vernon, J.[7]
		1694	March	Yard, R.
Trumbull	1695–7	1695	May	Tucker, J.
		1695	May	Ellis, J.
Vernon	1697–1702	1697	Dec.	Hopkins, T.
		1697	Dec.	Ellis, J.
		1700	Nov.	Yard, R. (v. Ellis)
Jersey	1699–1700	1699	May	Yard, R.
		1699	May	Prior, M.
Hedges	1700–1	1700	Nov.	Tucker, J.
		1700	Nov.	Ellis, J.
Manchester	1702	1702	Jan.	Ellis, J.
		1702	Jan.	Stanyan, A.
Nottingham	1702–4	1702	May	Warre, R.
		1702	May	Aglionby, W.
		1703	Oct.	Isham, J. (v. Aglionby)[8]
Hedges	1702–6	1702	May	Tucker, J.

[7] On Vernon's promotion to the secretaryship in Dec. 1697 his former position as Under Secretary to Shrewsbury appears to have been left vacant.

[8] The office formerly held by Aglionby remained vacant between Aug. 1702 and Oct. 1703.

Hedges	1702–6	1702	May	Ellis, J.
		1705	July	Addison, J. (v. Ellis)
Harley	1704–8	1704	May	Warre, R.
		1704	May	Lewis, E.
Sunderland	1706–10	1706	Dec.	Hopkins, T.
		1706	Dec.	Addison, J.
		1709	Jan.	Pringle, R. (v. Addison)
Boyle	1708–10	1708	Feb.	Walpole, H.
		1708	Feb.	Tilson, G.
Dartmouth	1710–13	1710	June	Warre, R.
		1710	June	Lewis, E.
St. John/ Bolingbroke	1710–14	1710	Sept.	Tilson, G.
		1710	Sept.	Hare, T.
Bromley	1713–14	1713	Aug.	Lewis, E.
		1713	Aug.	Stawell, Hon. E.
		(?) 1714		Holt, C. (v. Stawell)
Townshend	1714–16	1714	Sept.	Walpole, H.
		1714	Sept.	Tilson, G.
		1715	Oct.	Stanyan, T. (v. Walpole)
Stanhope	1714–17	1714	Sept.	Pringle, R.
		1714	Sept.	Stanhope, C.
Methuen[9]	1716–17	1716	Dec.	Tilson, G.
		(?) 1716	Dec.	Stanyan, T.
Sunderland	1717–18	1717	April	Tilson, G.
		1717	April	Delafaye, C.
Addison	1717–18	1717	April	Stanyan, T.
		1717	April	Tickell, T.
Stanhope	1718–21	1718	March	Tilson, G.
		1718	March	Delafaye, C.
Craggs	1718–21	1718	March	Stanyan, T.
		1718	March	Tickell, T.
Townshend	1721–30	1721	Feb.	Tilson, G.
		1721	Feb.	Delafaye, C.
		1724	April	Townshend, Hon. T. (v. Delafaye)
		1729	Sept.	Weston, E. (v. Townshend)
Carteret	1721–4	1721	March	Stanyan, T.
		1721	March	Tickell, T.
Walpole	1723			*No appointments traced*[10]

[9] As acting Secretary for the Southern Department from June to Dec. 1716 Methuen appears to have been served by Stanhope's Under Secretaries.

[10] As acting Secretary for both departments from May to Dec. 1723 Walpole appears to have been served by Townshend's and Carteret's Under Secretaries.

Newcastle	1724–54	1724	April	Stanyan, T.
		1724	April	Delafaye, C.
		1729	June	Couraud, J. (v. Stanyan)
		1734	July	Stone, A. (v. Delafaye)
		1743		Ramsden, T. (v. Couraud)
		1750	April	Amyand, C. (v. Ramsden)
		1751	April	Jones, H. V. (v. Stone)
		1751	June	Wallace, J. (v. Amyand)
Harrington	1730–42	1730	May	Tilson, G.
		1730	May	Weston, E.
		1739	May	Stanhope, Hon. T. (v. Tilson)
		1741	Nov.	Burnaby, J. (v. Stanhope)
Carteret/ Granville	1742–4	1742	Feb.	Weston, E.
		1742	Feb.	Balaguier, J. A.
Harrington	1744–6	1744	Nov.	Weston, E.
		1744	Nov.	Chetwynd, W. R.
Chesterfield	1746–8	1746	Oct.	Chetwynd, W. R.
		1746	Oct.	Potter, J.
Bedford	1748–51	1748	Feb.	Chetwynd, W. R.
		1748	Feb.	Potter, J.
		1748	April	Aldworth, R. N. (v. Chetwynd)
		1749	June	Leveson Gower, Hon. R. (v. Potter)
Holdernesse	1751–61	1751	June	Amyand, C.
		1751	June	Potenger, R.
		1754	March	Wallace, J. (v. Amyand)
		1759		Morin, P. M. (*Assistant*)[11]
		1759		Fraser, W. (*Assistant*)[11]
Robinson	1754–5	1754	March	Amyand, C.
		1754	March	Rivers, J.
Fox	1755–6	1755	Nov.	Amyand, C.
		1755	Nov.	Digby, H.
Pitt	1756–61	1756	Dec.	Wood, R.
		1756	Dec.	Rivers, J.
Bute	1761–2	1761	March	Weston, E.
		1761	March	Jenkinson, C.

[11] Morin and Fraser jointly filled the place left vacant by Wallace.

Egremont	1761–3	1761	Oct.	Wood, R.
		1761	Oct.	Rivers, J.
Grenville	1762	1762	June	Weston, E.
		1762	June	Morin, P. M. (*Assistant*)
		1762	June	Lloyd, C. (*Assistant*)
Halifax	1762–5	1762	Oct.	Weston, E.
		1762	Oct.	Morin, P. M. (*Assistant*)
		1762	Oct.	Lloyd, C. (*Assistant*)
		1763	Sept.	Sedgwick, E.[12]
		1764	May	Stanhope, L. (v. Weston)
Sandwich	1763–5	1763	Sept.	Phelps, R.
		1763	Sept.	Rivers, J.
Seymour Conway	1765–8	1765	July	Burke, W.
		1765	July	Morin, P. M. (*Assistant*)
		1765	July	Roberts, J. C. (*Assistant*)
		1766	May	Fraser, W.[13]
		1767	Feb.	Hume, D. (v. Burke)
Grafton	1765–6	1765	July	Stanhope, L.
		1765	July	Stonehewer, R.
		1765	July	Fraser, W. (v. Stanhope)
Richmond	1766	1766	May	Stonehewer, R.
		1766	May	Morin, P. M. (*Assistant*)
		1766	May	Roberts, J. C. (*Assistant*)
Shelburne	1766–8	1766	July	Sutton, R.
		1766	July	Morin, P. M. (*Assistant*)
		1766	July	Roberts, J. C. (*Assistant*)
		1766	Aug.	Macleane, L. (*Assistant*)[14]
		1766	Aug.	Morgann, M. (*Assistant*)[14]
		1768	July	Porten, S.[15]
Weymouth	1768–70	1768	Jan.	Wood, R.
		1768	Jan.	Fraser, W.
Rochford	1768–75	1768	Oct.	Sutton, R.
		1768	Oct.	Porten, S.
		1772	Oct.	Willes, F. (v. Sutton)
Sandwich	1770–1	1770	Dec.	Phelps, R.
		1770	Dec.	Fraser, W.
Halifax	1771	1771	Jan.	Sedgwick, E.
		1771	Jan.	Stanhope, L.

[12] Appointed Under Secretary for American affairs.

[13] On his transfer from the Southern to the Northern Department Seymour Conway appointed Fraser Under Secretary in place of his former Assistant Under Secretaries, Morin and Roberts, who remained in the Southern Department to serve Richmond, the incoming Secretary.

[14] Macleane and Morgann, who had special responsibilities for American affairs, jointly filled the position formerly held by Roberts.

[15] Appointed in place of Shelburne's three former Assistant Under Secretaries, Morin, Macleane and Morgann.

Halifax	1771	1771	March	Fraser, W. (v. Stanhope)
Suffolk	1771–9	1771	June	Whately, T.
		1771	June	Fraser, W.
		1772	June	Eden, W. (v. Whately)
		1778	Oct.	Oakes, R. (v. Eden)
Weymouth	1775–9	1775	Nov.	Chamier, A.
		1775	Nov.	Porten, Sir S.
Stormont	1779–82	1779	Oct.	Langlois, B.
		1779	Oct.	Fraser, W.
Hillsborough	1779–82	1779	Nov.	Chamier, A.
		1779	Nov.	Porten, Sir S.
		1781	Jan.	Bell, J. (v. Chamier)

SCOTTISH DEPARTMENT

Queensberry	1709–11	1709	Feb.	Montgomery, J.
		1709	Feb.	Rowe, N.
Mar	1713–14	1713	Sept.	Strahan, W.
Montrose	1714–15	1714	Sept.	Kennedy, C.
Roxburghe	1716–25	1716	Dec.	Scott, T.
Tweeddale	1742–6	1742	Feb.	Mitchell, A.

COLONIAL DEPARTMENT

Hillsborough	1768–72	1768	Jan.	Phelps, R.
		1768	June	Pownall, J. (v. Phelps)
		1770	June	Knox, W.[16]
Dartmouth	1772–5	1772	Aug.	Pownall, J.
		1772	Aug.	Knox, W.
Germain	1775–82	1775	Nov.	Pownall, J.
		1775	Nov.	Knox, W.
		1776	April	D'Oyly, C. (v. Pownall)
		1778	Jan.	de Grey, T. (v. D'Oyly)
		1780	July	Thompson, B. (v. de Grey)
		1781	Oct.	Fisher, J. (v. Thompson)
Ellis	1782	1782	Feb.	Knox, W.
		1782	Feb.	Fisher, J.

[16] Before the appointment of Knox there was only one Under Secretary in the Colonial Department.

Clerks 1660-1782

The Secretaries of State appear to have employed salaried Clerks as early as 1628.[1] In all probability the practice was resumed at the Restoration. It was certainly observed from the close of the seventeenth century until the end of the period. By 1702 it seems to have been accepted in principle that Clerks, once appointed, were entitled to remain in office until their death or resignation. Formally the Secretaries retained the power of dismissal but they exercised it only rarely and in practice their freedom of action was limited to the making of new appointments. Subject to this consideration the Secretaries were able to fix the number of Clerks in their offices at whatever level they wished. The practice of employing salaried Clerks was followed in the Scottish and Colonial Departments. In the latter part of the eighteenth century certain of the more senior Clerks in each department were distinguished by the designation 'Senior Clerks'.[2]

In the absence of satisfactory evidence it is impossible to give a complete account of the salaries paid by the Secretaries to their Clerks. They evidently varied considerably in amount at different times. Those in Middleton's office in 1684 received from £40 to £60 a year.[3] Trumbull and Vernon paid their Clerks £50 between 1695 and 1702.[4] Harley (1704-8) paid one of his Clerks £60 and the other four £50. In 1710 and 1717-18 Sunderland paid one of his Clerks £100 and the other four £50.[5] During his second term of office (1718-21) Stanhope paid one of his Clerks £100, three £50 and one £40.[6] Newcastle's usual practice between 1724 and 1733 was to pay his Clerks £30 or £40 on appointment and to increase these sums later to £50. A few received as much as £100 and one was eventually paid £150.[7] In 1737 one of Newcastle's Clerks claimed that the Secretaries of State in both departments had 'always distinguished their Senior Clerks by an additional £50'.[8] As a result of action taken by Egremont and Halifax at the beginning of the reign of George III salary scales in both the offices were considerably improved.[9] Egremont (1761-3) paid four of his Clerks £100, two £80 and one £60.[10] In 1767 Seymour Conway paid two of his Clerks £170, two £100, two £80 and three £50. In 1768 Shelburne paid three of his Clerks £120, two £100, one £80, four £50 and two £40.[11] There do not appear to have been any substantial changes in salary levels between this date and 1782.[12] Nothing is known of the salaries paid in the Scottish Department except that in 1746 Tweeddale paid his only Clerk, apart from his Chief Clerk, £50.[13] In the Colonial Department Dartmouth

---

[1] For Clerks generally, see pp. 16-18.   [2] For Senior Clerks, see p. 39.
[3] Evans, *Principal Secretary*, 193.   [4] Trumbull Add. MS 113; BM Add. MSS 40785, 40786.
[5] BM Loan 29/162; SP 34/12 f. 165; Sunderland MS D 1/36.   [6] Stanhope MS 76.
[7] MSS Rawlinson C 367, 123.   [8] Petition of E. Maskelyne (SP 36/43 ff. 19-21).
[9] Shelburne MS 134 p. 108.   [10] PRO 30/47/31/1-7.
[11] Shelburne MS 134 pp. 119, 147.
[12] Changes in salary arrangements in the Southern Department 1769-70 and the Northern Department 1770-6 may be studied in FO 95/591/1 ff. 5-6.
[13] Tweeddale MS Acc. 4862 Box 160/1 Bundle 4.

in 1774 paid his Clerks £170, £120, £80, £60, £50 and £40; while Ellis in 1782 paid one £170, one £120, two £60 and three £50.[14]

Originally the Clerks, like certain others of the Secretaries' officials, enjoyed the privilege of franking mail. This constituted a valuable addition to their salaries. The privilege was greatly curtailed in 1764.[15] After representations had been made on their behalf compensation was provided in 1769 in the form of £500 which was paid annually out of Post Office funds to each of the three Secretaries of State for distribution amongst their Clerks.[16]

LISTS OF APPOINTMENTS

NORTHERN AND SOUTHERN DEPARTMENTS

1663	Swaddell, J.	1699	Drift, A.
By 1666	{ Francis, R.	1699	de Lacombe de
	Leigh, R.		Vrigny, J.P.
By 1668	Yard, R.		{ Tilson, G.
By 1671	{ Ball, H.	By 1700	Watkins, F.
	Benson, F.		Delafaye, C.[19]
	Field, J.	By 1701	Hussey, W.
c. 1675	Le Pin, J.		{ Southern, S.
By 1683	de Paz, S.	By 1702	Gilbert, H.
	{ Carne, E.		Batchellor, T.
By 1684	Chute, E.	By 1704	Tooke, C.
	Widdows, —[17]		{ Borret, T.
By 1685	Tucker, J.	By 1706	Brocas, J.
	{ Armstrong, T.[18]		Pauncefort, T.
	Bernard, D.		Man, N.
By 1689	Bedingfield, E.	1706	Gregg, W.
	Knatchbull, E.	1706	Thomas, W.
	Morley, R.		{ Whittaker, —
	Champion, L.		Coling, —
By 1693	{ Stanyan, A.	By 1708	Stanyan, T.
	Egar, D.		Prevereau, D.
By 1694	{ Brown, —		Lowndes, W.
	Welby, A.	1709	Burch, J.
	{ Swinford, J.	By 1710	Newcomen, (?) T.
By 1695	Payzant, J.	1710	Davids, J.
	Dayrolle, J.	1710	Marshall, H.
1695	Woodeson, G.	By 1711	{ Weston, —
1696	Devenish, St. G.		Mauries, F.
By 1697	Rowley, W.	1711	Wace, J.
	{ Jones, W.	1713	Kineir, A.
By 1698	Roberts, P.	1713	Maskelyne, N.
	Vanbrugh, K.	1715	Shepherd, J.
	Weston, H.	By 1716	Armistead, M.

[14] Spector, *American Department*, 62 n. 2; T 1/579 Schedule 2. [15] 4 Geo. III, c 24, ss 1, 6.

[16] Shelburne MS 134 pp. 101–3; 9 Geo. III, c 35, s 5. For the distribution of these sums amongst Clerks, see FO 95/591/1 ff. 5–6; Spector, *American Department*, 62 n. 2.

[17] 'Writing Clerk'.   [18] Possibly Chief Clerk.   [19] Began service as 'Extraordinary' Clerk.

1716	Gedney, T.	By 1749	Money, J.
1716	Maskelyne, E.	1749	Digby, H.
By 1717	Couraud, J.	By 1750	Allen, W.
1717	Richardson, J.	1750	Sneyd, J.
1717	Woodward, G.	By 1751	Bell, C.
1718	Tickell, R.	1751	Fraser, W.
1718	Gregory, G.	1751	Noble, T.
1718	Bowes, G.	1752	Kluft, J. D.
1719	Griffin, J.	1752	Payzant, J.
1719	Shaftoe, G.	1752	Shelley, T.
1719	Milnes, J.	1753	Royer, J.
1721	Balaguier, J. A.[20]	1753	Diemar, G.
1722	Tigh, E.	1753	Jouvencel, P. C.
1724	Stepney, J.	1754	Draper, N.
1724	Wiggs, J.	c. 1755	Wright, J.
1725	Moore, H.	1756	Francis, P.
1725	Lawrey, A.	1756	Brietzcke, C.
1726	Pelham, T.[21]	1756	Haynes, J.
1726	West, G.	By 1757	Morrison, R.
By 1727	Dale, J.	1758	Shuckburgh, S.
1727	Burnaby, J.	1759	Kluft, J. D.
1727	Hutchinson, F. H.	1761	Larpent, J.
1727	Sandys, W.	1761	Featherstone, R.
1729	Price, J.	1761	Brummell, W.
1729	Trevor, Hon. R.	1761	Roberts, J. C.
1730	Ramsden, T.	By 1762	Taylor, W.
By 1731	Larpent, J.	1762	Broughton, B.
1734	Brown, G.	1762	Weston, F.
By 1736	Huxley, G.	1763	Pollock, W.
1736	Lister, J.	1763	Fenhoulet, J. J.
1737	Gage, T.	1763	Aust, G.
By 1741	Houghton, W.	1763	Cooke, G.
1741	Morin, P. M.	1765	Morin, J.
1742	Harling, W.	1766	Collins, C.
By 1743	Jones, H. V.	1766	Bidwell, T.
1744	Rivers, J.	1767	Deyverdun, G.
1744	Cranmer, T.	1767	Leautier, D.
1745	Wace, F.	1767	Stewart, T.
1745	Shadwell, R.	1767	Randall, G.
1746	Henricks, G.	1767	Shadwell, T.
1746	Duck, W.	1768	Carrington, G. W.
1747	Wallace, J.	1768	Daw, T.
1748	Sneyd, F.	1768	Higden, W. H.
1748	Aspinwall, S.[22]	1772	Carter, R.
1748	Pulse, P.	1772	Jenkins, J. W.

[20] Probably Private Secretary to Carteret rather than Clerk.
[21] Not a salaried Clerk.
[22] Described in 1749 as 'Assistant Secretary'.

1774	Colleton, J. N.	1780	Money, W.
1779	Chetwynd, Hon. R.	1780	Manby, J.

SCOTTISH DEPARTMENT

By 1710	{ Scott, T.	By 1717	Kineir, A.
	{ Gibbons, —	1742	Reid, G.

COLONIAL DEPARTMENT

1768	Sawer, W.	By 1777	Poplett, T.
	{ Hutchinson, J.	By 1779	Peace, C.
By 1769	{ Hanbury Williams, C.	By 1780	Palman, G. L.
	{ Pownall, J. L.	By 1782	{ Burrell, W.
By 1771	Allen, W.		{ Walsh, F. T.
By 1775	{ Wilmot, E.		
	{ Bayley, A. Y.		

Chief Clerks c. 1689-1782

In the eighteenth century it was the established practice for there to be a First or Chief Clerk in each of the Secretaries' offices, ranking immediately after the Under Secretaries. Considerable obscurity surrounds the origins of this office.[1] Such evidence as exists suggests that it evolved from the earlier position of Entering or Writing Clerk and that the Chief Clerks acquired their distinctive position at the head of each office about 1689. The term 'First' Clerk is not actually used until 1700 and the Chief Clerks were not regularly distinguished from their colleagues in lists until 1718. In consequence their identification in the earlier part of the period, and particularly in the years before 1700, must in many cases be tentative.

At first there was a tendency for the Chief Clerks, like the Under Secretaries, to go out of office with the Secretaries whom they were serving. However, from the time of the appointments of Jones in one office (1704) and Wace in the other (1717) it was accepted that the tenure of the Chief Clerks should not be affected by changes of Secretary and that they should remain in office until death or retirement.

In both the Scottish and the Colonial Departments Chief Clerks were appointed with the same rank and function as their counterparts in the older offices.

Unlike the other Clerks the Chief Clerks in the older offices received no salary from the Secretary of State. Their remuneration consisted principally in official fees. At some point during the eighteenth century they were accorded annual allowances of £25 from the Irish concordatum fund.[2] Since the Chief Clerks in the third office did not share in the arrangement for the pooling of the fees, their incomes from this source were smaller than those of their colleagues. It was probably for this reason that Tweeddale paid his Chief Clerk a salary of £100 and that successive Colonial Secretaries undertook to make up the deficiency in the event of the product of their Chief Clerk's fees falling below £250.[3] After 1769 the Chief Clerks in each of the three offices received shares of the money made available from Post Office funds.[4]

LISTS OF APPOINTMENTS

NORTHERN AND SOUTHERN DEPARTMENTS

(?) 1689 Feb.	Yard, R.		1698 May	Stanyan, A.
(?) 1689 March	Armstrong, T.		1699 March	Welby, A.
(?) 1690 Dec.	Tucker, J.		1699 May	Swinford, J.
(?) 1693 March	Stanyan, A.		1702 Jan.	Lewis, E.
(?) 1694 March	Bernard, D.		1702 May	Armstrong, T.
(?) 1697 Nov.	Vernon, J.		1702 May	Swinford, J.
1697 Dec.	Welby, A.		1704 May	Jones, W.

[1] For a discussion of the origin and development of this office, see pp. 13–16.
[2] *1st Rept. on Fees*, 6.
[3] Tweeddale MS Acc. 4862 Box 160/1 Bundle 4; Spector, *American Department*, 51.
[4] See p. 34.

1706 Dec.	Delafaye, C.		1746 May	Larpent, J.
1714 Sept.	Micklethwaite, J.		1766 May	Brown, G.
1717 April	Wace, J.		1769 April	Sneyd, J.
1719 Dec.	Prevereau, D.		1772 Oct.	Shadwell, R.
1745 March	Richardson, J.			

SCOTTISH DEPARTMENT

1709 Feb.	Stanyan, T.	1742 March	Patterson, W.
1716 Dec.	Paxton, N.		

COLONIAL DEPARTMENT

1768 Jan.   Pollock, W.

Senior Clerks c. 1763-1782

During the second half of the eighteenth century it was the practice, in each of the Secretaries' offices, for certain of the more senior Clerks below the rank of Chief Clerk to be designated 'Senior Clerks'. The reason for the introduction of this term is obscure and there is no evidence to suggest that the Senior Clerks undertook duties or responsibilities that were significantly different from those of other Clerks.[1] The term is first used in 1763 to distinguish two Clerks in one of the older offices.[2] There is no trace of its use in the other office until 1772 after which it was the practice for there to be two Senior Clerks in the Northern Department and three in the Southern. Two Senior Clerks were appointed in the Colonial Department on its establishment in 1768. Senior Clerks, like other Clerks below the rank of Chief Clerk, received their salaries from the Secretaries of State. After 1769 they received shares of the money made available from Post Office funds.[3]

LISTS OF APPOINTMENTS

NORTHERN AND SOUTHERN DEPARTMENTS

By 1763	{ Shadwell, R.	1772	Wright, J.
	{ Wace, F.	1776	Morin, J.
By 1772	(Duck, W.	1779	Broughton, B.
	{ Brietzcke, C.	1780	Aust, G.
	(Haynes, J.		

COLONIAL DEPARTMENT

1768	Larpent, J.	1776	Sawer, W.
1768	Serle, A.		

[1] This remained the case in 1786 (*1st Rept. on Fees*, 4).

[2] *CHOP 1760-5*, 302-3. Before 1770 these two Senior Clerks were attached to individual Secretaries regardless of the departments for which they had responsibility. The Secretaries in question were: Halifax 1763-5, Seymour Conway 1765-8, Weymouth 1768-70. From the appointment of Sandwich in 1770 the Northern Department was invariably the one to which two Senior Clerks were attached.

[3] For the salaries of Clerks generally, see pp. 33-4.

Office Keepers c. 1689-1782

In 1684 the 'Office Keeper' was amongst those of the Secretaries' officials who were entitled to fees.[1] Although Office or Chamber Keepers had undoubtedly been employed at an earlier date it is not until the reign of William III that they can be identified. Before 1698 their number seems to have varied. The poll tax assessment of 1689 suggests that there were then three in Shrewsbury's office and two in Nottingham's.[2] Trumbull appears to have employed three during his term of office 1695-7.[3] From 1698 it was the regular practice for there to be two in each of the older departments.[4] Only one was appointed in the Scottish and Colonial Departments. The Office Keepers appear to have enjoyed a tenure similar to that of the Clerks and to have remained in employment until death or voluntary resignation. On occasion they exercised their functions by deputy.[5]

In addition to their fees, the Office Keepers received salaries from the Secretaries of State. These were already fixed at £20 16s in 1695 and remained unchanged until the end of the period.[6]

LISTS OF APPOINTMENTS

NORTHERN AND SOUTHERN DEPARTMENTS

	Shorter, T.	By 1723	Ward, A.
	Robinson, J.		Noble, J.
By 1689	Wright, W.	1730	Sommer, J.
	Price, —	1732	Quin, W.
	Sedgwick, —	By 1748	White, J.
By 1695	Smith, T.	1752	Turner, R.
	Ramsey, B.	1759	Milburn, W.
By 1698	Turner, J.	c. 1769	Gorton, W.
1702	Goodridge, A.	c. 1770	Kirby, W.
By 1706	Mynatt, W.	1777	Doudiet, J.
By 1708	Marlow, —	c. 1782	Shaw, J.
By 1716	Blenner, J.		
	Burrows, I.		

[1] Evans, *Principal Secretary*, 193.
[2] LS 13/231 pp. 13-14.
[3] Trumbull Add. MS 113.
[4] BM Add. MS 40785 ff. 20, 34.
[5] *1st Rept. on Fees*, 7, 24-5, 32. The following deputies can be identified: Ancell, Brooke, Crowder, Longmore, Mitton, Phipps and, possibly, Evans and Pearson.
[6] Trumbull Add. MS 113; *1st Rept. on Fees*, 24-5, 32-3; Tweeddale MS Acc. 4862 Box 160/1 Bundle 4; Spector, *American Department*, 51.

Scottish Department

| By 1710 | Turner, J. | 1742 | Massey, J. |

Colonial Department

| By 1769 | Muly, J. P. | 1782 | Lackington, C. |

Necessary Women c. 1695-1782

The earliest evidence of the employment of a Necessary Woman or Cleaner dates from 1695 and relates to Trumbull's office.[1] From at least 1698 it was the regular practice for there to be one Necessary Woman in each of the older departments.[2] One was probably employed in the Scottish Department from the first although there is no evidence on the point until the time of Tweeddale's secretaryship (1742-6).[3] There was one Necessary Woman in the Colonial Department throughout its existence. Necessary Women held their places on a tenure that was similar to that of the Office Keepers.

The Necessary Women received their remuneration, which included a salary and an allowance for incidents, from the Secretaries of State. During the secretaryships of Trumbull and Vernon (1695-1702) this amounted to £9 10s a year.[4] Harley (1704-8) paid his Necessary Woman £12 a year. Sunderland and Stanhope paid theirs £14 between 1717 and 1720 as did Carteret and Newcastle between 1724 and 1733 and Egremont between 1761 and 1763.[5] In 1766 the Necessary Women in the offices of Shelburne and Seymour Conway were receiving £14 and £48 respectively.[6] The Necessary Woman in the Colonial Department was paid £48.[7]

LISTS OF APPOINTMENTS

NORTHERN AND SOUTHERN DEPARTMENTS

By 1695	Pope, —	By 1745	{ Turfery, E.
By 1698	Hill, —		{ Graham, M.
c. 1699	Ombee, —	By 1751	Shirley, P.
By 1717	Smart, E.	c. 1759	Southcott, M.
1724	Bickford, M.	c. 1765	Matthews, E.
		c. 1778	Emmitt, E.

SCOTTISH DEPARTMENT

| 1742 | Blenner, — |

COLONIAL DEPARTMENT

| By 1769 | Muly, E. |

---

[1] Trumbull Add. MS 113. It is possible that the Hill who was Necessary Woman to Shrewsbury in 1698 was identical with the person of the same name who was serving in some capacity in Nottingham's office in 1689 (LS 13/231 p. 14).

[2] BM Add. MS 40785 ff. 20, 34.   [3] Tweeddale MS Acc. 4862 Box 57/1b.

[4] Trumbull Add. MS 113; BM Add. MSS 40785, 40786.

[5] BM Loan 29/162; Sunderland MS D 1/36; Stanhope MS 76; MSS Rawlinson C 367, 123; PRO 30/47/31/1-7.

[6] Shelburne MS 134 p. 119.   [7] Spector, *American Department*, 51.

Embellisher of Letters 1660–c. 1800

The employment of individuals to embellish diplomatic letters and other documents, particularly those addressed to eastern princes, occurred during the early Stuart period and was continued after the Restoration.[1] From 1662 payments were made to a series of Embellishers for this work. These payments, usually at the rate of £10 a document, were made by the Treasurer of the Chamber on the authority of a warrant from one of the Secretaries of State. From 1707 to 1782 a regular salary of £60 was paid by the Treasurer of the Chamber.[2] Although in fact in the employment of the Secretaries of State, the Embellisher was from at least 1714 sworn by the Lord Chamberlain as an official of the Royal Household.[3] By 1797 the salary had been reduced to £25 16s carried on the Stationer's bill of the Foreign Office.[4] The last trace of the office occurs in 1800.[5]

LIST OF APPOINTMENTS

| By 1662 | Tomlin, G. | By 1704 | Brand, T. |
| By 1669 | Royer, G. | 1761 | Holland, J. |

[1] Evans, *Principal Secretary*, 200; *CSPD 1699–1700*, 330.
[2] *CTB*, xxi, 517; AO 1/219/426.   [3] LC 3/63 p. 49; LC 3/64 p. 57.
[4] *16th Rept. on Finance*, 320.   [5] FO 366/671 p. 144.

Writer of Gazette 1665-1863, Deputy Writer of Gazette c. 1751-1828 and French Translator of Gazette 1666-c. 1710

The publication of the *London Gazette* began in 1665.[1] It was at first prepared under the auspices of Williamson, Under Secretary to Arlington. On the appointment of Coventry as Secretary in 1672 an arrangement was made whereby the profits from its sale were equally divided between the two offices and from this date the *Gazette* may be regarded as common to the secretariat as a whole. The compilation of the *Gazette* was at first undertaken for brief periods by Muddiman and Perrott. By 1673 it had been entrusted to Yard, originally a Clerk in Arlington's office, during whose period of service the writership came to be recognised as a distinct office with a regular salary attached to it. Yard's successor, C. Delafaye, was placed under the supervision of the four Under Secretaries who were responsible for the contents of the *Gazette*.[2] This arrangement did not prove satisfactory and on the appointment of Steele in 1707 the Writer regained his former position. Originally the Writer was appointed by the Secretaries of State. In 1719, however, Buckley, who had originally been appointed in 1714, had the office conferred upon him by the crown by letters patent under the great seal.[3] Thereafter it was granted for life and the principal was empowered to exercise his functions by deputy. Between 1741 and 1828 the office was held by persons who were either officials or former officials of the Secretaries' offices who appointed Clerks in those offices as their deputies. Rolleston (1803–28), however, exercised his duties in person and was responsible for reorganising the office in 1811 following the expiry of the Printer's patent.[4] Gregson, the last Writer of the Gazette, also took an active part in the work at the beginning of his period of office (1829–63). During the course of the year 1848 a series of reforms were carried out with the object of transferring the busi-

[1] For the *London Gazette*, see Evans, *Principal Secretary*, 291–6; Nelson, *Home Office*, 146–9; J. G. Muddiman, *The King's Journalist* (London 1923), 174–93; L. Hanson, *Government and the Press* (Oxford 1936), 84–93; P. Fraser, *The Intelligence of the Secretaries of State 1660–88* (Cambridge 1956), 47–56; P. M. Handover, *The History of the London Gazette 1665–1965* (London 1965).

[2] Hist. MSS Comm. *Portland*, viii, 187–8; *House of Lords MSS*, new ser., v, 467–8. The annual allowance of £100 which the Under Secretaries received from the profits of the *Gazette* was probably paid to them in respect of this function (BM Loan 29/162).

[3] Letters patent of 7 May 1719 (C 66/3531). In 1828–9 the question of the right of nomination to the writership was the cause of a lengthy dispute between the Home and Foreign Offices. Peel, the Home Secretary, finally prevailed and nominated Gregson (FO 366/413).

[4] The printing of the *Gazette* was undertaken by Thomas Newcombe 1665–88, Edward Jones 1688–1706, Jacob Tonson 1707–10, Benjamin Tooke 1710–14 and Jacob Tonson from 1714. From 1716 to 1810 the printing and publishing were in the hands of patentees. Patents were granted as follows: to Samuel Buckley 16 April 1716 for 40 years (C 66/3514), to Edward Owen 26 March 1756 for 40 years (C 66/3651), to Edward Johnston 28 Nov. 1793 for 14 years from 1796 (C 66/3885). In 1811 Robert George Clarke was appointed Printer (FO 366/413). On his death in 1839 he was succeeded by Francis Watts.

ness connected with the printing and publishing of the *Gazette* from the Secretaries of State to the Treasury. The immediate direction of the *Gazette* was placed wholly in the hands of a Superintendent. Gregson was allowed to continue to receive his salary as Writer until his death when the office was finally abolished.[5]

The salary of the Writer of the Gazette was paid by the Printer who was responsible to the Secretaries of State for keeping the accounts of its sales. Yard's salary was £60 in 1679 and 1684. By 1695 it had risen to £100.[6] C. Delafaye received £60. Steele was appointed at £300 in 1707 and King and Ford at £200 in 1711 and 1712.[7] From the time of Buckley's appointment in 1714 the salary remained fixed at £300.[8] The salary of the deputy was £30 paid by the principal.[9]

In 1666 a French version of the *Gazette* began to be published, being prepared by a distinct official known as the French Translator who received a salary of £52 from the same source as the Writer. There is no trace of this office after 1710.[10]

LISTS OF APPOINTMENTS

WRITER OF GAZETTE

1665	Nov.	Muddiman, H.	1712	July	Ford, C.
1666	Feb.	Perrott, C.	1714	Sept.	Buckley, S.
By 1673		Yard, R.	1741	22 Nov.	Weston, E.
1702	May	Delafaye, C.	1770	13 July	Fraser, W.
1707	May	Steele, R.	1803	15 Jan.	Rolleston, S.
By 1711		Scott, —	1829	23 Sept.	Gregson, W.
1711	Dec.	King, W.			

DEPUTY WRITER OF GAZETTE

By 1751	Brown, G.	By 1791		Moore, F.
By 1770	Wace, F.	1797	30 Jan.	Rolleston, S.
By 1781	Aust, G.	By 1804		Rolleston, H.

FRENCH TRANSLATOR OF GAZETTE

1666	Morainville, —	By 1679	Delafaye, L.

[5] TM 27 June 1848 (T 29/522 pp. 443–4), 8 Aug. 1848 (T 29/524 pp. 162–4), 13 Oct. 1848 (T 29/526 pp. 215–22). The office of Superintendent was instituted 1839 and held by Francis Watts (1839–54), Thomas Lawrence Behan (1854–69) and Thomas Walker (1869–89).

[6] All Souls MS 204 f. 81c; BM Add. MS 41806 f. 64; Trumbull Add. MS 113.

[7] BM Loan 29/162; *Correspondence of Richard Steele*, ed. R. Blanchard (London 1941), 201; J. Swift, *Prose Works*, ed. F. Ryland and others (London 1898–1922), ii, 309, 374.

[8] SP 35/19 ff. 154–65; letters patent to Buckley of 7 May 1719 (C 66/3531).

[9] *1st Rept. on Fees*, 27, 29.

[10] A. Grey, *Debates of the House of Commons 1667–94* (London 1769), vi, 161; All Souls MS 204 f. 81c; BM Add. MS 41806 f. 64; Trumbull Add. MS 113; BM Loan 29/162; SP 34/12 f. 165.

Law Clerk 1743-74

This office was created in 1743.[1] Appointments were made by the crown by letters patent under the great seal granting it during pleasure. The function of its holders was 'to attend the Secretaries of State in order to take the depositions of such persons whom it may be necessary to examine upon affairs which may concern the Public and to do and perform all such matters relating thereto as may be committed to (their) care'.[2] The office was discontinued in 1774 on the resignation of Stanhope. It was, however, revived in 1791 and attached to the Home Office.[3]

The salary attached to the office in 1743 was £200, payable by the Paymaster of Pensions.[4] In 1747 it was raised to £300 payable by the Treasury Solicitor. It was further increased to £500 in 1761.[5]

LIST OF APPOINTMENTS

1743	10 Feb.	Waite, T.	1747	4 Aug.	Stanhope, L.

[1] For some account of this office, see Thomson, *Secretaries of State*, 136, 140–1.
[2] Letters patent to Waite 10 Feb. 1743 (C 66/3612).
[3] Nelson, *Home Office*, 59.
[4] *CTBP 1742–5*, 396; AO 3/789.
[5] AO 1/2324/62; AO 3/1102.

Secretary for Latin Tongue 1660-1832

This office originated in the early sixteenth century.[1] Appointments were made by the crown by letters patent under the great seal. It was held on a life tenure from 1661 to 1681 and during pleasure thereafter except for the years 1722–30 when it was again held for life.[2] The office appears to have become a sinecure by the beginning of the eighteenth century and it was discontinued on the revocation of Hobhouse's patent in 1832.

The patent salary attached to the office was £80. An additional salary of £200 was granted to Lee in 1722[3] and was continued to his successors. Both salaries were paid at the Exchequer.

LIST OF APPOINTMENTS

1661	12 Jan.	Fanshawe, Sir R.	1718	18 July	Lee, W.
1666	19 July	Oudart, N.	1730	27 Nov.	Couraud, J.
1682	2 March	Cooke, J.	1752	20 April	Ramsden, T.
1691	6 Nov.	Hill, R.	1792	15 Nov.	Bruce, J.
1714	22 Oct.	Hill, S.	1826	23 May	Hobhouse, H.

Secretary for French Tongue 1660-1700

This office originated in the fifteenth century.[4] Appointments were made by the crown by letters patent under the great seal. De Vic was appointed for life; Henshaw was at first appointed for life, in 1662, but received a new grant during pleasure in 1693.[5] The office appears to have been a sinecure from the Restoration until the death of Henshaw in 1700 when it was discontinued. The salary was £66 13s 4d payable at the Exchequer.

LIST OF APPOINTMENTS

1634	27 Sept.	de Vic, H.	1662	13 March	Henshaw, T.

[1] For this office, see *1st Rept. on Fees*, 34; Evans, *Principal Secretary*, 21, 170–3; Nelson, *Home Office*, 145–6.

[2] By letters patent 24 Jan. 1722 Lee, who had been appointed during pleasure in 1718, received a new grant of the office for life (C 66/3547). [3] Ibid.

[4] For this office, see J. Otway-Ruthven, *The King's Secretary and the Signet Office in the 15th Century* (Cambridge 1939), 89–105, 156; Evans, *Principal Secretary*, 19–21, 170–3.

[5] Letters patent to Henshaw, 4 May 1693 (C 66/3364).

Interpreter of Oriental Languages 1723-1835

This office originated in 1723.[1] Its holder was principally concerned with translation from Arabic. Appointments were made by the crown. Until 1782 it was attached to the secretariat generally. In that year it passed under the general authority of the Home Office, being transferred to the Colonial Office in 1804.[2] It was abolished in 1816 but was temporarily revived between 1823 and 1835.[3]

The salary attached to the office was paid by the Paymaster of Pensions from 1723 to 1770 and after 1784 from the contingent funds of the Home and Colonial Offices.[4] Until 1816 it was fixed at £80. The salary of Salamé, the last holder of the office, was £150 from 1823 to 1828 and £200 from 1828 to 1835.[5]

LIST OF APPOINTMENTS

1723	May	Negri, S.	1782	March	Cardozo Nunes, I.
1727	May	Didichi, T. R.	1784	May	Lucas, S.
1734	May	Massabeky, J.	1794	Jan.	Tully, R.
1739	July	Stamma, F.	1802	July	Costa, F.
1755	Sept.	Stonehewer, R.	1809	Sept.	Delagarde, C.
1763	June	Arbona, J.	1823	Jan.	Salamé, A. Y.
1767	Dec.	Logie, A.			
1769	May	Deceramis, A. X.			

[1] SP 44/123 p. 275; SP 44/124 pp. 30, 114. For this office after 1782, see Nelson, *Home Office*, 57–9; D. M. Young, *The Colonial Office in the Early 19th Century* (London 1961), 21, 74–5, 268, 269.

[2] HO 82/3; the Colonial Office became responsible for paying the salary of the Interpreter from 5 Jan. 1804 (CO 701/1 p. 48).

[3] CO 701/2 pp. 29, 109; CO 701/3 p. 62. Between 1854 and 1917 an Interpreter of Oriental Languages was attached to the Foreign Office. This post was held by John William Redhouse 1854–92 and Charles Wells 1892–1917 (*Foreign Office List* (1892), 179; ibid. (1893), 216; ibid. (1918), xxiv).

[4] T 52/33 p. 87; T 52/60 p. 355; TM 14 May 1784 (T 29/55 p. 239).

[5] T 52/33 p. 87; CO 701/2 pp. 29, 109, 142; CO 701/3 p. 62.

Translator of German Language 1735-1802

This office originated in 1735 with the appointment of a Decipherer, Zolman, who by the time of his death in 1748 had acquired the title of Translator of the German Language.[1] Until 1782 it was attached to the secretariat generally. From that date it passed under the authority of the Foreign Office, being formally included in its establishment in 1797. The office, which had probably become a sinecure by 1760, was abolished in 1802 on the death of Fraser.[2]

Until 1782 the salary attached to the office was, like those of the Decipherers, disbursed by the Secretary of the Post Office out of secret service money. From that year the Foreign Secretary was responsible for paying it out of the secret service money provided for his department. Zolman's salary, originally £200, was raised to £300 in 1744.[3] Wallace was appointed at £200 in 1748, his salary being increased to £400 between 1761 and 1763.[4] From the time of Howard's appointment in 1772 the salary remained fixed at £300.[5]

LIST OF APPOINTMENTS

1735	July	Zolman, P. H.	1772	March	Howard, Hon. C.
1748	Aug.	Wallace, J.	1773	Oct.	Fraser, W.

[1] *CTBP 1735–8*, 37. For this office, see Ellis, *Post Office*, 129–30, 133; *16th Rept. on Finance*, 311, 324.
[2] Order in council 21 June 1797 (PC 2/148 pp. 504–5). Between 1806 and 1809, however, the emoluments formerly attached to the office were shared by three persons, two of whom were Clerks on the establishment of the Foreign Office (*Public Record Office Handbook No. 13: The Records of the Foreign Office 1782–1939* (London 1969), 11).   [3] T 53/41 p. 466.
[4] T 53/43 p. 377; PRO 30/8/83 pt. i, Todd to Newcastle, 6 Jan. 1761; L. B. Namier, *The Structure of Politics at the Accession of George III*, 2nd ed. (London 1960), 193–4.
[5] *Correspondence of George III*, ed. Sir J. Fortescue (London 1927–8), iii, 38; *1st Rept. on Fees*, 27.

Translator of Southern Languages 1755–c. 1765

The office of Translator of Southern, or Italian and Spanish, Languages originated in 1755. It seems to have been created principally with the object of providing an allowance for Rivers who was temporarily removed from the position of Under Secretary in that year.[1] Rivers continued to hold it after his reappointment as Under Secretary in 1756.

The salary attached to the office was, like those of the Decipherers, disbursed by the Secretary of the Post Office out of secret service money. Originally £200 it was raised to £400 at some time between 1763 and 1765.[2] The last evidence of the payment of the salary is of the latter year although it is possible that Rivers continued to receive it as a form of retiring allowance until his death in 1807.[3]

APPOINTMENT

1755   Dec.   Rivers, J.

[1] T 53/45 p. 461; *Grenville Papers*, ed. W. J. Smith (London 1852–3), i, 180–1.

[2] Ellis, *Post Office*, 130, 133–4; L. B. Namier, *The Structure of Politics at the Accession of George III*, 2nd ed. (London 1960), 193; BM Add. MS 38339 f. 143.

[3] It may be significant that it was in 1807 or 1808 that an official with active functions and the title of Translator of the Spanish, Portuguese, Italian and Danish Languages was appointed and attached to the Foreign Office (*Public Record Office Handbook No. 13 : The Records of the Foreign Office 1782–1939* (London 1969), 11).

Decipherers 1701-1844

Although cryptography and translation were amongst the general responsibilities of the Secretaries of State from the Tudor period, it was only in the early eighteenth century that settled arrangements were made for the decipherment of letters and dispatches.[1] After the Restoration much of the work was entrusted to Wallis, who, until 1701, had no established position, being paid by the Secretaries of State for each commission that he executed. In that year, however, the Decipherers' office was placed on a permanent basis, Wallis and his grandson, Blencowe, being granted a regular salary by privy seal.[2] Blencowe was succeeded in 1713 by Keill who was himself succeeded in 1716 by the elder E. Willes. Between 1716 and the abolition of the office there were invariably between one and three members of this family serving as Decipherers. In 1715 a second salaried position was established and conferred upon Corbiere who at first appears to have worked under the immediate supervision of the Treasury.[3] Corbiere was succeeded by Scholing (1743-8) and he in turn by the brothers Neubourg (1750-3; 1753-62).[4]

Until 1722 the salaries of the Decipherers were paid at the Exchequer. From that year until 1782 they were disbursed by the Secretary of the Post Office from secret service money in the same manner as those of the officials of the secret department of that office with whom the Decipherers came to be closely associated.[5] Since no regular accounts of these disbursements exist it is in many cases impossible for the periods of service of Decipherers to be determined precisely. New appointments and changes in salary appear usually to have been a matter of oral communication of the King's pleasure to the Secretary of the Post Office.[6]

By 1723 a third salaried post of Decipherer had come into existence and was held by Ashfield who was succeeded by Lampe in 1729. On Lampe's death in 1755 his salary was divided between one of the Clerks in the secret department of the Post Office and the former Under Secretary, Rivers, who was given the title of Translator of the Southern, or Italian and Spanish, Languages.[7] In 1735 a salary was made available from secret service money for Zolman who was given particular responsibility for the translation of the German language.[8] From 1762 the Decipherers' office was staffed

---

[1] For these offices, see Ellis, *Post Office*, 66-8, 127-34, 138-42.

[2] *CTB*, xvi, 243.   [3] Ibid. xxx, 56.

[4] In 1762 the salary formerly paid to G. W. Neubourg was granted to the younger J. E. Bode, a Clerk in the secret department of the Post Office (PRO 30/8/232, Bode memorial, May 1786).

[5] Corbiere's salary was transferred to the Post Office on 29 March 1722 (T 29/24 pt. ii, 156). The last payment to the elder E. Willes was for the quarter to 25 March 1722 (T 53/29 p. 339). Until 1760 the Secretary of the Post Office paid these salaries out of secret service money issued out of the surplus revenue of that office; thereafter from secret service money issued to him at the Exchequer (Ellis, *Post Office*, 66-7).

[6] From 1745 to 1760, however, it appears to have been the invariable practice for alterations in the payments made out of the Post Office secret service money to be the subject of Treasury warrants to the Secretary.

[7] T 53/45 p. 461. For the office of Translator of Southern Languages, see p. 50.

[8] *CTBP 1735-8*, 37. For the office of Translator of the German Language, see p. 49.

exclusively by members of the Willes family.[9] Having been common to the secretariat as a whole until 1782 it passed in that year under the authority of the Foreign Secretary who became responsible for paying the salaries out of the secret service money provided for that department. The office was abolished on 1 October 1844.[10]

The salaries of the Decipherers varied considerably in amount. Wallis and Blencowe were granted £100 in 1701, Blencowe's salary being raised to £200 in 1709.[11] Keill was appointed at £100 in 1713.[12] The elder E. Willes' salary, originally £200, was raised to £250 in 1721.[13] Corbiere's salary began at £100 in 1715 and was raised to £200 in 1716, to £400 in 1721 and to £500 in 1722.[14] In 1742 the elder and the younger E. Willes were sharing £1000, Corbiere was receiving £800 and Lampe £500.[15] Scholing was appointed at £300 in 1743 and the elder W. Willes at £100 in 1744, the younger E. Willes also being granted an additional £100 in the latter year.[16] The two Neubourgs were successively appointed at £300 in 1750 and 1753.[17] In 1761 the elder E. Willes, now Bishop of Bath and Wells, was being paid £800, the younger E. Willes £300, G. W. Neubourg £300 and the elder W. Willes £200.[18] In 1763 the Bishop and the younger E. Willes were both receiving £500 and the elder F. Willes £300.[19] In 1775 the latter was advanced from £400 to £700 in consideration of his services as Under Secretary 1772–5.[20] In 1801–4 the salaries of the elder F. and the youngest E. Willes remained fixed at £700 and £500 respectively while the younger F. Willes was receiving £200.[21] In 1806 the elder F. Willes was receiving £900 and the younger F. Willes £500.[22] The salaries of the last Decipherers, the younger F. Willes and Lovell were £700 and £200 in 1844.[23]

LIST OF APPOINTMENTS

1701	{ Wallis, J.	1744	Willes, W.
	{ Blencowe, W.	1750	Neubourg, P. F.
1713	Keill, J.	1753	Neubourg, G. W.
1715	Corbiere, A.	By 1763	Willes, F.
1716	Willes, E.	By 1793	Willes, E.
By 1723	Ashfield, F.	1793	Willes, W.
1729	Lampe, J.	By 1801	Willes, F.
c. 1741	Willes, E.	By 1844	Lovell, W. W.
1743	Scholing, —		

[9] Lovell, who was one of the Decipherers in 1844, appears to have been a nephew of the younger F. Willes (Ellis, *Post Office*, 131).

[10] BM Add. MS 45520 ff. 53–4.   [11] *CTB*, xvi, 243; ibid. xxiii, 189–90.   [12] Ibid. xxvii, 88.

[13] Ibid. xxx, 252; T 53/29 p. 339.

[14] *CTB*, xxx, 56; ibid. xxxi, 7; T 53/29 p. 51; T 29/24 pt. ii, 156.

[15] *Commons Journals*, xxiv, 331.   [16] T 53/41 pp. 466–7.   [17] T 53/43 p. 491; T 53/45 p. 45.

[18] PRO 30/8/83 pt. ii, Todd to Newcastle, 6 Jan. 1761.

[19] L. B. Namier, *The Structure of Politics at the Accession of George III*, 2nd ed. (London 1960), 193; BM Add. MS 38339 f. 143.

[20] BM Add. MS 45519 ff. 58–9.   [21] Ibid. 38357 ff. 62–4, 180–2, 38358 ff. 24–6.

[22] Ibid. 51463 ff. 30, 31, 51464 f. 110.   [23] Ibid. 45520 ff. 53–4.

Keeper of State Papers 1660–1854

This office originated in 1578.[1] Appointments were made by the crown by letters patent under the great seal. The tenure of the office varied. It was held for life 1660–1701, during pleasure 1702–22, for life 1722–38,[2] during pleasure 1739–1800 and for life 1800–54.[3] Power to act by deputy was included in patents from 1702.[4] The office was practically a sinecure for much of the eighteenth century. With the appointment of Bruce in 1792, however, the Keeper became active and in 1800 the office was reorganised and given a new establishment.[5] The office was abolished on the death of Hobhouse in 1854 when its functions were transferred to the Public Record Office.

In 1660 the Keeper was receiving a salary of 3s 4d a day and an additional allowance of £100 a year. In 1661 a consolidated salary of £160 was provided payable at the Exchequer.[6] At the time of the reorganisation of 1800 this was increased to £500.[7]

LIST OF APPOINTMENTS

By 1660		Raymond, T.	1741	5 May	Stone, A.
1661	31 Dec.	Williamson, J.	1774	3 May	Porten, Sir S.
1702	16 July	Tucker, J.	1792	15 Nov.	Bruce, J.
1714	18 Nov.	Howard, H.	1826	23 May	Hobhouse, H.
1739	3 Feb.	Couraud, J.			

[1] For this office, see F. S. Thomas, *Notes of Materials for the History of Public Departments* (London 1846), 41–3, 111–44, 170–1; *30th Rept. of the Deputy Keeper of Public Records*, 212–93; *1st Rept. on Fees*, 33; Nelson, *Home Office*, 143–5.

[2] By letters patent 13 Dec. 1722 Howard, who had been appointed during pleasure in 1714, received a new grant of the office for life (C 66/3551).

[3] By letters patent 23 Sept. 1800 Bruce, who had been appointed during pleasure in 1792, received a new grant of the office for life (C 66/3963).

[4] J. Wace, one of the Clerks in the Secretaries' offices, acted as Deputy Keeper from at least 1718 until 1745.

[5] Royal warrant 4 March 1800 (SP 45/75). The establishment made provision for a Deputy or First Clerk, a Second Clerk, a Third Clerk, a Housekeeper and a Messenger. These subordinate officials have not been included in the lists. Details of their appointments and remuneration may be found in the establishment books of the State Paper Office 1800–54 (ibid.).

[6] Letters patent to Raymond 20 July 1640 (C 66/2873), to Williamson 31 Dec. 1661 (C 66/2980).

[7] SP 45/75.

Collector of State Papers 1725-1848

This office, the full title of which was Collector and Transmitter of State Papers, was created in 1725.[1] Appointments were made by the crown by letters patent under the great seal. Except for the years 1739–41 when it was granted during pleasure the office was always held for life. Between 1739 and 1751 it was occupied by joint holders. The nominal function of the office, which was a sinecure almost from the time of its creation, was to collect records from the offices of the Secretaries of State and to transmit them to the Keeper of State Papers. It passed under the general authority of the Foreign Office in 1782 and was formally included in its establishment in 1795.[2] It was discontinued on the death of Goddard in 1848.

The remuneration attached to the office was £500, composed of a salary of £400 and an allowance of £100 for Clerks and incidents. This sum was disbursed by the Secretary of the Post Office until 1782 when the Foreign Secretary became responsible for its payment.[3]

LIST OF APPOINTMENTS

1725	20 Jan.	Tilson, G.
1739	18 May	{ Weston, E. / Stone, A.
1741	26 June	{ Weston, E. / Couraud, J.
1742	4 Jan.	{ Couraud, J. / Ramsden, T.
1796	6 Jan.	Goddard, C.

[1] For this office, see *1st Rept. on Fees*, 34; Nelson, *Home Office*, 144.
[2] Order in council 21 Oct. 1795 (*16th Rept. on Finance*, 34); TM 28 July 1796 (T 29/69 p. 303).
[3] Ellis, *Post Office*, 133; *1st Rept. on Fees*, 34.

Methodisers of State Papers 1764-1800

The offices of Methodisers of State Papers, which were usually three in number, were created in 1764.[1] Appointments were made by the crown by warrant under sign manual. The Methodisers of State Papers also held the distinct offices of Methodisers of the records of the Court of Exchequer which had been created in 1763 and which were abolished in 1789.[2] The offices of Methodisers of State Papers were abolished in 1800 when that of Keeper of State Papers was reorganised.[3]

In 1764 the Methodisers were accorded salaries of £100 each, an allowance of £100 for Clerks and a further allowance of £100 for incidents.[4] This was in addition to their remuneration for their work in the Exchequer. When this work was discontinued in 1789 a new arrangement was adopted. One Methodiser, the elder Astle, served without salary and the remaining two, Topham and the younger Astle, were given salaries of £200 each. At the same time allowances of £100 for Clerks, £100 for incidents and £50 for a Housekeeper were also provided.[5] In addition to their ordinary remuneration the Methodisers also shared £1000 from the secret service money. This payment does not appear to have been continued after 1782.[6]

LIST OF APPOINTMENTS

1764	16 July	Ayloffe, Sir J. Ducarel, A. C. Astle, T.	1789	26 June	Astle, T. Topham, J. Astle, T.
1781	30 April	Ducarel, A. C. Astle, T. Topham, J.			

---

[1] For these offices, see *1st Rept. on Fees*, 34–5; Nelson, *Home Office*, 143–5.

[2] Treasury constitutions 22 July 1763, 12 June 1765 and royal warrant 26 June 1789 (T 54/39 pp. 181–6, 492–3; T 52/78 pp. 55–7).

[3] Royal warrant 7 March 1800 (T 52/85 pp. 473–4).

[4] Royal warrant 16 July 1764 (T 52/56 p. 99).

[5] Royal warrant 26 June 1789 (T 52/78 pp. 55–7).

[6] Ellis, *Post Office*, 133; *1st Rept. on Fees*, 34–5.

Clerks of the Signet, Deputy Clerks of the Signet and Office Keepers of the Signet Office 1660-1851

The number of the Clerks of the Signet was fixed at four from the sixteenth century.[1] The Clerks were appointed by the crown by letters patent under the great seal.[2] Between 1660 and 1807 grants of the offices were invariably for life and until 1678 reversionary in character.[3] After 1678 appointments were usually made only when one of the offices fell vacant.[4] Although the patents did not authorise the Clerks to act by deputy, it is clear that by the end of the seventeenth century most of the work had in fact been delegated to deputies or 'Clerks for the Business of the Office'.[5] From the early eighteenth century it was the usual practice for those Clerks who wished to act by deputy to secure from the crown a commission under the privy seal authorising them to do so.[6] Deputies, who occasionally acted for more than one principal at the same time, were frequently selected from amongst the Clerks in the Secretaries' offices.

In 1817 the offices were regulated by act which required that Clerks appointed thereafter should exercise their duties in person subject to such conditions as the Treasury should lay down.[7] In 1832 the Treasury was given statutory authority to reduce the number of clerkships when it saw fit.[8] Under this authority one office was abolished in 1833 and another in 1846.[9] The remaining two clerkships were abolished by act in 1851 which transferred to the Home Office the residual functions connected with the signet.[10]

Originally the Clerks of the Signet received no salary, being dependent on dividends of the fees arising from signet business for the greater part of their remuneration. During the Tudor and early Stuart period they had been entitled to diet as members of the Household. In the latter part of the seventeenth century this privilege was

[1] For these offices, see J. Otway-Ruthven, *The King's Secretary and the Signet Office in the 15th Century* (Cambridge 1939), 106-42, 157-9, 180-9; Evans, *Principal Secretary*, 194-209; Nelson, *Home Office*, 153-6; *Rept. of Committee on the Signet and Privy Seal Offices 1849* (HC 1849, xxii); HO 39/6, 12.

[2] With the single exception of Nicholas who was admitted a Clerk of the Signet to Charles II in exile in 1655 without a patent and was allowed to retain office at the Restoration, to the prejudice of the existing reversioners (*CSPD Addenda 1660-85*, 471; *CSPD 1660-1*, 304).

[3] After the Restoration there were three cases in which reversioners did not come into possession: Robert Reade (27 Nov. 1638), George Castle (17 Dec. 1645) and Nicholas Oudart (28 April 1662).

[4] Six further reversions were, however, granted: C. and T. Delafaye (1720), Wilkinson (1767), Morin (1767), Wilmot (1783), Bentinck (1801) and Gage (1803).

[5] Chamberlayne, *Present State* (1682), pt i., 194.

[6] As early as 1692 the younger Trumbull was formally authorised to act by deputy (Trumbull Add. MS 90) but this appears to be an isolated case.

[7] 57 Geo. III, c 63, ss 1, 2.   [8] 2 & 3 Will. IV, c 49, s 1.

[9] Treasury warrants 16 April 1833 (T 54/56 pp. 260-2), 7 Dec. 1846 (T 54/58 p. 401). The fees of the abolished clerkships were carried to the consolidated fund.

[10] 14 & 15 Vict., c 82, ss 3, 5.

commuted for board wages of £30 a year each payable by the Cofferer.[11] In 1825, under the authority of the act of 1817, the Treasury substituted a fixed salary of £300 in place of all other emoluments for Clerks appointed thereafter.[12] Until the early nineteenth century the remuneration of the deputies appears to have been a matter for private negotiation between them and their principals. From at least 1834, however, the deputies received a recognised share of the fees arising from signet business.[13]

An Office Keeper of the Signet Office first occurs in 1689. Until 1790 he was also Office Keeper of the Privy Seal Office. During the eighteenth century he occasionally acted as a Deputy Clerk of the Signet as well. In 1814 the Office Keeper was also appointed Receiver of Fees.[14] A second Office Keeper was appointed about 1828 and from about 1833 these two officials were described as Record Keepers and Receivers of Fees.

LISTS OF APPOINTMENTS

CLERKS OF THE SIGNET

By 1660	Warwick, Sir P.	1729	13 Nov.	Weston, E.
	Windebanke,	1736	7 May	Moyle, J.
	Sir T.[15]	1746	22 May	Blair, W.
	Trumbull, W.	1762	22 Dec.	Rivers, J.
	Nicholas, J.	1770	15 July	Wilkinson, M.
By 1678	Bere, S.	1781	16 April	Morin, J.
1678	Morrice, N.	1782	4 March	Fraser, W.
1683 15 Jan.	Trumbull, W.	1797	June	Wilmot, E.
c.1684	Gauntlet, J.	1801	24 Jan.	Taylor, B.
1705 9 Jan.	Cooke, W.	1802	11 Dec.	Bentinck, W. H. E.
1708 25 Aug.	Moyle, J.	1807	19 March	Gage, J.
1716 18 Feb.	Alexander, Hon. P.	1807	30 Oct.	Powlett, T. N.
1716 2 Oct.	Fry, G.	1825	26 Feb.	Cockburn, A.
1728 28 May	Delafaye, C.	1826	8 May	Stapleton, A. G.
	Delafaye, T.	1847	26 Jan.	Grey, C. S.

DEPUTY CLERKS OF THE SIGNET

By 1682	Gauntlet, J.	By 1722	Richardson, J.
	Williamson, R.	By 1723	Haynes, H.
	Woodeson, G.	1725	Marwood, W.
	Tench, J.	1725	Fisher, T.
By 1701	Gregson, R.[16]	By 1735	Davids, J.
By 1716	Fry, G.	1735	Moyle, J.

[11] *Household Ordinances* (Society of Antiquaries of London 1790), 406.
[12] Treasury warrant 2 Feb. 1825 (T 54/55 pp. 187–8).
[13] See Signet Office Apportionment Book 1834–51 (SO 5/43).
[14] Deed of 26 April 1814 (HO 39/6).
[15] Windebanke, a papist, never succeeded in making good his claim to be admitted although his legal title to office continued to be recognised in patents until 1674. The duties of this clerkship were in fact undertaken by Bere who was provisionally admitted a Clerk at the Restoration and confirmed in his position by order in council 3 Sept. 1662 (PC 2/56 p. 123).
[16] Usually described as 'Clerk of Dispatches'.

1735	Maskelyne, E.	1795	Jones, C. P.
1740	Richardson, J.	1795	Higden, W. H.
1740	Haynes, T.	1801	Williams Wynn, H. W.
1744	Brown, G.	By 1804	Bidwell, T.
1761	Haynes, J.	1808	Canning, S.
1769	Shadwell, R.	1814	Canning, C. F.
1769	Brietzcke, C.	1816	Venables, T.
1776	Jones, J.	1837	Plasket, T. H.
1776	Brietzcke, C.	1841	Taylor, B.
1785	Pollock, W.	1850	Scott, H. D.

OFFICE KEEPERS OF THE SIGNET OFFICE

By 1689	Littlefield, G.	By 1783	Jones, E. D.
By 1702	Fountain, N.	By 1789	Jones, C. P.
1735	Richardson, T.	By 1828	Jones, E. D.
1773	Routledge, J.	1832	Sanders, H. W.

Periodic Lists of Officials

LIST OF OFFICIALS AT ACCESSION OF ANNE
8 MARCH 1702

NORTHERN
DEPARTMENT
Secretary of State
  Vernon, J.
Under Secretaries
  Yard, R.
  Hopkins, T.
Chief Clerk
  Welby, A.
Clerks
  Egar, D.
  Jones, W.
  Weston, H.
  Tilson, G.
  Delafaye, C.
Office Keepers
  Shorter, T.
  Turner, J.
Necessary Woman
  Ombee, —

SOUTHERN
DEPARTMENT
Secretary of State
  Manchester, Earl of
Under Secretaries
  Ellis, J.
  Stanyan, A.
Chief Clerk
  (?) Lewis, E.
Clerks
  Chetwynd, J.
  Payzant, J.
  Roberts, P.
  Vanbrugh, K.
Office Keepers
  Smith, T.
  Ramsey, B.
Necessary Woman
  (Name unknown)

Embellisher of Letters
  Royer, G.
Writer of Gazette
  Yard, R.

*French Translator of
Gazette*
  Delafaye, L.
*Secretary for Latin
Tongue*
  Hill, R.
Decipherers
  Wallis, J.
  Blencowe, W.
Keeper of State Papers
  (Vacant)
Clerks of Signet
  Nicholas, Sir J.
  Morrice, N.
  Trumbull, Sir W.
  Gauntlet, J.
Deputy Clerks of Signet
  Woodeson, G.
  Gregson, R.
*Office Keeper of Signet
Office*
  Fountain, N.

LIST OF OFFICIALS AT ACCESSION OF GEORGE I
1 AUGUST 1714

NORTHERN
DEPARTMENT
Secretary of State
  Bromley, W.
Under Secretaries
  Lewis, E.
  (?) Holt, C.
Chief Clerk
  (Name unknown)

Clerks
  Payzant, J.
  (?) Weston, —
  Wace, J.
  (?) Mauries, —
Office Keepers
  (?) Smith, T.
  (?) Marlow, —
(?) *Deputy Office Keeper*
  (?) Pearson, —

Necessary Woman
  (Name unknown)

SOUTHERN
DEPARTMENT
Secretary of State
  Bolingbroke, Viscount
Under Secretaries
  Tilson, G.
  Hare, T.

Chief Clerk
  Jones, W.
Clerks
  Prevereau, D.
  Davids, J.
  Marshall, H.
  Maskelyne, N.
Office Keepers
  Shorter, T.
  (?) Mynatt, W.
Necessary Woman
  Ombee, —

SCOTTISH
DEPARTMENT
Secretary of State
  Mar, Earl of

Under Secretary
  Strahan, W.
Chief Clerk
  (?) Stanyan, T.
Clerks
  (Names unknown)
Office Keepers
  (Names unknown)
Necessary Woman
  (Name unknown)

Embellisher of Letters
  Brand, T.
Writer of Gazette
  Ford, C.

Secretary for Latin Tongue
  Hill, R.
Decipherer
  Keill, J.
Keeper of State Papers
  Tucker, J.
Clerks of Signet
  Trumbull, Sir W.
  Gauntlet, J.
  Cooke, W.
  Moyle, J.
Deputy Clerk of Signet
  Woodeson, G.
Office Keeper of Signet Office
  Fountain, N.

LIST OF OFFICIALS AT ACCESSION OF GEORGE II
11 JUNE 1727

NORTHERN
DEPARTMENT
Secretary of State
  Townshend, Viscount
Under Secretaries
  Tilson, G.
  Townshend, Hon. T.
Chief Clerk
  Wace, J.
Clerks
  Payzant, J.
  Richardson, J.
  Lawrey, A.
  West, G.
  Dale, J.
  Burnaby, J.
Office Keepers
  Smith, T.
  Burrows, I.
Necessary Woman
  Smart, E.

SOUTHERN
DEPARTMENT
Secretary of State
  Newcastle, Duke of

Under Secretaries
  Stanyan, T.
  Delafaye, C.
Chief Clerk
  Prevereau, D.
Clerks
  Couraud, J.
  Davids, J.
  Maskelyne, E.
  Stepney, J.
  Moore, H.
  Hutchinson, F. H.
  Sandys, W.
Office Keepers
  Ward, A.
  Noble, J.
Necessary Woman
  Bickford, M.

Embellisher of Letters
  Brand, Sir T.
Writer of Gazette
  Buckley, S.
Secretary for Latin Tongue
  Lee, W.

Interpreter of Oriental Languages
  Didichi, T. R.
Decipherers
  Corbiere, A.
  Willes, E.
  Ashfield, F.
Keeper of State Papers
  Howard, H.
Deputy Keeper of State Papers
  Wace, J.
Collector of State Papers
  Tilson, G.
Clerks of Signet
  Cooke, W.
  Moyle, J.
  Alexander, P.
  Fry, G.
Deputy Clerks of Signet
  Marwood, W.
  Fisher, T.
Office Keeper of Signet Office
  Fountain, N.

LIST OF OFFICIALS AT ACCESSION OF GEORGE III
25 OCTOBER 1760

NORTHERN
DEPARTMENT
Secretary of State
  Holdernesse, Earl of
Under Secretary
  Potenger, R.
*Assistant Under
Secretaries*
  Morin, M. P.
  Fraser, W.
Chief Clerk
  Larpent, J.
Clerks
  Stepney, J.
  Shadwell, R.
  Wace, F.
  Noble, T.
  Kluft, J. D.
  Wright, J.
  Brietzcke, C.
  Morrison, R.
Office Keepers
  Turner, R.
  Milburn, W.
Deputy Office Keeper
  Ancell, T.
Necessary Woman
  Southcott, M.

SOUTHERN
DEPARTMENT
Secretary of State
  Pitt, W.

Under Secretaries
  Wood, R.
  Rivers, J.
Chief Clerk
  Richardson, J.
Clerks
  Brown, G.
  Duck, W.
  Sneyd, J.
  Jouvencel, P. C.
  Francis, P.
  Haynes, J.
  Shuckburgh, S.
Office Keepers
  Sommer, J.
  White, J.
Necessary Woman
  Barrington, P.

Embellisher of Letters
  Brand, Sir T.
Writer of Gazette
  Weston, E.
Deputy Writer of Gazette
  Brown, G.
Law Clerk
  Stanhope, L.
*Secretary for Latin
Tongue*
  Ramsden, T.
*Interpreter of Oriental
Languages*
  Stonehewer, R.

*Translator of German
Language*
  Wallace, J.
*Translator of Southern
Languages*
  Rivers, J.
Decipherers
  Bath and Wells,
    Bishop of
  Willes, E.
  Willes, W.
  Neubourg, G. W.
Keeper of State Papers
  Stone, A.
Collector of State Papers
  Ramsden, T.
Clerks of Signet
  Delafaye, C.
  Weston, E.
  Moyle, J.
  Blair, W.
Deputy Clerks of Signet
  Haynes, T.
  Brown, G.
  Haines, J.
*Office Keeper of Signet
Office*
  Richardson, T.

LIST OF OFFICIALS ON EVE OF REORGANISATION
27 MARCH 1782

NORTHERN
DEPARTMENT
Secretary of State
  Stormont, Viscount
Under Secretaries
  Langlois, B.
  Fraser, W.

Chief Clerk
  Sneyd, J.
Senior Clerks
  Broughton, B.
  Aust, G.
Clerks
  Bidwell, T.

  Carter, R.
  Jenkins, J. W.
  Money, W.
  Manby, J.
Office Keepers
  Turner, R.
  (?) Shaw, J.

61

Deputy Office Keeper
  Ancell, T.
Necessary Woman
  Southcott, M.

SOUTHERN
DEPARTMENT
Secretary of State
  Hillsborough, Earl of
Under Secretaries
  Porten, Sir S.
  Bell, J.
Chief Clerk
  Shadwell, R.
Senior Clerks
  Duck, W.
  Brietzcke, C.
  Morin, J.
Clerks
  Randall, G.
  Higden, W. H.
  Carrington, G. W.
  Daw, T.
  Colleton, J. N.
  Chetwynd, Hon. R.
Office Keepers
  Kirby, W.
  Doudiet, J.
Necessary Woman
  Emmitt, E.

COLONIAL
DEPARTMENT
Secretary of State
  Ellis, W.
Under Secretaries
  Knox, W.
  Fisher, J.
Chief Clerk
  Pollock, W.
Senior Clerks
  Larpent, J.
  Sawer, W.
Clerks
  Wilmot, E.
  Peace, C.
  Palman, G. L.
  Burrell, W.
  Walsh, F. T.
Office Keeper
  Lackington, C.
Deputy Office Keeper
  Crowder, N.
Necessary Woman
  Muly, E.

Embellisher of Letters
  Holland, J.
Writer of Gazette
  Fraser, W.
Deputy Writer of Gazette
  Aust, G.

Secretary for Latin Tongue
  Ramsden, T.
Interpreter of Oriental Languages
  Cardozo Nunes, I.
Translator of German Language
  Fraser, W.
Decipherers
  Willes, E.
  Willes, F.
Keeper of State Papers
  Porten, Sir S.
Collector of State Papers
  Ramsden, T.
Methodisers of State Papers
  Ducarel, A. C.
  Astle, T.
  Topham, J.
Clerks of Signet
  Rivers, J.
  Wilkinson, M.
  Morin, J.
  Fraser, W.
Deputy Clerks of Signet
  Shadwell, R.
  Brietzcke, C.
Office Keeper of Signet Office
  Routledge, J.

Alphabetical List of Officials

Addison, Joseph *Under Secretary* (Hedges) July 1705–Dec. 1706; (Sunderland) Dec. 1706–Jan. 1709. *Secretary of State* (South) 12 April 1717–14 March 1718.

App. Under Secretary by Hedges July 1705 (Luttrell, *Hist. Relation*, v, 569), by Sunderland Dec. 1706 (ibid. vi, 112). Left office Jan. 1709 on app. as Chief Secretary to Lord Lieutenant, Ireland (ibid. 391). App. Secretary of State 12 April 1717 (*CTB*, xxxi, 274). Left office 14 March 1718 (ibid. xxxii, 329).

Aglionby, William *Under Secretary* (Nottingham) May–Aug. 1702.

App. by Nottingham May 1702 (*Post Man* no. 964). Left office Aug. 1702 on app. as Envoy to Swiss Cantons (*CSPD 1702–3*, 497; *Post Man* no. 998).

Aldworth, Richard Neville *Under Secretary* (Bedford) April 1748–June 1751.

App. by Bedford April 1748 (*Gent. Mag.* (1748), xviii, 188); app. notified 10 May 1748 (SP 44/129 p. 467).

Alexander, Hon. Peter *Clerk of Signet* 18 Feb. 1716–1 Nov. 1729.

App. 18 Feb. 1716 (C 66/3513). D. 1 Nov. 1729 (*Hist. Reg. Chron.* (1729), xiv, 61).

Allen, William *Clerk* (Newcastle) c. 1750.

Occ. from 16 April to 4 Nov. 1750 (T 52/45 p. 324).

Allen, William *Clerk* (Hillsborough) c. 1771–Aug. 1772; (Dartmouth) Aug. 1772–Nov. 1775; (Germain) Nov. 1775–c. 1781.

Occ. as Clerk to Hillsborough from 1771 to 1772 (*Royal Kal.* (1771), 116; ibid. (1772), 116), to Dartmouth from 1773 to 1775 (ibid. (1773), 116; ibid. (1775), 107), to Germain from 1776 to 1781 (ibid. (1776), 109; ibid. (1781), 110). Superannuated by March 1782 (T 1/579 Schedule 2).

Amyand, Claudius *Under Secretary* (Newcastle) April 1750–June 1751; (Holdernesse) June 1751–March 1754; (Robinson) March 1754–Nov. 1755; (Fox) Nov. 1755–Nov. 1756.

App. by Newcastle April 1750 (*Gent. Mag.* (1750), xx, 189; SP 45/27); received fees as Under Secretary to Holdernesse from June 1751 to March 1754 (SP 45/28); app. by Robinson March 1754 (*Gent. Mag.* (1754), xxiv, 143), by Fox Nov. 1755 (ibid. (1755), xxv, 523).

Ancell, Thomas *Deputy Office Keeper* (Newcastle) Jan. 1752–March 1754; (Holdernesse) March 1754–March 1761; (Bute) March 1761–May 1762; (Grenville) June–Oct. 1762; (Halifax) Oct. 1762–July 1765; (Seymour Conway) July 1765–Jan. 1768; (Weymouth) Jan. 1768–Dec. 1770; (Rochford) Dec. 1770–Nov. 1775; (Suffolk) Nov. 1775–March 1779; (Stormont) Oct. 1779–March 1782.

Deputy to R. Turner; received his fees as Office Keeper to Newcastle and Holdernesse from Jan. 1752 to Nov. 1756 (SP 45/27); probably continuously in office as Turner's deputy thereafter; occ. as Deputy Office Keeper to Halifax from 1764 to 1765 (*Court and City Reg.* (1764), 106; ibid. (1765), 110), to Seymour Conway from 1766 to 1768 (ibid. (1766), 107; *Royal Kal.* (1768), 118; Shelburne MS 134 p. 119), to Weymouth from 1769 to 1771 (sic) (*Royal Kal.* (1769), 117; ibid.

(1771), 115); probably became Deputy Office Keeper to Rochford on his transfer to Southern Department Dec. 1770 and to Suffolk on Weymouth's app. Nov. 1775; occ. as Deputy Office Keeper to Rochford from 1772 to 1775 (ibid. (1772), 115; ibid. (1775), 107), to Suffolk from 1776 to 1779 (ibid. (1776), 109; ibid. (1779), 109), to Stormont from 1780 to 1782 (ibid. (1780), 110; ibid. (1782), 110). Transferred to Foreign Office March 1782 (*1st Rept. on Fees*, 32).

Arbona, Jaime *Interpreter of Oriental Languages* June 1763–4 Sept. 1767.

App. notified 15 June 1763 (*CHOP 1760–5*, 289). D. 4 Sept. 1767 (T 52/59 pp. 161–2).

Arlington, Lord and Earl of *see* **Bennet,** Sir Henry

Armistead, Michael *Clerk* (Stanhope) c. 1716–April 1717; (Sunderland) April–Sept. 1717.

Occ. as Clerk to Stanhope from 6 July 1716 to 19 Jan. 1717 (*CTB*, xxx, 312; ibid. xxxi, 138–9); pd. as Clerk to Sunderland from 12 April to 29 Sept. 1717 (Sunderland MS D 1/36). Left office by 7 Oct. 1717 (SP 35/10 f. 16).

Armstrong, Thomas (?) *Chief Clerk* (Nottingham) March 1689–June 1690. *Clerk* (Nottingham) June 1690–Nov. 1693. *Chief Clerk* (Nottingham) May 1702–April 1704.

Heads list of Nottingham's Clerks July 1689 (LS 13/231 p. 14); possibly his Chief Clerk until replacement by Yard June 1690. Occ. as Clerk to Nottingham 1694 (sic) (Chamberlayne, *Present State* (1694), 243). Heads lists of Nottingham's Clerks from 1702 to 1704 (*Compleat History* (1702), 69; Chamberlayne, *Present State* (1704), 530). Kept Nottingham's accounts throughout both his periods of office (Finch MS DG 7/1/19a).

Ashfield, Frederick *Decipherer* c. 1723–24 Dec. 1728.

Occ. 23 Nov. 1723 (SP 35/46 f. 124). D. 24 Dec. 1728 (*Hist. Reg. Chron.* (1729), xiv, 4).

Aspinwall, Stanhope *Clerk* (Newcastle) May 1748–Aug. 1752.

App. by Newcastle notified 2 May 1748 (SP 44/148); described as 'Assistant Secretary' 1749 (*Court and City Reg.* (1749), 106); last occ. as Clerk 18 Nov. 1752 (T 52/46 p. 147). Probably left office 1752 on app. as Consul at Algiers (*Gent. Mag.* (1752), xxii, 385).

Astle, Thomas *Methodiser of State Papers* 16 July 1764–7 March 1800.

App. 16 July 1764 (T 52/56 p. 99; T 52/69 pp. 374–5; T 52/78 pp. 55–7). Office abolished 7 March 1800 (T 52/85 pp. 473–4).

Astle, Thomas *Methodiser of State Papers* 26 June 1789–7 March 1800.

App. 26 June 1789 (T 52/78 pp. 55–7). Office abolished 7 March 1800 (T 52/85 pp. 473–4).

Aust, George *Clerk* (Halifax) Sept. 1763–July 1765; (Seymour Conway) July 1765–Jan. 1768; (Weymouth) Jan. 1768–Dec. 1770; (Sandwich) Dec. 1770–Jan. 1771; (Halifax) Jan.–June 1771; (Suffolk) June 1771–March 1779; (Stormont) Oct. 1779–c. July 1780. *Senior Clerk* (Stormont) c. July 1780–March 1782.

Deputy Writer of Gazette c. 1781–90.

Probably app. Clerk by Halifax; presence in office notified as Clerk to Halifax 13 Sept. 1763, 30 April 1764 (*CHOP 1760–5*, 302–3, 407), to Seymour Conway 15 Aug. 1766 (*CHOP 1766–9*, 67), to Weymouth 20 Jan. 1768 (ibid. 293), to Sandwich 21 Dec. 1770 (*CHOP 1770–2*, 70), to Halifax 22 Jan., 20 March 1771 (ibid. 193, 225), to Suffolk 12 June 1771, 2 Oct. 1772 (ibid. 265, 556), to Stormont 9 Nov. 1779,

(FO 366/669 p. 16). Probably app. Senior Clerk in succession to F. Wace c. July 1780 (ibid. 27); first occ. as such 1781 (*Royal Kal.* (1781), 110). Transferred to Foreign Office March 1782 (*1st Rept. on Fees*, 29). Occ. as Deputy Writer of Gazette from 1781 to 1790 (*Royal Kal.* (1781), 110; ibid. (1790), 104).

Ayloffe, Sir Joseph, 6th Bart.   *Methodiser of State Papers* 16 July 1764–19 April 1781.

App. 16 July 1764 (T 52/56 p. 99). D. 19 April 1781 (T 53/55 p. 299).

Balaguier, John Anthony   (?) *Private Secretary* (Carteret) May 1721–April 1724. *Under Secretary* (Carteret/Granville) Feb. 1742–Nov. 1744.

App. by Carteret, probably as Private Secretary, notified 9 May 1721 (SP 44/147); acted as Under Secretary to Carteret abroad from 3 June to 30 Dec. 1723 (T 52/33 pp. 23, 51, 79, 275). App. by Carteret as Under Secretary notified 16 Feb. 1742 (SP 44/129 p. 285).

Ball, Henry   *Clerk* (Arlington) c. 1671–Sept. 1674; (Williamson) Sept. 1674–Dec. 1675.

Clerk in Arlington's office attached to Williamson; later Clerk to Williamson as Secretary of State; occ. from 2 Feb. 1671 to 2 Nov. 1675 (*CSPD 1671*, 65; *CSPD 1675-6*, 379). Left office c. Dec. 1675 on app. as Rose Rouge Pursuivant (H.S. London, *The College of Arms* (London 1963), 175–6).

Barrington *see* **Shirley**

Batchellor, Thomas   *Clerk* (Hedges) c. 1702–4.

Occ. from 1702 to 1704 (*Compleat History* (1702), 69—'Batcheam'; Chamberlayne, *Present State* (1704), 530). Had obtained employment in Ireland by April 1707 (BM Add. MS 28893 f. 243).

Bath and Wells, Bishop of *see* **Willes**, Edward

Bayly, Anselm Yates   *Clerk* (Dartmouth) c. 1775; (Germain) Nov. 1775–c. 1779.

Occ. as Clerk to Dartmouth 1775 (*Royal Kal.* (1775), 107), to Germain from 1776 to 1779 (ibid. (1776), 109; ibid. (1779), 109).

Bedford, John (Russell) 4th Duke of   *Secretary of State* (South) 13 Feb. 1748–14 June 1751.

App. 13 Feb. 1748 (T 53/42 p. 523). Left office 14 June 1751 (T 53/44 p. 102).

Bedingfield, Edmund   *Clerk* (Shrewsbury) c. 1689.

Occ. July 1689 (LS 13/231 p. 13).

Bell, Charles   *Clerk* (Bedford) c. 1751.

Occ. 1751 (*Court and City Reg.* (1751), 109).

Bell, John   *Under Secretary* (Hillsborough) Jan. 1781–March 1782.

App. by Hillsborough notified 4 Jan. 1781 (SP 44/143 p. 189). Transferred to Home Office March 1782 (SP 45/35).

Bennet, Sir Henry, kt. (cr. Lord **Arlington** 14 March 1665; Earl of **Arlington** 22 April 1672)   *Secretary of State* (South) 15 Oct. 1662–c. 11 Sept. 1674.

App. 15 Oct. 1662 (PC 2/56 p. 174). Left office by 11 Sept. 1674 (app. of Williamson).

Benson, Francis   *Clerk* (Arlington) c. 1671–Sept. 1674; (Williamson) Sept. 1674–Feb. 1679; (Sunderland) Feb. 1679–Feb. 1681; (Conway) Feb. 1681–Jan. 1683; (Sunderland) Jan. 1683–April 1686.

Clerk in Arlington's office attached to Williamson; later Clerk to Williamson as Secretary of State; occ. from 13 June 1671 to 8 Oct. 1678 (*CSPD 1671*, 318; *CSPD 1678*, 450); occ. as Clerk to Sunderland from 25 Sept. 1679 to 12 Oct. 1680 (*CSPD 1679-80*, 251; BM Add. MS 28875 f. 135), to Conway from 17 Jan. to 27

June 1682 (BM Add. MS 37983 ff. 24, 232), to Sunderland from 29 Dec. 1683 to d. (ibid. 28875 f. 328). D. April 1686 (*Ellis Corr.*, i, 115).

Bentinck, William Harry Edward *Clerk of Signet* 11 Dec. 1802–7 Aug. 1851.
 Grant in reversion 20 Aug. 1801 (C 66/3997); succ. 11 Dec. 1802 (d. of Fraser). Office abolished 7 Aug. 1851 (14 & 15 Vict., c 82, s 3).

Bere, Sidney *Clerk of Signet* c. 1678–84.
 Grant in reversion 5 Aug. 1641 (C 66/2890); admitted to office provisionally 1660–1 (*CSPD 1660–1*, 445; *CSPD 1661–2*, 3); following trial at law with Windebanke authorised by order in council 3 Sept. 1662 to continue to execute duties (PC 2/56 p. 123); came fully into possession of office between 12 June 1674 (grant of reversion to Gauntlet) and 2 May 1678 (grant of reversion to W. Cooke). D. by 26 July 1684 (Prob 11/376 f. 86).

Bernard, Daniel *Clerk* (Nottingham) March 1689–Nov. 1693. (?) *Chief Clerk* (Shrewsbury) March 1694–Nov. 1697.
 Occ. as Clerk to Nottingham from July 1689 to 1694 (sic) (LS 13/231 p. 14; Chamberlayne, *Present State* (1694), 243). Possibly Chief Clerk to Shrewsbury; recorded as receiving his official fees 5 Aug. 1697 (BM Add. MS 35107 f. 43). Dis. Nov. 1697 (Luttrell, *Hist. Relation*, iv, 301).

Bickford, Mary *Necessary Woman* (Carteret) Jan.–April 1724; (Newcastle) April 1724–c. 1743.
 App. by Carteret; pd. as Necessary Woman to Carteret from 31 Jan. to 3 April 1724 (MS Rawlinson C 367), to Newcastle from 4 April 1724 to 24 June 1733 (MSS Rawlinson C 367, 123); last occ. 1743 (Chamberlayne, *Present State* (1743), pt. ii, 32).

Bidwell, Thomas *Clerk* (Seymour Conway) Aug. 1766–Jan. 1768; (Weymouth) Jan. 1768–Dec. 1770; (Sandwich) Dec. 1770–Jan. 1771; (Halifax) Jan.–June 1771; (Suffolk) June 1771–March 1779; (Stormont) Oct. 1779–March 1782.
 Probably app. by Seymour Conway; presence in office notified as Clerk to Seymour Conway 15 Aug. 1766 (*CHOP 1766–9*, 67), to Weymouth 20 Jan. 1768 (ibid. 293), to Sandwich 21 Dec. 1770 (*CHOP 1770–2*, 103), to Halifax 22 Jan., 20 March 1771 (ibid. 193, 225), to Suffolk 12 June 1771, 2 Oct. 1772 (ibid. 265, 556), to Stormont 9 Nov. 1779 (FO 366/669 p. 16). Transferred to Foreign Office March 1782 (*1st Rept. on Fees*, 30).

Bidwell, Thomas *Deputy Clerk of Signet* c. 1804–March 1841.
 Deputy to Brook Taylor; first occ. 1804 (*Royal Kal.* (1804), 133). Res. March 1841 (SO 5/43; HO 39/12, Taylor to Jones and Sanders, 11 April 1841).

Blair, William *Private Secretary* (Harrington) June 1730–Feb. 1742; Nov. 1744–Oct. 1746.
 Clerk of Signet 22 May 1746–c. 4 March 1782.
 First occ. as Private Secretary to Harrington 10 June 1730 (T 52/37 p. 122); app. as such notified 17 Feb. 1733 (SP 44/122 p. 457), 27 Nov. 1744 (SP 44/129 p. 369). App. Clerk of Signet 22 May 1746 (C 66/3618). D. by 4 March 1782 (app. of Fraser).

Blathwayt, William *Under Secretary* (Conway) Feb. 1681–Jan. 1683.
 Occ. as Under Secretary to Conway 1682 (*Memoirs of Thomas, Earl of Ailesbury* (London 1890), i, 63); his letter book as Under Secretary contains copies of letters dated from 8 Feb. 1681 to 19 Jan. 1683 (BM Add. MS 35104 ff. 2, 85).

Blencowe, William *Decipherer* April 1701–25 Aug. 1712.
 App. April 1701 (*CTB*, xvi, 243). D. 25 Aug. 1712 (ibid. xxvii, 527).

Blenner, — *Necessary Woman* (Tweeddale) Feb. 1742–Jan. 1746.

App. by Tweeddale probably Feb. 1742; occ. from 1743 to 1 Jan. 1746 (Chamberlayne, *Present State* (1743), pt. ii, 32; Tweeddale MS Acc. 4862 Box 57/1b).

Blenner (Bloomer), John *Office Keeper* (Townshend) c. 1716; (Methuen) Dec. 1716–April 1717; (Addison) April 1717–c. 1718.

Occ. as Office Keeper to Townshend 1716 (Chamberlayne, *Present State* (1716), 527–8—'Blenner'); probably continued in office by Methuen; occ. as Office Keeper to Addison 1718 (ibid. (1718), pt. ii, 31—'Bloomer').

Bloomer *see* **Blenner,** John

Bolingbroke, Viscount *see* **St. John,** Hon. Henry

Borret, Thomas *Clerk* (Hedges) c. 1706; (Sunderland) Dec. 1706–June 1710.

Occ. as Clerk to Hedges 1707 (sic) (Chamberlayne, *Present State* (1707), 513), to Sunderland from 1708 to 1710 (ibid. (1708), 585; ibid. (1710), 515–16; SP 34/12 f. 165).

Bowes, George *Clerk* (Craggs) March 1718–c. 1719.

Probably app. by Craggs; presence in office first notified 29 March 1718 (SP 44/147); last notified 18 Dec. 1719 (ibid.).

Boyle, Hon. Henry *Secretary of State* (North) 13 Feb. 1708–20 Sept. 1710.

App. 13 Feb. 1708 (*CTB*, xxii, 301). Left office 20 Sept. 1710 (ibid. xxiv, 480).

Brand, Thomas (ktd. 14 Jan. 1718) *Embellisher of Letters* c. 1704–6 Nov. 1761.

Occ. from 11 April 1704 to d. (*CTB*, xix, 191; AO 1/420/199). D. 6 Nov. 1761 (AO 1/420/199).

Brereton, Thomas *Clerk* (Stanhope) c. 1716–17.

Occ. from 6 July 1716 to 19 Jan. 1717 (*CTB*, xxx, 312; ibid. xxxi, 138–9).

Bridgeman, William *Under Secretary* (Arlington) c. 1667–Sept. 1674; (Williamson) Sept. 1674–Feb. 1679; (Sunderland) Feb. 1679–Feb. 1681; Jan. 1683–Oct. 1688; (Middleton) Nov.–Dec. 1688; (Sydney) Dec. 1690–March 1692; (Trenchard) March 1693–July 1694.

Probably app. by Arlington in succession to Godolphin (*CSPD 1667–8*, 500); occ. as Under Secretary to Arlington from 9 June 1667 to 28 May 1674 (*CSPD 1667*, 163; *CSPD 1673–5*, 265), to Williamson from 6 Feb. 1675 to 16 Dec. 1678 (*CSPD 1673–5*, 573; *CSPD 1678*, 576), to Sunderland from 18 Oct. 1679 to 25 May 1680 (Hist. MSS Comm. *Ormonde*, iv, 545; *CSPD 1679–80*, 492); reapp. by Sunderland Jan. 1683 (Hist. MSS Comm. *7th Rept.*, 362); app. by Middleton Nov. 1688 (*Ellis Corr.*, ii, 287); the statement made by Ailesbury that he served as 'first secretary' to Shrewsbury 1689–90 (*Memoirs of Thomas, Earl of Ailesbury* (London 1890), i, 246–7) is not supported by any other evidence; app. by Sydney Dec. 1690 (*CSPD 1690–1*, 195; Luttrell, *Hist. Relation*, ii, 149), by Trenchard March 1693 (Luttrell, *Hist. Relation*, iii, 61). Left office July 1694 on app. as Secretary to Admiralty (ibid. 341).

Brietzcke, Charles *Clerk* (Holdernesse) April 1756–March 1761; (Bute) March 1761–May 1762; (Grenville) June–Oct. 1762; (Halifax) Oct. 1762–July 1765; (Seymour Conway) July 1765–May 1766; (Richmond) May–July 1766; (Shelburne) July 1766–Oct. 1768; (Rochford) Oct. 1768–c. 1772. *Senior Clerk* (Rochford) c. 1772–Nov. 1775; (Weymouth) Nov. 1775–Nov. 1779; (Hillsborough) Nov. 1779–March 1782.

Deputy Clerk of Signet 1769–70; 1776–95.

App. Clerk by Holdernesse 29 April 1756 (*Notes and Queries*, ccvi (1961), 147); app. notified 9 May 1757 (SP 44/148); occ. as Clerk to Holdernesse to 1761 (*Court and City Reg.* (1761), 106), to Bute 1762 (ibid. (1762), 106); presence in office notified as Clerk to Grenville 12 July 1762 (*CHOP 1760-5*, 189), to Halifax 8 Nov. 1762, 13 Sept. 1763, 30 April 1764 (ibid. 202, 302, 407); occ. as Clerk to Seymour Conway 1766 (*Court and City Reg.* (1766), 107); presence in office notified as Clerk to Richmond 28 June 1766 (*CHOP 1766-9*, 54), to Shelburne 27 July 1768 (ibid. 434), to Rochford 4 Nov. 1768 (ibid. 435). First occ. as Senior Clerk 1772 (*Royal Kal.* (1772), 115); presence in office as Senior Clerk to Weymouth notified 30 Nov. 1775 (*CHOP 1773-5*, 556); occ. as Senior Clerk to Weymouth to 1779 (*Royal Kal.* (1779), 109), to Hillsborough from 1780 to 1782 (ibid. (1780), 110; ibid. (1782), 110). Transferred to Home Office March 1782 (*1st Rept. on Fees*, 21). Occ. as Deputy Clerk of Signet to Weston from May 1769 to June 1770 (SO 5/3), to Blair from June 1776 to Feb. 1782 (SO 5/4); app. deputy to Fraser 21 March 1782 (Ind. 6767). Left office by 11 March 1795 (app. of Higden).

Brisbane, John   *Under Secretary* (Williamson) Sept. 1674–Sept. 1676.

App. by Williamson probably Sept. 1674; occ. 26 April 1675 (*CSPD 1675-6*, 80). Probably left office Sept. 1676 on app. as Agent in Paris (*CSPD 1676-7*, 318, 330).

Brocas, John   *Clerk* (Hedges) c. 1706; (Sunderland) Dec. 1706–June 1710.

Occ. as Clerk to Hedges 1707 (sic) (Chamberlayne, *Present State* (1707), 513), to Sunderland from 1708 to 1710 (ibid. (1708), 585; ibid. (1710), 515-16; SP 34/12 f. 165).

Bromley, William   *Secretary of State* (North) 17 Aug. 1713–22 Sept. 1714.

App. 17 Aug. 1713 (*CTB*, xxviii, 78). Left office 22 Sept. 1714 (ibid. xxix, 693).

Brooke, John   *Deputy Office Keeper* c. 1730–3.

Deputy to Sommer; received fees from March 1730 to Dec. 1733 (SP 45/26).

Broughton, Bryan   *Clerk* (Grenville) July–Oct. 1762; (Halifax) Oct. 1762–July 1765; (Seymour Conway) July 1765–Jan. 1768; (Weymouth) Jan. 1768–Dec. 1770; (Sandwich) Dec. 1770–Jan. 1771; (Halifax) Jan.–June 1771; (Suffolk) June 1771–March 1779. *Senior Clerk* (Stormont) Nov. 1779–March 1782.

App. as Clerk by Grenville notified 16 July 1762 (*CHOP 1760-5*, 190); presence in office notified as Clerk to Halifax 8 Nov. 1762, 13 Sept. 1763, 30 April 1764 (ibid. 202, 302-3, 407), to Seymour Conway 15 Aug. 1766 (*CHOP 1766-9*, 67), to Weymouth 20 Jan. 1768 (ibid. 293), to Sandwich 21 Dec. 1770 (*CHOP 1770-2*, 103), to Halifax 22 Jan., 20 March 1771 (ibid. 193, 225), to Suffolk 12 June 1771, 2 Oct. 1772 (ibid. 265, 556); occ. as Clerk to Suffolk to 1779 (*Royal Kal.* (1779), 109). Presence in office as Senior Clerk to Stormont notified 9 Nov. 1779 (FO 366/669 p. 16). Transferred to Foreign Office March 1782 (*1st Rept. on Fees*, 29).

Brown, —   *Clerk* (Trenchard) c. 1694.

Occ. 1694 (Chamberlayne, *Present State* (1694), 243).

Brown, George   *Clerk* (Harrington) Nov. 1734–Feb. 1742; (Carteret/Granville) Feb. 1742–Nov. 1744; (Harrington) Nov. 1744–Oct. 1746; (Chesterfield) Oct. 1746–Feb. 1748; (Bedford) Feb. 1748–June 1751; (Holdernesse) June 1751–March 1754; (Robinson) March 1754–Nov. 1755; (Fox) Nov. 1755–Nov. 1756; (Pitt) Dec. 1756–Oct. 1761; (Egremont) Oct. 1761–Aug. 1763; (Sandwich) Sept. 1763–July 1765; (Grafton) July 1765–May 1766. *Chief Clerk* (Grafton) May 1766; (Richmond) May–July 1766; (Shelburne) July 1766–Oct. 1768; (Rochford) Oct. 1768–10 April 1769. *Deputy Clerk of Signet* 1744–10 April 1769.

Deputy Writer of Gazette c. 1751–10 April 1769.

App. as Clerk by Harrington notified 20 Nov. 1734 (SP 44/122 p. 509); occ. as Clerk to Harrington to 1741 (Chamberlayne, *Present State* (1741), pt. ii, 47), to Carteret 1743 (ibid. (1743), pt. ii, 32), to Harrington 1745 (ibid. (1745), pt. ii, 32); presence in office as Clerk to Chesterfield notified 21 Nov. 1746 (SP 44/129 p. 428); occ. as Clerk to Bedford from 1748 to 1751 (Chamberlayne, *Present State* (1748), pt. ii, 52; *Court and City Reg.* (1751), 108), to Holdernesse from 1752 to 1754 (*Court and City Reg.* (1752), 107; ibid. (1754), 106), to Robinson from 1755 to 1756 (sic) (Chamberlayne, *Present State* (1755), pt. ii, 53; *Court and City Reg.* (1756), 107); probably continued in office by Fox; presence in office notified as Clerk to Pitt 17 Dec. 1756 (SP 44/136 p. 399), to Egremont 13 Oct. 1761 (*CHOP 1760–5*, 70), to Sandwich 9 Sept. 1763, 30 April 1764 (ibid. 302, 408), to Grafton 23 July 1765 (ibid. 580). App. as Chief Clerk by Grafton notified 10 May 1766 (*CHOP 1766–9*, 42); presence in office notified as Chief Clerk to Richmond 28 June 1766 (ibid. 54), to Shelburne 27 July 1768 (ibid. 434), to Rochford 4 Nov. 1768 (ibid. 435). Occ. as Deputy Clerk of Signet to Delafaye from July 1744 to Dec. 1762 (SO 5/2–3), to Weston from Aug. 1749 to Jan. 1769 (ibid.). Occ. as Deputy Writer of Gazette from 1751 to 1769 (*Court and City Reg.* (1751), 108; *Royal Kal.* (1769), 118). D. 10 April 1769 (*Gent. Mag.* (1769), xxxix, 215).

Bruce, John   *Secretary for Latin Tongue* 15 Nov. 1792–16 April 1826.

Keeper of State Papers 15 Nov. 1792–16 April 1826.

App. Secretary for Latin Tongue 15 Nov. 1792 (C 66/3885), Keeper of State Papers 15 Nov. 1792 (C 66/3885, 3963). D. 16 April 1826 (*Gent. Mag.* (1826), xcvi (2), 87).

Brummell, William   *Clerk* (Bute) March 1761–May 1762.

Probably app. by Bute March 1761; occ. 1762 (*Court and City Reg.* (1762), 106). Left office May 1762 (*Notes and Queries*, cciv (1959), 283).

Buckley, Samuel   *Writer of Gazette* Sept. 1714–8 Sept. 1741.

App. notified 24 Sept. 1714 (SP 44/147); grant for life 7 May 1719 (C 66/3531). D. 8 Sept. 1741 (*Gent. Mag.* (1741), xi, 500).

Burch, Joseph   *Clerk* (Boyle) Sept. 1709–Sept. 1710; (St. John/Bolingbroke) Sept. 1710–c. 1711.

App. by Boyle notified 1 Sept. 1709 (SP 44/107 p. 280); presence in office as Clerk to St. John notified 23 Nov. 1710 (SP 44/109); occ. as Clerk to St. John 1711 (Boyer, *Political State* (1711), 377). Probably left office 1712 on app. as Secretary to Lord Lexington, Ambassador to Spain (*Dip. Rep.*, 131).

Burke, William   *Under Secretary* (Seymour Conway) July 1765–Feb. 1767.

App. by Seymour Conway notified 15 July 1765 (*CHOP 1760–5*, 576). Res. by 21 Feb. 1767 (*CHOP 1766–9*, 161).

Burnaby, John   *Clerk* (Townshend) Feb. 1727–1729. *Under Secretary* (Harrington) Nov. 1741–Feb. 1742.

App. as Clerk by Townshend notified 2 Feb. 1727 (SP 44/122 p. 313); last occ. 13 Sept. 1729 (T 52/36 p. 403). Left office 1729 on app. as Secretary to Earl Waldegrave, Ambassador to Empire (BM Add. MSS 32689 f. 289, 33057 ff. 49–50; *Dip. Rep.*, 35). App. as Under Secretary by Harrington notified 24 Nov. 1741 (SP 44/129 p. 275).

Burniston, Charles   *Clerk* (Dartmouth) c. 1711.

D. in office by 26 April 1711 (SP 44/110 p. 8).

Burrell, Walter   *Clerk* (Germain) c. 1782; (Ellis) Feb.–March 1782.

Occ. as Clerk to Germain 1782 (*Royal Kal.* (1782), 110); continued in office by Ellis. Left office March 1782 on abolition of Colonial Department (T 1/579 Schedule 2).

Burrows, Isaac   *Office Keeper* (Stanhope) c. 1716–April 1717; (Sunderland) April 1717–March 1718; (Stanhope) March 1718–Feb. 1721; (Townshend) Feb. 1721–May 1730; (Harrington) May 1730–March 1732.

Occ. as Office Keeper to Stanhope from 6 July 1716 to 19 Jan. 1717 (*CTB*, xxx, 312; ibid. xxxi, 138–9); pd. as Office Keeper to Sunderland from April 1717 to March 1718 (Sunderland MS D 1/36), to Stanhope from 29 Sept. 1718 to 29 Sept. 1720 (Stanhope MS 76); occ. as Office Keeper to Townshend 1723 (Chamberlayne, *Present State* (1723), 483); received fees as Office Keeper to Townshend from Jan. 1727 to May 1730 and to Harrington from June 1730 to April 1732 (SP 45/26). Left office March 1732 on app. as Poor Knight, Windsor (*Gent. Mag.* (1732), ii, 680).

Bute, John (Stuart) 3rd Earl of   *Secretary of State* (North) 25 March 1761–27 May 1762.

App. 25 March 1761 (T 53/48 p. 3). Left office 27 May 1762 (ibid.).

Butler, —   *Office Keeper* (Holdernesse) c. 1760.

Occ. 1760 (*Court and City Reg.* (1760), 106).

Canning, Charles Fox   *Deputy Clerk of Signet* July 1814–18 June 1815.

Deputy to Powlett; took oath as such 21 July 1814 (HO 39/6). D. 18 June 1815 (*Gent. Mag.* (1815), lxxxv (2), 180).

Canning, Stratford   *Deputy Clerk of Signet* Jan. 1808–July 1814.

App. Deputy to Powlett 29 Jan. 1808 (Ind. 6770). Left office by 21 July 1814 (app. of C. F. Canning).

Cardozo Nunes, Isaac   *Interpreter of Oriental Languages* March 1782–c. 24 Feb. 1784.

App. March 1782 (HO 42/5, Cardozo Nunes to Sydney, 3 Nov. 1784). Dis. by 24 Feb. 1784 (HO 42/16, Lucas to Grenville, 22 Aug. 1790).

Carne, Edward   *Clerk* (Middleton) c. 1684.

'Mr. Carne'; probably identical with Edward Carne (Hist. MSS Comm. *1st Rept.*, 56). Occ. 1684 (Evans, *Principal Secretary*, 192–3).

Carrington, George William   *Clerk* (Shelburne) 1768; (Rochford) Oct. 1768–Nov. 1775; (Weymouth) Nov. 1775–Nov. 1779; (Hillsborough) Nov. 1779–March 1782.

App. by Shelburne 1768 (Shelburne MS 134 p. 147); presence in office notified as Clerk to Rochford 4 Nov. 1768 (*CHOP 1766–9*, 435), to Weymouth 30 Nov. 1775 (*CHOP 1773–5*, 556); occ. as Clerk to Weymouth to 1779 (*Royal Kal.* (1779), 109), to Hillsborough from 1780 to 1782 (ibid. (1780), 110; ibid. (1782), 110). Transferred to Home Office March 1782 (*1st Rept. on Fees*, 22).

Carter, Richard   *Clerk* (Suffolk) Feb. 1772–March 1779; (Stormont) Oct. 1779–March 1782.

App. by Suffolk notified 5 Feb. 1772 (*CHOP 1770–2*, 426); presence in office notified as Clerk to Suffolk 2 Oct. 1772 (ibid. 556), to Stormont 9 Nov. 1779 (FO 366/669 p. 16). Transferred to Foreign Office March 1782 (*Royal Kal.* (1783), 110).

Carteret, John (Carteret) 2nd Lord (succ. as 2nd Earl **Granville** 18 Oct. 1744) *Secretary of State* (South) 4 March 1721–3 April 1724; (North) 12 Feb. 1742–24 Nov. 1744.

App. 4 March 1721 (T 53/29 p. 347). Left office 3 April 1724 (T 53/31 p. 191).
App. 12 Feb. 1742 (*CTBP 1742-5*, 170). Left office 24 Nov. 1744 (ibid. 795).

Chamier, Anthony   *Under Secretary* (Weymouth) Nov. 1775–Nov. 1779; (Hillsborough) Nov. 1779–12 Oct. 1780.

App. by Weymouth notified 30 Nov. 1775 (*CHOP 1773-5*, 556); received fees as Under Secretary to Hillsborough from Nov. 1779 to Oct. 1780 (SP 45/34-5). D. 12 Oct. 1780 (*Gent. Mag.* (1780), l, 495).

Champion, Lewis   *Clerk* (Shrewsbury) c. 1689.

Occ. July 1689 (LS 13/231 p. 13). Probably left office 1689 on app. as Secretary to Alexander Stanhope, Envoy Extraordinary to Spain (*Dip. Rep.*, 127-8).

Champneys, William   *Clerk* (Trumbull) c. 1695-7.

'Mr. Champneys'; probably identical with William Champneys app. 1697 to service of Sir Joseph Williamson, Envoy to United Provinces (BM Add. MS 28899 ff. 218, 418). Pd. as Clerk to Trumbull from 3 Nov. 1695 to 3 Feb. 1697 (Trumbull Add. MS 113).

Changuion, —   *Private Secretary* (Richmond) Oct. 1765.

App. Private Secretary by Richmond Oct. 1765 (Hist. MSS Comm. *10th Rept.*, 396).

Chesterfield, Philip Dormer (Stanhope) 4th Earl of   *Secretary of State* (North) 19 Oct. 1746–6 Feb. 1748.

App. 19 Oct. 1746 (T 53/42 p. 290). Left office 6 Feb. 1748 (ibid. p. 523).

Chetwynd, John   *Clerk* (Manchester) c. 1702.

Occ. 1701 (sic) (*Compleat History* (1701), 98).

Chetwynd, Hon. Richard   *Clerk* (Weymouth) June–Nov. 1779; (Hillsborough) Nov. 1779–March 1782.

App. by Weymouth notified 10 June 1779 (SP 44/143 p. 166); occ. as Clerk to Hillsborough from 1780 to 1782 (*Royal Kal.* (1780), 110; ibid. (1782), 110). Transferred to Home Office March 1782 (*1st Rept. on Fees*, 23).

Chetwynd, William Richard   *Under Secretary* (Harrington) Dec. 1744–Oct. 1746; (Chesterfield) Oct. 1746–Feb. 1748; (Bedford) Feb.–April 1748.

App. notified by Harrington 3 Dec. 1744 (SP 44/129 p. 370), by Chesterfield 21 Nov. 1746 (ibid. p. 428); continued in office by Bedford. Res. April 1748 (*Gent. Mag.* (1748), xviii, 188).

Chute, Edward   *Clerk* (Jenkins) (?)–April 1684; (Godolphin) April–Aug. 1684; (Middleton) Aug. 1684–Sept. 1685.

App. by Jenkins (Hist. MSS Comm. *Downshire*, i, 44); continued in office by Godolphin and Middleton (Evans, *Principal Secretary*, 192-3). Left office Sept. 1685 on app. as Secretary to Sir William Trumbull, Ambassador to France (Hist. MSS Comm. *Downshire*, i, 45).

Cockburn, Alexander   *Clerk of Signet* 26 Feb. 1825–8 May 1826.

App. 26 Feb. 1825 (C 66/4284). Grant revoked 8 May 1826 (app. of Stapleton).

Coling, —   *Clerk* (Sunderland) c. 1708.

Occ. 1708 (Chamberlayne, *Present State* (1708), 585).

Colleton, James Nassau   *Clerk* (Rochford) Oct. 1774–Nov. 1775; (Weymouth) Nov. 1775–Nov. 1779; (Hillsborough) Nov. 1779–March 1782.

App. by Rochford notified 1 Oct. 1774 (*CHOP 1773-5*, 245); presence in office notified as Clerk to Weymouth 30 Nov. 1775 (ibid. 556); occ. as Clerk to Weymouth to 1779 (*Royal Kal.* (1779), 109), to Hillsborough from 1780 to 1782 (ibid. (1780),

110; ibid. (1782), 110). Transferred to Home Office March 1782 (*1st Rept. on Fees*, 23).

Collins, Charles *Clerk* (Grafton) March–May 1766; (Richmond) May–July 1766; (Shelburne) 1766.

App. by Grafton notified 14 March 1766 (*CHOP 1766–9*, 24); presence in office notified as Clerk to Richmond 28 June 1766 (ibid. 54); last occ. as Clerk to Shelburne 1766 (Shelburne MS 134 p. 119).

Conway, Edward (Conway) 1st Earl of *Secretary of State* (North) 2 Feb. 1681–28 Jan. 1683.

App. 2 Feb. 1681 (PC 2/69 p. 203). Left office 28 Jan. 1683 (Hist. MSS Comm. *7th Rept.*, 362).

Conway *see also* **Seymour Conway**

Cooke, George *Clerk* (Halifax) Sept. 1763–July 1765; (Seymour Conway) July 1765–Jan. 1768; (Weymouth) Jan. 1768–Dec. 1770; (Sandwich) Dec. 1770–Jan. 1771; (Halifax) Jan.–June 1771; (Suffolk) June 1771–Nov. 1776.

Probably app. by Halifax; presence in office notified as Clerk to Halifax 13 Sept. 1763, 30 April 1764 (*CHOP 1760–5*, 302–3, 407), to Seymour Conway 15 Aug. 1766 (*CHOP 1766–9*, 67), to Weymouth 20 Jan. 1768 (ibid. 293), to Sandwich 21 Dec. 1770 (*CHOP 1770–2*, 103), to Halifax 22 Jan., 20 March 1771 (ibid. 193, 225), to Suffolk 12 June 1771, 2 Oct. 1772 (ibid. 265, 556). Res. 27 Nov. 1776 on app. as Consul at Tripoli (FO 95/591/1 f. 6; *Royal Kal.* (1777), 94).

Cooke, John *Under Secretary* (Morrice) May 1660–Sept. 1668; (Trevor) Sept. 1668–May 1672; (Coventry) July 1672–April 1680; (Jenkins) April 1680–April 1684; (Godolphin) April–Aug. 1684; (Middleton) Aug. 1684–Oct. 1688.

Secretary for Latin Tongue 2 March 1682–19 Sept. 1691.

App. Under Secretary by Morrice probably May 1660; occ. as such from 10 Aug. 1662 to 28 July 1668 (*CSPD 1661–2*, 457; *CSPD 1667–8*, 509); app. Under Secretary by Trevor Sept. 1668 (Coventry MS 119 f. 1); occ. as such from 2 Nov. 1668 to 9 Jan. 1672 (*CSPD 1668–9*, 47; BM Add. MS 56240, Cooke to Blathwayt, 9 Jan. 1672); occ. as Under Secretary to Coventry from 31 Oct. 1672 to 10 Feb. 1680 (*CSPD 1672–3*, 105; *CSPD 1679–80*, 388), to Jenkins from 17 Sept. 1680 to 23 March 1684 (*CSPD 1680–1*, 23; *CSPD 1683–4*, 337); continued in office by Godolphin and Middleton (Evans, *Principal Secretary*, 192). Left office Oct. 1688 on transfer of Middleton to Southern Department (BM Add. MS 45731 f. 38; Hist. MSS Comm. *7th Rept.*, 422). App. Secretary for Latin Tongue 2 March 1682 (C 66/3230, 3262). D. 19 Sept. 1691 (*Westminster Abbey Registers*, ed. J. L. Chester (London 1876), 229 note 3).

Cooke, William *Clerk of Signet* 9 Jan. 1705–28 May 1728.

Grant in reversion 2 May 1678 (C 66/3201); succ. 9 Jan. 1705 (d. of Sir J. Nicholas). Left office 28 May 1728 (SO 5/2).

Copley *see* **Moyle**, Joseph (d. 1781)

Corbiere, Anthony *Decipherer* Sept. 1715–21 May 1743.

Pd. from 29 Sept. 1715 (*CTB*, xxx, 56). D. 21 May 1743 (T 53/41 p. 466).

Cosby, Dudley Alexander Sydney *Private Secretary* (Halifax) Nov. 1762–Aug. 1763.

App. by Halifax notified 9 Nov. 1762 (*CHOP 1760–5*, 202).

Costa, Francis *Interpreter of Oriental Languages* July 1802–30 Nov. 1806.

Pd. from 5 July 1802 to 30 Nov. 1806 (HO 82/3; CO 701/1 pp. 48, 62). D. 30 Nov. 1806 (CO 701/1 p. 62).

Couraud, John *Clerk* (Sunderland) April 1717–March 1718; (Stanhope) March 1718–Feb. 1721; (Townshend) Feb. 1721–Sept. 1724; (Newcastle) Sept. 1724–June 1729. *Under Secretary* (Newcastle) June 1729–1743.

Secretary for Latin Tongue 27 Nov. 1730–19 Feb. 1751.

Keeper of State Papers 3 Feb. 1739–5 May 1741. *Collector of State Papers* 26 June 1741–19 Feb. 1751.

Pd. as Clerk to Sunderland from April 1717 to March 1718 (Sunderland MS D 1/36), to Stanhope from 29 Sept. 1718 to 29 Sept. 1720 (Stanhope MS 76); occ. as Clerk to Townshend from 30 May to 30 Dec. 1723 (T 52/32 p. 361; T 52/33 pp. 23, 51, 79, 275); pd. as Clerk to Newcastle from 5 Sept. 1724 to 24 June 1729 (MS Rawlinson C 367). App. Under Secretary by Newcastle June 1729 (BM Add. MS 32687 f. 346); last occ. 1 April 1742 (SP 44/148). Probably left office 1743 (J. Haydn, *Book of Dignities*, 3rd ed. (London 1894), 225). App. Secretary for Latin Tongue 27 Nov. 1730 (C 66/3582), Keeper of State Papers 3 Feb. 1739 (C 66/3599), Collector of State Papers 26 June 1741 (C 66/3606, 3611). D. 19 Feb. 1751 (T 53/43 p. 4).

Coventry, Hon. Henry *Secretary of State* (North) 3 July 1672–Sept. 1674; (South) Sept. 1674–c. 26 April 1680.

App. 3 July 1672 (PC 2/63 p. 275). Left office by 26 April 1680 (app. of Jenkins).

Craggs, James *Secretary of State* (South) 15 March 1718–16 Feb. 1721.

App. 15 March 1718 (*CTB*, xxxii, 270). D. 16 Feb. 1721 (*Hist. Reg. Chron.* (1721), vi, 9).

Cranmer, Thomas *Clerk* (Newcastle) July 1744–c. 1746.

App. by Newcastle notified 20 July 1744 (SP 44/148). D. by 1746 (*Court and City Reg.* (1746), 99).

Crowder, Nathaniel *Deputy Office Keeper* (Dartmouth) c. 1774–Nov. 1775; (Germain) Nov. 1775–Feb. 1782; (Ellis) Feb.–March 1782.

Deputy to Muly; occ. as Deputy Office Keeper to Dartmouth from 1774 to 1775 (*Royal Kal.* (1774), 116; ibid. (1775), 107), to Germain from 1776 to 1782 (ibid. (1776), 109; ibid. (1782), 110), to Ellis March 1782 (T 1/579 Schedule 2). Transferred to Home Office March 1782 (*Royal Kal.* (1783), 110).

Dale, John *Clerk* (Townshend) c. 1727–May 1730; (Harrington) May 1730–c. 1731.

Occ. as Clerk to Townshend from 31 May 1727 to 14 May 1729 (T 52/35 p. 2; T 52/36 pp. 330–1), to Harrington 1731 (Miège, *Present State* (1731), 173).

Dartmouth, William (Legge) 2nd Lord (cr. Earl of **Dartmouth** 5 Sept. 1711) *Secretary of State* (South) 14 June 1710–16 Aug. 1713.

App. 14 June 1710 (*CTB*, xxiv, 371). Left office 16 Aug. 1713 (ibid. xxvii, 523).

Dartmouth, William (Legge) 2nd Earl of *Secretary of State* (Colonies) 15 Aug. 1772–10 Nov. 1775.

App. 15 Aug. 1772 (T 53/52 p. 367). Left office 10 Nov. 1775 (T 53/53 p. 143).

Davids, James *Clerk* (St. John/Bolingbroke) Nov. 1710–Aug. 1714; (Townshend) Sept. 1714–Dec. 1716; (Methuen) Dec. 1716–April 1717; (Addison) April 1717–March 1718; (Craggs) March 1718–Feb. 1721; (Carteret) March 1721–April 1724; (Newcastle) April 1724–c. Sept. 1737.

Deputy Clerk of Signet c. 1735.

Probably app. Clerk by St. John; presence in office notified as Clerk to St. John 23 Nov. 1710 (SP 44/109), to Townshend 30 Sept. 1714 (SP 44/116); probably continued in office by Methuen; occ. as Clerk to Addison 1718 (Miège, *Present*

State (1718), pt. i, 362); presence in office notified as Clerk to Craggs 29 March 1718, 18 Dec. 1719 (SP 44/147); pd. as Clerk to Carteret from 29 Sept. 1723 to 3 April 1724 (MS Rawlinson C 367), to Newcastle from 4 April 1724 to 24 June 1733 (MSS Rawlinson C 367, 123); last occ. 1736 (Chamberlayne, *Present State* (1736), pt. ii, 47). D. by 24 Sept. 1737 (SP 36/43 ff. 19–21). Occ. as Deputy Clerk of Signet 1735 (Chamberlayne, *Present State* (1735), pt. ii, 43).

Daw, Thomas   *Clerk* (Shelburne) 1768; (Rochford) Oct. 1768–Nov. 1775; (Weymouth) Nov. 1775–Nov. 1779; (Hillsborough) Nov. 1779–March 1782.

App. by Shelburne 1768 (Shelburne MS 134 p. 147); presence in office notified as Clerk to Rochford 4 Nov. 1768 (*CHOP 1766–9*, 435), to Weymouth 30 Nov. 1775 (*CHOP 1773–5*, 556); occ. as Clerk to Weymouth to 1779 (*Royal Kal.* (1779), 109), to Hillsborough from 1780 to 1782 (ibid. (1780), 110; ibid. (1782), 110). Transferred to Home Office March 1782 (*1st Rept. on Fees*, 23).

Dayrolle, James   *Clerk* (Trumbull) c. 1695–7.

'Mr. Dayrolle'; probably identical with James Dayrolle, Secretary to Sir William Trumbull as Ambassador to Turkey (*Dip. Rep.*, 150). Pd. as Clerk from 3 Nov. 1695 to 3 Feb. 1697 (Trumbull Add. MS 113).

Deceramis, Alexander Xerxes   *Interpreter of Oriental Languages* May 1769.

App. notified 11 May 1769 (*CHOP 1766–9*, 557); no further occ.

de Grey, Thomas   *Under Secretary* (Germain) Jan. 1778–Oct. 1780.

Pd. from 5 Jan. 1778 to 10 Oct. 1780 (SP 45/32).

de Lacombe de Vrigny, James Philip   *Clerk* (Vernon) June 1699–1702.

'M. de Vrigny'; probably identical with James Philip de Lacombe de Vrigny (*Letters of Denization and Acts of Naturalization for Aliens in England and Ireland 1603–1700*, ed. W. A. Shaw (Huguenot Soc. Publications, xviii, 1911), 296). App. by Vernon June 1699 (Hist. MSS Comm. *Bath*, iii, 366); pd. from 2 June 1699 to 25 Dec. 1701 (BM Add. MSS 40785 f. 43; 40786 f. 28); received payment 13 Feb. 1702 probably for quarter to 25 March 1702 (BM Add. MS 40786 f. 33). Left office 1702 on app. to service of James Vernon, jun., Envoy to Denmark (*British Diplomatic Instructions 1689–1789*, iii (Denmark), ed. J. F. Chance (Camden 3rd ser., xxxvi, 1926), 22).

Delafaye, Charles   *Clerk* (Jersey) c. 1700; (Vernon) Nov. 1700–May 1702; (Nottingham) May 1702–April 1704; (Hedges) May 1704–Dec. 1706. *Chief Clerk* (Sunderland) Dec. 1706–June 1710; (Dartmouth) June 1710–Aug. 1713. *Under Secretary* (Sunderland) April 1717–March 1718; (Stanhope) March 1718–Feb. 1721; (Townshend) Feb. 1721–April 1724; (Newcastle) April 1724–July 1734.

Writer of Gazette May 1702–May 1707.

Clerk of Signet 28 May 1728–11 Dec. 1762.

Question of app. as Clerk to Shrewsbury mentioned 21 Dec. 1697 (*CSPD 1697*, 523); occ. as 'Extraordinary' Clerk to Jersey 1700 (Chamberlayne, *Present State* (1700), 502); probably became Clerk to Vernon on his transfer to Southern Department Nov. 1700; occ. as such 1701 (Miège, *New State* (1701), pt. iii, 109); not one of Vernon's salaried Clerks (BM Add. MSS 40785–6); occ. as Clerk to Nottingham from 1702 to 1704 (*Compleat History* (1702), 69; Chamberlayne, *Present State* (1704), 530); probably became Clerk to Hedges on his transfer to Southern Department May 1704; occ. as such 1707 (sic) (Chamberlayne, *Present State* (1707), 513). Probably app. Chief Clerk by Sunderland Dec. 1706; heads lists of Clerks to Sunderland from 1708 to 1710 (ibid. (1708), 585; ibid. (1710), 515–16), to Dartmouth 1711 (Boyer, *Political State* (1711), 377); apparently kept Dartmouth's accounts as Secretary of State (Dartmouth MS D 1778 I, ii no. 444). Left office Sept. 1713 on app. as Private Secretary to Duke of Shrewsbury as Lord Lieutenant, Ireland (ibid. no. 425). App. Under Secretary by Sunderland April 1717 (*Hist. Reg. Chron.* (1717), ii, 20; SP 44/120 p. 157); occ. as Under Secretary to Stanhope from 11 April 1718 to 6 Aug. 1720 (SP 44/120 pp. 316, 523), to Townshend from 17 Feb. 1721 to April 1724 (SP 44/122 p. 8; *Hist. Reg. Chron.* (1724), ix, 20); app. Under Secretary by Newcastle April 1724 (*Hist. Reg. Chron.* (1724), ix, 20). Left office July 1734 (*Gent. Mag.* (1734), iv, 392). Probably app. Writer of Gazette May 1702 in succession to Yard (Hist. MSS Comm. *Portland*, viii, 187–8); first occ. 23 March 1704 (*House of Lords MSS*, new ser., v, 467–8); pd. from 15 Nov. 1706 to 1707 (BM Loan 29/162). Left office May 1707 on app. of Steele (ibid.). Grant of clerkship of signet in reversion jointly with T. Delafaye 2 March 1720 (C 66/3533); succ. 28 May 1728 (SO 5/2). D. 11 Dec. 1762 (SO 5/3).

Delafaye, Lewis   *French Translator of Gazette* c. 1679–1710.
Pd. from 1679 to 1710 (All Souls MS 204 f. 81c; Trumbull Add. MS 113; BM Loan 29/162; SP 34/12 f. 165).

Delafaye, Thomas   *Clerk of Signet* 28 May 1728–c. March 1747.
Grant in reversion jointly with C. Delafaye (C 66/3533); succ. 28 May 1728 (SO 5/2). D. by 30 March 1747 (LC 3/65 p. 208).

Delagarde, Charles   *Interpreter of Oriental Languages* Sept. 1809–April 1816.
Pd. from 16 Sept. 1809 to 5 April 1816 (CO 701/1 p. 77; CO 701/2 p. 29).

Delaval *see* **Shaftoe**

de Paz, Samuel   *Clerk* (Jenkins) c. 1683–April 1684; (Godolphin) April–Aug. 1684; (Middleton) Aug. 1684–c. 1687.
Occ. as Clerk to Jenkins 28 June 1683 (Hist. MSS Comm. *7th Rept.*, 365); continued in office by Godolphin and Middleton (Evans, *Principal Secretary*, 192–193); last occ. 30 July 1687 (*Ellis Corr.*, i, 334; *CSPD 1697*, 52).

Devenish, St. George   *Clerk* (Trumbull) May 1696–c. 1697.
'Mr. Devenish'; probably identical with St. George Devenish, son of Robert Devenish and Elizabeth, sister of John Tucker, Clerk and Under Secretary (*CSPD 1696*, 452; R. J. Devenish and C. H. McLaughlin, *Historical and Genealogical Records of the Devenish Families of England and Ireland* (Chicago 1948), 211–12). Pd. as Clerk from 3 May 1696 to 3 Feb. 1697 (Trumbull Add. MS 113).

de Vic, Sir Henry, 1st Bart.   *Secretary for French Tongue* 27 Sept. 1634–c. Dec. 1661.
App. 27 Sept. 1634 (C 66/2680, 2950). Surrendered office by 12 Dec. 1661 (*CSPD 1661–2*, 178).

de Vrigny *see* **de Lacombe de Vrigny**

Deyverdun, George   *Clerk* (Seymour Conway) March 1767–Jan. 1768; (Weymouth) Jan. 1768–c. 1769.
App. by Seymour Conway notified 4 March 1767 (*CHOP 1766–9*, 162); presence in office notified as Clerk to Weymouth 20 Jan. 1768 (ibid. 293); last occ. 1769 (*Royal Kal.* (1769), 117).

Didichi, Theocaris Rali   *Interpreter of Oriental Languages* May 1727–9 April 1734.
App. notified 30 May 1727 (SP 44/125 pp. 107, 204). D. 9 April 1734 (*Gent. Mag.* (1734), iv, 218).

Diemar, George   *Clerk* (Newcastle) Nov. 1753–March 1754; (Holdernesse) March 1754–c. 1755.

App. by Newcastle notified 13 Nov. 1753 (SP 44/148); occ. as Clerk to Holdernesse 1755 (Chamberlayne, *Present State* (1755), pt. ii, 53).

Digby, Henry   *Clerk* (Bedford) May 1749–c. 1750. *Under Secretary* Nov. 1755–Nov. 1756.

App. as Clerk by Bedford notified 8 May 1749 (SP 44/129 p. 520); last occ. 1750 (Millan, *Universal Register* (1750), 80). App. Under Secretary by Fox Nov. 1755 (*Gent. Mag.* (1755), xxv, 523).

Doudiet, John   *Office Keeper* (Weymouth) June 1777–Nov. 1779; (Hillsborough) Nov. 1779–March 1782.

App. by Weymouth; received fees as Office Keeper to Weymouth from June 1777 to Nov. 1779 (SP 45/34), to Hillsborough from Nov. 1779 to March 1782 (SP 45/34–35). Transferred to Home Office March 1782 (*1st Rept. on Fees*, 25).

D'Oyly, Christopher   *Under Secretary* (Germain) April 1776–Jan. 1778.

Pd. from 5 April 1776 to 5 Jan. 1778 (SP 45/32).

Draper, Nathan   *Clerk* (Robinson) Sept. 1754–Nov. 1755; (Fox) Nov. 1755–April 1756.

App. by Robinson notified 11 Sept. 1754 (SP 44/136 p. 295); occ. as Clerk to Robinson from 1755 to 1756 (sic) (Chamberlayne, *Present State* (1755), pt. ii, 53; *Court and City Reg.* (1756), 107). Removal from office by Fox notified 8 April 1756 (SP 44/136 p. 358).

Drift, Adrian   *Clerk* (Jersey) May 1699–June 1700.

Occ. Nov. 1698 in service of Jersey, Ambassador to Paris (BM Add. MS 28902 ff. 86, 134); probably entered office as Clerk on Jersey's app. as Secretary May 1699; occ. as such 9 Dec. 1699, 1700 (Hist. MSS Comm. *Bath*, iii, 385; Chamberlayne, *Present State* (1700), 502); pd. by Vernon during vacancy following Jersey's res. from 24 June to 24 Sept. 1700 (BM Add. MS 40785 f. 66). App. Clerk, Board of Trade 6 Aug. 1700 (CO 389/36 pp. 106–7).

Ducarel, Andrew Coltee   *Methodiser of State Papers* 16 July 1764–29 May 1785.

App. 16 July 1764 (T 52/56 p. 99; T 52/69 pp. 374–5). D. 29 May 1785 (T 53/58 p. 95).

Duck, William   *Clerk* (Chesterfield) Nov. 1746–Feb. 1748; (Bedford) Feb. 1748–June 1751; (Holdernesse) June 1751–March 1754; (Robinson) March 1754–Nov. 1755; (Fox) Nov. 1755–Nov. 1756; (Pitt) Dec. 1756–Oct. 1761; (Egremont) Oct. 1761–Aug. 1763; (Sandwich) Sept. 1763–July 1765; (Grafton) July 1765–May 1766; (Richmond) May–July 1766; (Shelburne) July 1766–Oct. 1768; (Rochford) Oct. 1768–c. 1772. *Senior Clerk* (Rochford) c. 1772–Nov. 1775; (Weymouth) Nov. 1775–Nov. 1779; (Hillsborough) Nov. 1779–March 1782.

Probably app. Clerk by Chesterfield; presence in office as such notified 21 Nov. 1746 (SP 44/129 p. 428); occ. as Clerk to Bedford from 1748 to 1751 (Chamberlayne, *Present State* (1748), pt. ii, 52; *Court and City Reg.* (1751), 108), to Holdernesse from 1752 to 1754 (*Court and City Reg.* (1752), 108; ibid. (1754), 106), to Robinson from 1755 to 1756 (sic) (Chamberlayne, *Present State* (1755), pt. ii, 53; *Court and City Reg.* (1756), 107); probably continued in office by Fox; presence in office notified as Clerk to Pitt 17 Dec. 1756 (SP 44/136 p. 399), to Egremont 13 Oct. 1761 (*CHOP 1760–5*, 70), to Sandwich 9 Sept. 1763, 30 April 1764 (ibid. 302, 408), to Grafton 23 July 1765 (ibid. 580), to Richmond 28 June 1766 (*CHOP 1766–9*, 54), to Shelburne 27 July 1768 (ibid. 434), to Rochford 4 Nov. 1768 (ibid. 435). First occ. as Senior Clerk 1772 (*Royal Kal.* (1772), 115); presence in office as Senior

Clerk to Weymouth notified 30 Nov. 1775 (*CHOP 1773-5*, 556); occ. as Senior Clerk to Weymouth to 1779 (*Royal Kal.* (1779), 109), to Hillsborough from 1780 to 1782 (ibid. (1780), 110; ibid. (1782), 110). Probably left office March 1782 on formation of Home Office; does not occ. in list of that office for 1783 (ibid. (1783), 110).

Eden, William *Under Secretary* (Suffolk) June 1772–Oct. 1778.

App. by Suffolk notified 17 June 1772 (*CHOP 1770-2*, 512). Left office by 28 Oct. 1778 (app. of Oakes).

Egar, David *Clerk* (Nottingham) (?)–Nov. 1693; (Shrewsbury) March 1694–Dec. 1698; (Jersey) May 1699–June 1700; (Vernon) Nov. 1700–May 1702; (Nottingham) May 1702–April 1704; (Harley) May 1704–Feb. 1708; (Boyle) Feb. 1708–Sept. 1710; (St. John/Bolingbroke) Sept. 1710–c. 1711.

Occ. as Clerk to Nottingham 1694 (sic) (Chamberlayne, *Present State* (1694), 243); probably continued in office by Shrewsbury March 1694; in his service Dec. 1698; pd. by Vernon during vacancy following Shrewsbury's res. from 25 Dec. 1698 to 25 March 1699 (BM Add. MS 40785 f. 34); probably continued in office by Jersey May 1699; in his service 1700 (Chamberlayne, *Present State* (1700), 502); pd. by Vernon during vacancy following Jersey's res. from 24 June to 24 Sept. 1700 (BM Add. MS 40785 f. 65); transferred to Vernon's service Nov. 1700; pd. from 29 Sept. 1700 to 25 March 1702 and on 1 May 1702 for quarter to 24 June 1702 (BM Add. MSS 40785 f. 70; 40786 ff. 35, 37); occ. as Clerk to Nottingham from 1702 to 1704 (*Compleat History* (1702), 69; Chamberlayne, *Present State* (1704), 530); pd. as Clerk to Harley from 16 Feb. 1706 to 3 Sept. 1707 (BM Loan 29/162); presence in office notified as Clerk to Boyle 23 Feb. 1708 (SP 44/107 p. 4), to St. John 23 Nov. 1710 (SP 44/109); last occ. 1711 (Boyer, *Political State* (1711), 377).

Egremont, Charles (Wyndham) 2nd Earl of *Secretary of State* (South) 9 Oct. 1761–21 Aug. 1763.

App. 9 Oct. 1761 (T 53/48 p. 227). D. 21 Aug. 1763.

Ellis, John *Under Secretary* (Trumbull) May 1695–Dec. 1697; (Vernon) Dec. 1697–Nov. 1700; (Hedges) Nov. 1700–Dec. 1701; (Manchester) Jan.–May 1702; (Hedges) May 1702–May 1705.

App. by Trumbull May 1695 (Luttrell, *Hist. Relation*, iii, 468), by Vernon Dec. 1697 (ibid. iv, 316), by Hedges Nov. 1700 (ibid. 705), by Manchester Jan. 1702 (ibid. v, 127), by Hedges May 1702 (ibid. 169). Dis. May 1705 (ibid. 555).

Ellis, Welbore *Secretary of State* (Colonies) 11 Feb.–27 March 1782.

App. 11 Feb. 1782 (T 53/55 p. 212). Left office 27 March 1782 (ibid. p. 388).

Emmitt, Elizabeth *Necessary Woman* (Weymouth) c. 1778–Nov. 1779; (Hillsborough) Nov. 1779–March 1782.

Occ. as Necessary Woman to Weymouth from 1778 to 1779 (*Royal Kal.* (1778), 109; ibid. (1779), 109), to Hillsborough from 1780 to 1782 (ibid. (1780), 110; ibid. (1782), 110). Transferred to Home Office March 1782 (*1st Rept. on Fees*, 25).

Evans, Morgan (?) *Office Keeper* (Boyle) c. 1708–10.

Possibly Deputy Office Keeper; occ. from 1708 to 1710 (Chamberlayne, *Present State* (1708), 586; ibid. (1710), 516).

Fanshawe, Sir Richard, 1st Bart. *Secretary for Latin Tongue* 12 Jan. 1661–16 June 1666.

App. 12 Jan. 1661 (C 66/2936). D. 16 June 1666.

Faye *see* **Delafaye**

Featherstone, Ralph *Clerk* (Bute) March 1761–May 1762.
Probably app. by Bute March 1761; occ. 1762 (*Court and City Reg.* (1762), 106). Left office May 1762 (*Notes and Queries*, cciv (1959), 283). App. Supernumerary Clerk, Treasury 21 July 1762 (T 29/34 p. 328).

Fenhoulet, John James *Clerk* (Egremont) April–Aug. 1763; (Sandwich) Sept. 1763–July 1765; (Grafton) July 1765–May 1766; (Richmond) May–July 1766; (Shelburne) July 1766–Oct. 1768; (Rochford) Oct. 1768–c. Oct. 1774.
App. by Egremont; pd. as his Clerk from 5 April to 5 July 1763 (PRO 30/47/31/4); presence in office notified as Clerk to Sandwich 9 Sept. 1763, 30 April 1764 (*CHOP 1760–5*, 302, 408), to Grafton 23 July 1765 (ibid. 580), to Richmond 28 June 1766 (*CHOP 1766–9*, 54), to Shelburne 27 July 1768 (ibid. 434), to Rochford 4 Nov. 1768 (ibid. 435). Res. by 1 Oct. 1774 (*CHOP 1773–5*, 245).

Field, John *Clerk* (Trevor) c. 1671–May 1672; (Coventry) July 1672–c. 1677.
Occ. as Clerk to Trevor 26 Sept. 1671 (BM Add. MS 56240, Field to Blathwayt, 26 Sept. 1671), to Coventry 25 Jan. 1677 (BM Add. MS 25118 f. 156).

Finch, Hon. Edward *Under Secretary* (Nottingham) March 1689–April 1693.
App. by Nottingham probably March 1689; occ. July 1689 (LS 13/231 p. 14). Left office April 1693 (Finch MSS Box V Bundle 16, Finch to Nottingham, 17 April 1693; Luttrell, *Hist. Relation*, iii, 81).

Fisher, John *Under Secretary* (Germain) Oct. 1781–Feb. 1782; (Ellis) Feb.–March 1782.
Pd. from 5 Oct. 1781 (SP 45/32). Left office March 1782 on abolition of Colonial Department (T 1/579 Schedule 2).

Fisher, Thomas *Deputy Clerk of Signet* c. 1725–35.
Occ. as Deputy to Moyle from March 1725 to Jan. 1735 (SO 5/1–2), to Cooke from Nov. 1727 to April 1728 (ibid.).

Ford, Charles *Writer of Gazette* July 1712–Sept. 1714.
App. July 1712 (J. Swift, *Prose Works*, ed. F. Ryland and others (London 1898–1922), ii, 374). Left office Sept. 1714 (SP 44/147, Walpole to Ford, 24 Sept. 1714).

Fountain, Nicholas *Office Keeper of Signet Office* c. 1702–35.
Occ. from 1702 to 1735 (Chamberlayne, *Present State* (1702), 481; ibid. (1735), pt. ii, 43).

Fox, Henry *Secretary of State* (South) 14 Nov. 1755–13 Nov. 1756.
App. 14 Nov. 1755 (T 53/45 p. 468). Left office 13 Nov. 1756 (ibid.).

Francis, Philip *Clerk* (Fox) April–Nov. 1756; (Pitt) Dec. 1756–Oct. 1761; (Egremont) Oct. 1761–Jan. 1763.
App. by Fox notified 8 April 1756 (SP 44/136 p. 358); presence in office notified as Clerk to Pitt 17 Dec. 1756 (ibid. p. 399), to Egremont 13 Oct. 1761 (*CHOP 1760–5*, 70); pd. to 5 Jan. 1763 (PRO 30/47/31/5). Left office c. Jan. 1763 on app. as First Clerk, War Office (*Notes and Queries*, ccv (1960), 455; J. Parkes and H. Merrivale, *Memoirs of Sir Philip Francis* (London 1867), i, 64–5).

Francis, Robert *Clerk* (Arlington) c. 1666–74.
Clerk in Arlington's office attached to Williamson; occ. from 6 July 1666 to 20 Feb. 1674 (*CSPD 1665–6*, 503; *CSPD 1673–5*, 173).

Fraser, William *Clerk* (Holdernesse) July 1751–1759. *Assistant Under Secretary* (Holdernesse) 1759–March 1761. *Private Secretary* (Grafton) July 1765. *Under Secretary* (Grafton) July 1765–May 1766; (Seymour Conway) May 1766–Jan. 1768; (Weymouth) Jan. 1768–Dec. 1770; (Sandwich) Dec. 1770–Jan. 1771;

(Halifax) March–June 1771; (Suffolk) June 1771–March 1779; (Stormont) Oct. 1779–March 1782.

Writer of Gazette 13 July 1770–11 Dec. 1802.

Translator of German Language 6 Oct. 1773–11 Dec. 1802.

Clerk of Signet 4 March 1782–11 Dec. 1802.

App. as Clerk by Holdernesse notified 31 July 1751 (SP 44/136 p. 180). App. Assistant Under Secretary by Holdernesse probably c. April 1759 (*Grenville Papers*, ed. W. J. Smith (London 1852–3), i, 290–1); occ. as such 1761 (*Court and City Reg.* (1761), 106). App. Private Secretary by Grafton July 1765 (Hist. MSS Comm. *10th Rept.*, 392). App. as Under Secretary by Grafton notified 23 July 1765 (*CHOP 1760–5*, 579); received fees as Under Secretary to Seymour Conway from May 1766 (SP 45/31); app. as Under Secretary notified by Weymouth 20 Jan. 1768 (*CHOP 1766–9*, 293), by Sandwich 21 Dec. 1770 (*CHOP 1770–2*, 103), by Halifax 20 March 1771 (ibid. 225), by Suffolk 12 June 1771 (ibid. 556), by Stormont 9 Nov. 1779 (FO 366/669 p. 16). Transferred to Foreign Office March 1782 (*1st Rept. on Fees*, 27). App. Writer of Gazette 13 July 1770 (C 66/3727), Translator of German Language 6 Oct. 1773 (*CHOP 1773–5*, 87), Clerk of Signet 4 March 1782 (C 66/3791). D. 11 Dec. 1802 (*Gent. Mag.* (1802), lxxii (2), 1171).

Fry, Gauntlet *Deputy Clerk of Signet* c. 1716. *Clerk of Signet* 2 Oct. 1716–7 May 1746.

Occ. as Deputy Clerk of Signet 1716 (Chamberlayne, *Present State* (1716), 525). App. Clerk of Signet 2 Oct. 1716 (C 66/3517). D. 7 May 1746 (SO 5/3).

Gage, John *Clerk of Signet* 19 March 1807–24 Dec. 1846.

Grant in reversion 26 Aug. 1803 (C 66/4021); succ. 19 March 1807 (d. of Tirel Morin). D. 24 Dec. 1846 (*Gent. Mag.* (1847), cxx, 308).

Gage, Thomas *Clerk* (Newcastle) Nov. 1737–c. 1741.

App. by Newcastle notified 25 Nov. 1737 (SP 44/148); last occ. 1741 (Chamberlayne, *Present State* (1741), pt. ii, 47).

Gauntlet, John *Deputy Clerk of Signet* c. 1682. *Clerk of Signet* c. 1684–20 Sept. 1716.

Occ. as Deputy Clerk of Signet 1682 (Chamberlayne, *Present State* (1682), pt. i, 194). Grant of clerkship of signet in reversion 12 June 1674 (C 66/3156); probably succ. c. 1684 (d. of Bere); occ. 1687 (Chamberlayne, *Present State* (1687), pt. i, 169). Surrendered office 20 Sept. 1716 (surrender recited in grant to Fry).

Gedney, Thomas *Clerk* (Townshend) May–Dec. 1716; (Methuen) Dec. 1716–April 1717; (Addison) April 1717–c. 1718.

App. by Townshend notified 5 May 1716 (SP 44/118); probably continued in office by Methuen; occ. as Clerk to Addison 1718 (Miège, *Present State* (1718), 362 —'John Gedney').

Germain, Lord George *Secretary of State* (Colonies) 10 Nov. 1775–10 Feb. 1782.

App. 10 Nov. 1775 (T 53/53 p. 359). Left office 10 Feb. 1782 (T 53/55 p. 212).

Gibbons, — *Clerk* (Queensberry) c. 1710.

Occ. 1710 (Chamberlayne, *Present State* (1710), 515).

Gilbert, Humphrey *Clerk* (Hedges) c. 1702–4.

Occ. from 1702 to 1704 (*Compleat History* (1702), 69; Chamberlayne, *Present State* (1704), 530).

Goddard, Charles *Collector of State Papers* 6 Jan. 1796–21 Jan. 1848.

App. 6 Jan. 1796 (C 66/3913). D. 21 Jan. 1848 (*Gent. Mag.* (1848), cxx, 555).

Godolphin, Sidney *Secretary of State* (North) 17 April–c. 24 Aug. 1684.

App. 17 April 1684 (PC 2/70 p. 142). Left office by 24 Aug. 1684 (ibid. p. 220).

Godolphin, William *Under Secretary* (Bennet/Arlington) Oct. 1662–Dec. 1665.

Occ. from 21 Oct. 1662 to 24 Sept. 1665 (*CSPD 1661–2*, 524; *CSPD 1664–5*, 571). Left office Dec. 1665 on app. as Secretary to Earl of Sandwich, Ambassador to Spain (Hist. MSS Comm. *Heathcote*, 219).

Goodridge, Anthony *Office Keeper* (Nottingham) May 1702–April 1704.

Occ. from 1702 to 1704 (*Compleat History* (1702), 69; Chamberlayne, *Present State* (1704), 530); a footman of Nottingham's who served as Office Keeper only while his master was in office (Finch MS DG 7/1/19a).

Gorton, William *Office Keeper* (Rochford) c. 1769.

Occ. 1769 (*Royal Kal.* (1769), 118).

Gower *see* **Leveson Gower**

Grafton, Augustus Henry (Fitzroy) 3rd Duke of *Secretary of State* (North) 11 July 1765–23 May 1766.

App. 11 July 1765 (T 53/50 p. 13). Left office 23 May 1766 (ibid.).

Graham, Fergus *Under Secretary* (Preston) Nov.–Dec. 1688.

App. by Preston Nov. 1688 (*Ellis Corr.*, ii, 287).

Graham, Mary *Necessary Woman* (Newcastle) c. 1745–March 1754; (Holdernesse) March 1754–c. 1758.

Occ. as Necessary Woman to Newcastle from 1745 to 1754 (Chamberlayne, *Present State* (1745), pt. ii, 31–2; *Court and City Reg.* (1754), 106), to Holdernesse from 1755 to 1758 (Chamberlayne, *Present State* (1755), pt. ii, 52–3; *Court and City Reg.* (1758), 106).

Granville, Earl *see* **Carteret,** Lord

Gregg, William *Clerk* (Harley) April 1706–Jan. 1708.

App. 16 April 1706 (*Lords Journals*, xviii, 518). Left office 1 Jan. 1708 on being taken into custody (Luttrell, *Hist. Relation*, vi, 252).

Gregory, George *Clerk* (Craggs) March 1718–Feb. 1721; (Carteret) March 1721–April 1724; (Newcastle) April 1724–June 1725.

Probably app. by Craggs; presence in office notified as Clerk to Craggs 29 March 1718, 18 Dec. 1719 (SP 44/147); pd. as Clerk to Carteret from 29 Sept. 1723 to 3 April 1724 (MS Rawlinson C 367), to Newcastle from 4 April 1724 to 24 June 1725 (MSS Rawlinson C 367, 123).

Gregson, Richard *Deputy Clerk of Signet* c. 1701–10.

Occ. as Deputy Clerk of Signet 1701 (Miège, *New State* (1701), pt. iii, 109). Occ. as 'Clerk of Dispatches' in Signet Office from 1707 to 1710 (Chamberlayne, *Present State* (1707), 514; ibid. (1710), 516).

Gregson, William *Writer of Gazette* 23 Sept. 1829–1869.

App. 23 Sept. 1829 (C 66/4356). D. 1869 (*Gent. Mag.* (1869), clii, 666).

Grenville, Hon. George *Secretary of State* (North) 5 June–14 Oct. 1762.

App. 5 June 1762 (T 53/48 p. 388). Left office 14 Oct. 1762 (ibid.).

Grey, Charles Samuel *Clerk of Signet* 26 Jan. 1847–7 Aug. 1851.

App. 26 Jan. 1847 (C 66/4802). Office abolished 7 Aug. 1851 (14 & 15 Vict., c 82, s 3).

Grey *see also* **de Grey**

Griffin, John *Clerk* (Stanhope) 1719–Feb. 1721; (Townshend) Feb. 1721–c. 1723.

App. by Stanhope; pd. as his Clerk from 29 Sept. 1719 to 29 Sept. 1720 (Stanhope MS 76); occ. as Clerk to Townshend 1723 (Miège, *Present State* (1723), 69).

Gwyn, Francis *Under Secretary* (Conway) Feb. 1681–Jan. 1683.

Occ. as Under Secretary to Conway 1682 (Chamberlayne, *Present State* (1682), pt. i, 193; *Memoirs of Thomas, Earl of Ailesbury* (London 1890), i, 63); Conway's fee book, formerly in Gwyn's possession, contains entries dating from Feb. 1681 to Jan. 1683 (Folger MS V.b.302).

Halifax, George (Dunk Montagu) 2nd Earl of *Secretary of State* (North) 14 Oct. 1762–Aug. 1763; (South) Aug. 1763–10 July 1765; (North) 22 Jan.–8 June 1771.

App. 14 Oct. 1762 (T 53/48 p. 442). Left office 10 July 1765 (T 53/50 p. 12). App. 22 Jan. 1771 (T 53/52 p. 118). D. 8 June 1771.

Hanbury Williams, Charles *Clerk* (Hillsborough) c. 1769–Aug. 1772; (Dartmouth) Aug. 1772–Nov. 1775; (Germain) Nov. 1775–c. 1781.

Occ. as Clerk to Hillsborough from 1769 to 1772 (*Royal Kal.* (1769), 118; ibid. (1772), 116), to Dartmouth from 1773 to 1775 (ibid. (1773), 116; ibid. (1775), 107), to Germain from 1776 to 1781 (ibid. (1776), 109; ibid. (1781), 110).

Hare, Thomas *Under Secretary* (St. John/Bolingbroke) Sept. 1710–Aug. 1714.

App. by St. John Sept. 1714 (Luttrell, *Hist. Relation*, vi, 635).

Harley, Robert *Secretary of State* (North) 16 May 1704–11 Feb. 1708.

App. 16 May 1704 (*CTB*, xix, 270). Left office 11 Feb. 1708 (ibid. xxii, 217).

Harling, William *Clerk* (Carteret/Granville) June 1742–Nov. 1744; (Harrington) Nov. 1744–Oct. 1746; (Chesterfield) Oct. 1746–Feb. 1748; (Bedford) 1748.

App. by Carteret notified 10 June 1742 (SP 44/129 p. 296); occ. as Clerk to Carteret to 15 Nov. 1743 (T 52/42 p. 324), to Harrington from 1 May to 31 Aug. 1745 (T 52/43 pp. 134, 213); presence in office as Clerk to Chesterfield notified 21 Nov. 1746 (SP 44/129 p. 428); last occ. 1748 as Clerk to Bedford (Chamberlayne, *Present State* (1748), pt. ii, 52).

Harrington, William (Stanhope) 1st Lord (cr. Earl of **Harrington** 9 Feb. 1742) *Secretary of State* (North) 16 May 1730–12 Feb. 1742; 24 Nov. 1744–19 Oct. 1746.

App. 16 May 1730 (T 53/35 p. 398). Left office 12 Feb. 1742 (*CTBP 1742–5*, 169). App. 24 Nov. 1744 (ibid. 804). Left office 19 Oct. 1746 (T 53/42 p. 143).

Haynes, H. *Deputy Clerk of Signet* c. 1723–4.

Occ. as Deputy to Moyle from March 1723 to Nov. 1724 (SO 5/1).

Haynes, John *Clerk* (Pitt) Dec. 1756–Oct. 1761; (Egremont) Oct. 1761–Aug. 1763; (Sandwich) Sept. 1763–July 1765; (Grafton) July 1765–May 1766; (Richmond) May–July 1766; (Shelburne) July 1766–Oct. 1768; (Rochford) Oct. 1768–c. 1772. *Senior Clerk* (Rochford) c. 1772–Nov. 1775; (Weymouth) Nov. 1775–c. April 1776. *Deputy Clerk of Signet* 1761–76.

Probably app. Clerk by Pitt; presence in office notified as Clerk to Pitt 17 Dec. 1756 (SP 44/136 p. 399), to Egremont 13 Oct. 1761 (*CHOP 1760–5*, 70), to Sandwich 9 Sept. 1763, 30 April 1764 (ibid. 302, 408), to Grafton 23 July 1765 (ibid. 580), to Richmond 28 June 1766 (*CHOP 1766–9*, 54), to Shelburne 27 July 1768 (ibid. 434), to Rochford 4 Nov. 1768 (ibid. 435). First occ. as Senior Clerk 1772 (*Royal Kal.* (1772), 115); presence in office as Senior Clerk to Weymouth notified 30 Nov. 1775 (*CHOP 1773–5*, 556). App. Deputy Clerk of Signet to Moyle March 1761 (Ind. 6764); last occ. Jan. 1776 (SO 5/4). D. April or May 1776 (*Gent. Mag.* (1776), xlvi, 240; *Lond. Mag.* (1776), xlv, 278).

Haynes, Thomas *Deputy Clerk of Signet* 1740–64.

Occ. as Deputy to Fry from March 1740 to April 1746 (SO 5/2–3); app. Deputy by Blair Aug. 1746 (Ind. 6763); last occ. 1764 (*Court and City Reg.* (1764), 107).

Hedges, Sir Charles, kt. *Secretary of State* (North) 5 Nov. 1700–29 Dec. 1701; 2 May 1702–May 1704; (South) May 1704–3 Dec. 1706.

App. 5 Nov. 1700 (PC 2/78 p. 95). Left office 29 Dec. 1701 (BM Add. MS 40786 f. 29). App. 2 May 1702 (PC 2/78 p. 110). Left office 3 Dec. 1706 (*CTB*, xxi, 157).

Henricks, Gerard *Clerk* (Harrington) June–Oct. 1746; (Chesterfield) Oct. 1746–Feb. 1748; (Bedford) Feb. 1748–June 1751; (Holdernesse) June 1751–c. 1752.

App. by Harrington notified 2 June 1746 (SP 44/129 p. 414); presence in office as Clerk to Chesterfield notified 21 Nov. 1746 (ibid. p. 428); occ. as Clerk to Bedford from 1748 to 1751 (Chamberlayne, *Present State* (1748), pt. ii, 52; *Court and City Reg.* (1751), 108); last occ. as Clerk to Holdernesse 1752 (*Court and City Reg.* (1752), 108).

Henshaw, Thomas *Secretary for French Tongue* 13 March 1662–2 Jan. 1700.

App. 13 March 1662 (C 66/3013, 3264). D. 2 Jan. 1700 (J. Le Neve, *Monumenta Anglicana 1680–99* (London 1718), 205–6; Prob 11/454 f. 8).

Higden, William Henry *Clerk* (Rochford) Nov. 1768–Nov. 1775; (Weymouth) Nov. 1775–Nov. 1779; (Hillsborough) Nov. 1779–March 1782.

Private Secretary (Rochford) c. 1769.

Deputy Clerk of Signet March 1795–Dec. 1802.

Probably app. Clerk by Rochford; presence in office notified as Clerk to Rochford 4 Nov. 1768 (*CHOP 1766–9*, 435), to Weymouth 30 Nov. 1775 (*CHOP 1773–5*, 556); occ. as Clerk to Weymouth to 1779 (*Royal Kal.* (1779), 109), to Hillsborough from 1780 to 1782 (ibid. (1780), 110; ibid. (1782), 110). Transferred to Home Office March 1782 (*1st Rept. on Fees*, 22). Occ. as Private Secretary to Rochford 1769 (*Court and City Reg.* (1769), 118). Deputy Clerk of Signet to Fraser; took oath as such 11 March 1795 (HO 38/6 p. 239); occ. from April 1795 to Dec. 1802 (SO 5/20).

Hill, — (?) *Necessary Woman* (Nottingham) c. 1689. *Necessary Woman* (Shrewsbury) (?)–Dec. 1698; (Jersey) May 1699–June 1700; (Hedges) Nov. 1700.

Possibly Necessary Woman to Nottingham July 1689 (LS 13/231 p. 14); in Shrewsbury's service as such Dec. 1698; pd. by Vernon during vacancy following Shrewsbury's res. from 25 Dec. 1698 to 25 March 1699 (BM Add. MS 40785 f. 34); probably continued in office by Jersey May 1699; in his service June 1700; pd. by Vernon during vacancy following Jersey's res. from 24 June to 5 Nov. 1700 (ibid. ff. 65, 67); probably continued in office by Hedges Nov. 1700.

Hill, Richard *Secretary for Latin Tongue* 6 Nov. 1691–22 Oct. 1714.

App. 6 Nov. 1691 (C 66/3347, 3432). Grant determined 22 Oct. 1714 (app. of S. Hill).

Hill, Samuel *Secretary for Latin Tongue* 22 Oct. 1714–16 July 1718.

App. 22 Oct. 1714 (C 66/3509). Grant determined 16 July 1718 (app. of Lee).

Hillsborough, Wills (Hill) 1st Earl of *Secretary of State* (Colonies) 21 Jan. 1768–15 Aug. 1772; (South) 25 Nov. 1779–27 March 1782.

App. 21 Jan. 1768 (T 53/51 p. 21). Left office 15 Aug. 1772 (T 53/52 p. 404). App. 25 Nov. 1779 (T 53/54 p. 437). Left office 27 March 1782 (T 53/55 p. 213).

Hobhouse, Henry *Secretary for Latin Tongue* 23 May 1826–19 July 1832.

Keeper of State Papers 23 May 1826–13 April 1854.

App. Secretary for Latin Tongue 23 May 1826 (C 66/4306, 4374). Grant determined 19 July 1832 (C 66/4408). App. Keeper of State Papers 23 May 1826 (C 66/4306). D. 13 April 1854 (*Gent. Mag.* (1854), cxxxv, 79).

Holdernesse, Robert (Darcy) 4th Earl of *Secretary of State* (South) 21 June 1751–March 1754; (North) March 1754–25 March 1761.

App. 21 June 1751 (PC 2/102 p. 251). Left office 25 March 1761 (T 53/47 pp. 560–1).

Holland, John *Embellisher of Letters* Nov. 1761–c. 1800.

App. Nov. 1761 (AO 1/420/199); last occ. 15 July 1800 (FO 366/671 p. 144).

Holt, Charles (?) *Under Secretary* (Bromley) 1714.

In Bromley's service apparently as Under Secretary; occ. from 13 Feb. to 21 Aug. 1714 (SP 44/115 pp. 168, 277); letter of 5 Nov. 1714 enquiring about Bromley's papers suggests that he remained in office until Sept. 1714 (SP 35/1 f. 184).

Hopkins, Thomas *Under Secretary* (Trenchard) April 1694–April 1695; (Vernon) Dec. 1697–May 1702; (Sunderland) Dec. 1706–June 1710.

App. by Trenchard April 1694 (Luttrell, *Hist. Relation*, iii, 300), by Vernon Dec. 1697 (ibid. iv, 316), by Sunderland Dec. 1706 (ibid. vi, 112).

Houghton, William *Clerk* (Harrington) c. 1741.

Occ. 1741 (Chamberlayne, *Present State* (1741), pt. ii, 47).

Howard, Hon. Charles *Translator of German Language* March 1772–Sept./Oct. 1773.

App. 28 March 1772 (*CHOP 1773–5*, 87). D. Sept. or Oct. 1773 (*Correspondence of George III*, ed. Sir J. Fortescue (London 1927–8), iii, 38; *Gent. Mag.* (1773), xliii, 527).

Howard, Hugh *Keeper of State Papers* 18 Nov. 1714–17 March 1738.

App. 18 Nov. 1714 (C 66/3499, 3551). D. 17 March 1738 (*CTBP 1735–8*, 606).

Hume, David *Under Secretary* (Seymour Conway) Feb. 1767–Jan. 1768.

App. by Seymour Conway notified 21 Feb. 1767 (*CHOP 1766–9*, 161).

Hussey, W. *Clerk* (Hedges) c. 1701.

Occ. 1701 (Miège, *New State* (1701), pt. iii, 109). Probably not continued in office by Manchester (BM Add. MS 28888 ff. 3, 24).

Hutchinson, Francis Howard *Clerk* (Newcastle) Aug. 1727–22 June 1752.

App. by Newcastle notified 7 Aug. 1727 (SP 44/148). D. 22 June 1752 (*Gent. Mag.* (1752), xxii, 289).

Hutchinson, John *Clerk* (Hillsborough) c. 1769–Aug. 1772; (Dartmouth) Aug. 1772–c. 1774.

Occ. as Clerk to Hillsborough from 1769 to 1772 (*Royal Kal.* (1769), 118; ibid. (1772), 116), to Dartmouth from 1773 to 1774 (ibid. (1773), 116; ibid. (1774), 116).

Huxley, George *Clerk* (Harrington) c. 1736–Feb. 1742; (Carteret/Granville) Feb. 1742–Nov. 1744; (Harrington) Nov. 1744–c. 1745.

Occ. as Clerk to Harrington 18 May 1736 (T 52/39 p. 164); app. as such notified 4 Jan. 1737 (SP 44/129 p. 45); occ. as Clerk to Carteret from 18 April to 15 Nov. 1743 (T 52/42 pp. 205, 324), to Harrington 1745 (Chamberlayne, *Present State* (1745), pt. ii, 32).

Isham, John *Under Secretary* (Nottingham) April–Nov. 1693; Oct. 1703–April 1704.

App. by Nottingham April 1693 (Finch MSS Box V Bundle 16, Finch to Nottingham, 17 April 1693; Luttrell, *Hist. Relation*, iii, 81), Oct. 1703 (*Daily Courant* no. 467; Isham MSS nos. 2205, 2206).

Jenkins, John Warham *Clerk* (Suffolk) Oct. 1772–March 1779; (Stormont) Oct. 1779–March 1782.

App. by Suffolk notified 2 Oct. 1772 (*CHOP 1770–2*, 556); presence in office as Clerk to Stormont notified 9 Nov. 1779 (FO 366/669 p. 16). Transferred to Foreign Office March 1782 (*1st Rept. on Fees*, 30).

Jenkins, Sir Leoline, kt. *Secretary of State* (North) 26 April 1680–Feb. 1681; (South) Feb. 1681–c. 17 April 1684.

App. 26 April 1680 (PC 2/68 p. 489). Left office by 17 April 1684 (PC 2/70 p. 142).

Jenkinson, Charles *Under Secretary* (Bute) March 1761–May 1762.

App. by Bute March 1761 (*Gent. Mag.* (1761), xxxi, 189).

Jersey, Edward (Villiers) 1st Earl of *Secretary of State* (South) 13 May 1699–25 June 1700.

App. 13 May 1699 (Hist. MSS Comm. *Bath*, iii, 344–5). Left office 25 June 1700 (BM Add. MS 40784 f. 31).

Jones, Charles Pleydell *Office Keeper of Signet Office* c. 1789–1832. *Deputy Clerk of Signet* Jan. 1795–June 1797.

Occ. as Office Keeper of Signet Office from 1789 to 1832 (*Royal Kal.* (1789), 104; ibid. (1832), 139). App. Deputy Clerk of Signet to Wilkinson 2 Jan. 1795 (Ind. 6768); last occ. 1797 (*Royal Kal.* (1797), 104). Probably ceased to act June 1797 on d. of Wilkinson.

Jones, E. D. *Office Keeper of Signet Office* c. 1783–8.

Occ. from 1783 to 1788 (*Royal Kal.* (1783), 109; ibid. (1788), 104).

Jones, Edward Drewe *Office Keeper of Signet Office* c. 1828–49.

Occ. from 1828 to 1849 (*Royal Kal.* (1828), 137; ibid. (1849), 165).

Jones, Hugh Valence *Clerk* (Newcastle) c. 1743–April 1751. *Under Secretary* (Newcastle) April 1751–March 1754.

Occ. as Clerk from 1743 to 1751 (Chamberlayne, *Present State* (1743), pt. ii, 32; *Court and City Reg.* (1751), 108); probably acting as Private Secretary from 13 May to 23 Nov. 1748 (T 52/44 pp. 372, 386, 502) and from 16 April to 4 Nov. 1750 (T 52/45 pp. 162, 324). App. Under Secretary by Newcastle April 1751; received fees as such from April 1751 to March 1754 (SP 45/27).

Jones, John *Deputy Clerk of Signet* May 1776–April 1781.

App. Deputy to Copley 1 May 1776 (SP 44/143 pp. 69–70); last occ. 1781 (*Royal Kal.* (1781), 108). Probably ceased to act April 1781 on d. of Copley.

Jones, William *Clerk* (Vernon) c. 1698–May 1702; (?) (Nottingham) May 1702–April 1704. *Chief Clerk* (Harley) May 1704–Feb. 1708; (Boyle) Feb. 1708–Sept. 1710; (St. John/Bolingbroke) Sept. 1710–Aug. 1714; (Townshend) Sept. 1714–Dec. 1716; (Methuen) Dec. 1716–April 1717; (Addison) April 1717–March 1718; (Craggs) March 1718–7 Dec. 1719.

Pd. as Clerk to Vernon from 2 June 1698 to 25 March 1702 and on 1 May 1702 for quarter to 24 June 1702 (BM Add. MSS 40785 f. 20; 40786 ff. 35, 37); possibly continued in office by Nottingham. App. Chief Clerk by Harley probably May 1704; occ. as such 5 Feb. 1705 (*Lords Journals*, xviii, 517); heads list of Harley's Clerks 1707 (Chamberlayne, *Present State* (1707), 513–14); presence in office notified as most senior Clerk to Boyle 23 Feb. 1708 (SP 44/107 p. 4), to St. John 23 Nov. 1710 (SP 44/109), to Townshend 30 Sept. 1714 (SP 44/116); probably continued in office by Methuen; occ. as Chief Clerk to Addison 1718 (Chamberlayne, *Present State* (1718), pt. ii, 31); presence in office as most senior Clerk to Craggs notified 29 March 1718 (SP 44/147). D. 7 Dec. 1719 (*Hist. Reg. Chron.* (1719), iv, 42).

Jouvencel, Peter Cuchet *Clerk* (Holdernesse) Nov. 1753–March 1754; (Robinson) March 1754–Nov. 1755; (Fox) Nov. 1755–Nov. 1756; (Pitt) Dec. 1756–Oct. 1761; (Egremont) Oct. 1761–Aug. 1763; (Sandwich) Sept. 1763–July 1765; (Grafton) July 1765–May 1766; (Seymour Conway) 1766.

Private Secretary (Grafton) July 1765–May 1766.

App. as Clerk by Holdernesse notified 16 Nov. 1753 (SP 44/136 p. 269); occ. as Clerk to Robinson from 1755 to 1756 (sic) (Chamberlayne, *Present State* (1755), pt. ii, 53; *Court and City Reg.* (1756), 107); probably continued in office by Fox; presence in office notified as Clerk to Pitt 17 Dec. 1756 (SP 44/136 p. 399), to Egremont 13 Oct. 1761 (*CHOP 1760–5*, 70), to Sandwich 9 Sept. 1763, 30 April 1764 (ibid. 302, 408), to Grafton 23 July 1765 (ibid. 580), to Seymour Conway 15 Aug. 1766 (*CHOP 1766–9*, 67). Probably left office 1766 on app. as Secretary to Earl of Chatham as Lord Privy Seal (*Royal Kal.* (1767), 112). App. Private Secretary by Grafton July 1765 (*Gent. Mag.* (1765), xxxv, 348).

Keill, John *Decipherer* Jan. 1713–June 1716.

App. Jan. 1713 (*CTB*, xxvii, 88). Left office June 1716 (ibid. xxx, 252).

Kennedy, Cornelius *Under Secretary* (Montrose) Sept. 1714–Aug. 1715.

App. Under Secretary by Montrose probably Sept. 1714; occ. from 9 Oct. 1714 to 1716 (sic) (SP 55/4 pp. 1, 40; Miège, *Present State* (1716), pt. i, 391).

Kineir, Andrew *Clerk* (Bolingbroke) April 1713–Aug. 1714; (Roxburghe) c. 1717.

App. by Bolingbroke notified 16 April 1713 (SP 44/114); in service of Roxburghe probably as Clerk; occ. 10 April 1717 (SP 55/7 p. 10).

King, William *Writer of Gazette* Dec. 1711–c. July 1712.

App. Dec. 1711 (J. Swift, *Prose Works*, ed. F. Ryland and others (London 1898–1922), ii, 309, 374). Left office by July 1712 (app. of Ford).

Kirby, William *Office Keeper* (Rochford) c. 1770; (Sandwich) Dec. 1770–Jan. 1771; (Halifax) Jan.–June 1771; (Suffolk) June 1771–Nov. 1775; (Weymouth) Nov. 1775–Nov. 1779; (Hillsborough) Nov. 1779–March 1782.

Occ. as Office Keeper to Rochford from 1770 to 1771 (sic) (*Royal Kal.* (1770), 115; ibid. (1771), 115); probably remained in Northern Department Dec. 1770 on Rochford's transfer to the Southern and continued in office under Sandwich and Halifax; received fees as Office Keeper to Suffolk from Jan. 1772 to Nov. 1775 (SP 45/33), to Weymouth from Nov. 1775 to Nov. 1779 (SP 45/33–4), to Hillsborough from Nov. 1779 to March 1782 (SP 45/34–5). Transferred to Home Office March 1782 (*1st Rept. on Fees*, 24).

Kluft, Jacob Daniel *Clerk* (Holdernesse) Jan. 1752–c. 1754; Dec. 1759–March 1761; (Bute) March 1761–c. 1762.

Private Secretary (Bute) April 1761.

App. as Clerk by Holdernesse notified 8 Jan. 1752 (SP 44/148); last occ. 1754 (*Court and City Reg.* (1754), 106); reapp. by Holdernesse notified 20 Dec. 1759 (SP 44/148); occ. as Clerk to Holdernesse to 1761 (*Court and City Reg.* (1761), 106), to Bute 1762 (ibid. (1762), 106). App. Private Secretary by Bute April 1761 (*Notes and Queries*, cc (1955), 247).

Knatchbull, Edward *Clerk* (Nottingham) c. 1689.

Occ. July 1689 (LS 13/231 p. 14).

Knox, William *Under Secretary* (Hillsborough) June 1770–Aug. 1772; (Dartmouth) Aug. 1772–Nov. 1775; (Germain) Nov. 1775–Feb. 1782; (Ellis) Feb.–March 1782.

Pd. from 25 June 1770 (SP 45/32). Left office March 1782 on abolition of Colonial Department (T 1/579 Schedule 2).

Lackington, Charles *Office Keeper* (Ellis) Feb.–March 1782.

Received fees as Office Keeper to Ellis from 12 Feb. to 27 March 1782 (SP 45/32). Left office March 1782 on abolition of Colonial Department (T 1/579 Schedule 2).

Lacombe de Vrigny *see* **de Lacombe de Vrigny**

Lampe, John *Decipherer* Jan. 1729–c. 12 Dec. 1755.

App. Jan. 1729 (*CTBP 1729–30*, 5, 183). D. by 12 Dec. 1755 (T 53/45 p. 461).

Langlois, Benjamin *Under Secretary* (Stormont) Nov. 1779–March 1782.

App. by Stormont notified 9 Nov. 1779 (FO 366/669 p. 16).

Larpent, John *Clerk* (Harrington) c. 1731–Feb. 1742; (Carteret/Granville) Feb. 1742–Nov. 1744; (Harrington) Nov. 1744–May 1746. *Chief Clerk* (Newcastle) May 1746–March 1754; (Holdernesse) March 1754–March 1761; (Bute) March 1761–May 1762; (Grenville) June–Oct. 1762; (Halifax) Oct. 1762–July 1765; (Seymour Conway) July 1765–Jan. 1768; (Weymouth) Jan. 1768–Dec. 1770; (Sandwich) Dec. 1770–Jan. 1771; (Halifax) Jan.–June 1771; (Suffolk) June 1771–c. Oct. 1772.

First occ. as Clerk to Harrington 10 June 1731 (T 52/37 p. 319); app. as such notified 8 Dec. 1732 (SP 44/122 p. 454); occ. as Clerk to Harrington to 20 Oct. 1741 (T 52/41 p. 350), to Carteret from 17 Sept. 1742 to 15 Nov. 1743 (T 52/42 pp. 82, 324), to Harrington from 3 May to 31 Aug. 1745 (T 52/43 p. 213). App. Chief Clerk by Newcastle May 1746 (*Gent. Mag.* (1746), xvi, 273); occ. as Chief Clerk to Newcastle to 1754 (*Court and City Reg.* (1754), 106), to Holdernesse from 1755 to 1761 (Chamberlayne, *Present State* (1755), pt. ii, 53; *Court and City Reg.* (1761), 106), to Bute 1762 (*Court and City Reg.* (1762), 106); presence in office notified as Chief Clerk to Grenville 12 July 1762 (*CHOP 1760–5*, 189), to Halifax 8 Nov. 1762, 13 Sept. 1763, 30 April 1764 (ibid. 202, 302–3, 407), to Seymour Conway 15 Aug. 1766 (*CHOP 1766–9*, 67), to Weymouth 20 Jan. 1768 (ibid. 293), to Sandwich 21 Dec. 1770 (*CHOP 1770–2*, 103), to Halifax 22 Jan., 20 March 1771 (ibid. 193, 225), to Suffolk 12 June 1771 (ibid. 265). Left office by 2 Oct. 1772 (ibid. 556).

Larpent, John *Clerk* (Holdernesse) March 1761; (Bute) March 1761–May 1762; (Grenville) June–Sept. 1762. *Senior Clerk* (Hillsborough) Feb. 1768–Aug. 1772; (Dartmouth) Aug. 1772–Nov. 1775; (Germain) Nov. 1775–Feb. 1782; (Ellis) Feb.–March 1782.

App. as Clerk by Holdernesse notified 14 March 1761 (*CHOP 1760–5*, 26); occ. as Clerk to Bute 1762 (*Court and City Reg.* (1762), 106); presence in office as Clerk to Grenville notified 12 July 1762 (*CHOP 1760–5*, 189). Res. Sept. 1762 on app. as Secretary to Bedford, Ambassador to France (*Notes and Queries*, ccv (1960), 344–5). App. 'Secretary' (Senior Clerk) by Hillsborough Feb. 1768 (*Gent. Mag.* (1768), xxxviii, 95); occ. as Senior Clerk to Hillsborough to 1772 (*Royal Kal.* (1772), 116), to Dartmouth from 1773 to 1775 (ibid. (1773), 116; ibid. (1775), 107), to Germain from 1776 to 1782 (ibid. (1776), 109; ibid. (1782), 110); continued in office by Ellis. Left office March 1782 on abolition of Colonial Department (T 1/579 Schedule 2).

Lawrey, Adam *Clerk* (Townshend) March 1725–c. 1727.

App. by Townshend notified 27 March 1725 (SP 44/122 p. 276); last occ. 1727 (Chamberlayne, *Present State* (1727), pt. ii, 29).

Leautier, Daniel *Clerk* (Shelburne) Sept. 1767–Oct. 1768; (Rochford) Oct. 1768–c. 1770.

App. by Shelburne notified 25 Sept. 1767 (*CHOP 1766–9*, 187); presence in office notified as Clerk to Shelburne 27 July 1768 (ibid. 434), to Rochford 4 Nov. 1768 (ibid. 435); last occ. 1770 (*Royal Kal.* (1770), 115).

Lee, William *Secretary for Latin Tongue* 16 July 1718–11 Nov. 1730.

App. 16 July 1718 (C 66/3526, 3574). Surrendered office 11 Nov. 1730 (surrender recited in grant to Couraud).

Leigh, Robert *Clerk* (Arlington) c. 1666–8.

Clerk in Arlington's office attached to Williamson; occ. from 18 Dec. 1666 to 25 Aug. 1668 (*CSPD 1666–7*, 356; *CSPD 1667–8*, 552).

Le Pin, Jeremiah *Clerk* (Coventry) c. 1675–7; (Shrewsbury) Feb. 1689–June 1690; (Sydney) Dec. 1690–March 1692.

App. c. 1675 (*CSPD 1693*, 255); occ. as Clerk to Coventry 25 Jan. 1677 (BM Add. MS 25118 ff. 155–6); occ. as Clerk in one of the offices Dec. 1685 (Hist. MSS Comm. *Downshire*, i, 73; *CTB*, viii, 462); occ. as Clerk to Shrewsbury July 1689 (LS 13/231 p. 13); app. by Sydney Dec. 1690 (*CSPD 1690–1*, 195); not retained in office by Trenchard March 1693 (*CSPD 1693*, 255).

Leveson Gower, Hon. Richard *Under Secretary* (Bedford) June 1749–June 1751.

App. by Bedford notified 29 June 1749 (SP 44/129 p. 529).

Lewis, Erasmus (?) *Chief Clerk* (Manchester) Jan. May 1702. *Under Secretary* (Harley) May 1704–Feb. 1708; (Dartmouth) June 1710–Aug. 1713; (Bromley) Aug. 1713–Sept. 1714.

Probably app. Chief Clerk by Manchester Jan. 1702; heads list of his Clerks 1701 (sic) (*Compleat History* (1701), 98). App. Under Secretary by Harley May 1704 (Luttrell, *Hist. Relation*, v, 428), by Dartmouth June 1710 (ibid. vi, 595), by Bromley Aug. 1713 (*Post Boy* no. 2852).

Lister, John *Clerk* (Newcastle) July 1736–c. 1737.

App. by Newcastle notified 12 July 1736 (SP 44/148); last occ. 29 Oct. 1737 (T 52/40 p. 7).

Littlefield, George *Office Keeper of Signet Office* c. 1689–1700.

Occ. from July 1689 to 1700 (LS 13/231 p. 14; Chamberlayne, *Present State* (1700), 456).

Lloyd, Charles *Assistant Under Secretary* (Grenville) June–Oct. 1762; (Halifax) Oct. 1762–c. 1763.

App. by Grenville June 1762 (*Notes and Queries*, cciv (1959), 284); app. notified 12 July 1762 (*CHOP 1760–5*, 189); app. by Halifax notified 8 Nov. 1762 (ibid. 202); last occ. Sept. 1763 (ibid. 309). Left office by 30 April 1764 (ibid. 407).

Logie, Alexander *Interpreter of Oriental Languages* Dec. 1767–1770.

App. notified 16 Dec. 1767 (*CHOP 1766–9*, 274). Salary discontinued 28 Feb. 1770 by warrant 12 March 1770 (T 52/60 p. 355).

Longmore, Henry *Deputy Office Keeper* (Sandwich) c. 1764–July 1765; (Grafton) July 1765–May 1766; (Richmond) May–July 1766; (Shelburne) July 1766–Oct. 1768; (Rochford) Oct. 1768–Dec. 1770; (Sandwich) Dec. 1770–Jan. 1771; (Halifax) Jan.–June 1771; (Suffolk) June 1771–10 April 1773.

Deputy to Sommer; occ. as Deputy Office Keeper to Sandwich from 1764 to 1765 (*Court and City Reg.* (1764), 106; ibid. (1765), 110), to Grafton 1766 (ibid. (1766), 107), to Shelburne from 1766 to 1768 (Shelburne MS 134 p. 119; *Royal Kal.* (1768), 117), to Rochford from 1769 to 1771 (sic) (*Royal Kal.* (1769), 117; ibid. (1771), 115); probably remained in Northern Department Dec. 1770 on Rochford's transfer to Southern and continued in office under Sandwich and Halifax; occ. as Deputy

Office Keeper to Suffolk from 1772 to 1773 (ibid. (1772), 115; ibid. (1773), 115). D. 10 April 1773 (*Lond. Mag.* (1773), xlii, 205).

Lovell, William Willes *Decipherer* (?)–1 Oct. 1844.
'Mr. Lovell'; probably identical with William Willes Lovell (Ellis, *Post Office*, 131). Occ. 31 Aug. 1844 (BM Add. MS 45520 ff. 53–4). Office abolished 1 Oct. 1844 (ibid.).

Lowndes, William *Clerk* (Boyle) c. 1708–10.
Presence in office first notified 23 Feb. 1708 (SP 44/107 p. 4); last occ. 1710 (Chamberlayne, *Present State* (1710), 516).

Lucas, Simon *Interpreter of Oriental Languages* May 1784–Dec. 1792.
App. notified 12 May 1784 (HO 36/4 p. 64); pd. to 24 Dec. 1792 (HO 82/3).

Macleane, Lauchlan *Assistant Under Secretary* (Shelburne) Oct. 1766–c. July 1768.
App. by Shelburne notified 8 Oct. 1766 (*CHOP 1766–9*, 84). Left office by 27 July 1768 (ibid. 434).

Man, Nicholas *Clerk* (Harley) c. 1706–7.
Pd. from 16 Feb. 1706 to 3 Sept. 1707 (BM Loan 29/162); last occ. 1707 (Chamberlayne, *Present State* (1707), 513–14). Left office by Feb. 1708 (*Lords Journals*, xviii, 518).

Manby, James *Clerk* (Stormont) Aug. 1780–March 1782.
App. by Stormont notified 15 Aug. 1780 (FO 366/669 p. 31). Transferred to Foreign Office March 1782 (*1st Rept. on Fees*, 31).

Manchester, Charles (Montagu) 4th Earl of *Secretary of State* (South) 3 Jan.–2 May 1702.
App. 3 Jan. 1702 (BM Add. MS 40803 f. 2). Left office 2 May 1702 (*CTB*, xviii, 228).

Mar, John (Erskine) 22nd Earl of *Secretary of State* (Scotland) 9 Sept. 1713–c. 24 Sept. 1714.
App. 9 Sept. 1713 (*CTB*, xxviii, 78). Left office by 24 Sept. 1714 (app. of Montrose).

Marlow, — *Office Keeper* (Sunderland) c. 1708–June 1710; (Dartmouth) June 1710–Aug. 1713; (Bromley) Aug. 1713–Sept. 1714; (Stanhope) Sept. 1714–c. 1716.
Occ. as Office Keeper to Sunderland from 1708 to 1710 (Chamberlayne, *Present State* (1708), 585; ibid. (1710), 515–16; SP 34/12 f. 165), to Dartmouth 1711 (Boyer, *Political State* (1711), 377); probably continued in office by Bromley; last occ. as Office Keeper to Stanhope 1716 (Miège, *Present State* (1716), pt. i, 391).

Marshall, Henry *Clerk* (St. John/Bolingbroke) Nov. 1710–Aug. 1714; (Townshend) Sept. 1714–c. May 1716.
Probably app. by St. John; presence in office notified as Clerk to St. John 23 Nov. 1710 (SP 44/109), to Townshend 30 Sept. 1714 (SP 44/116). Left office by 5 May 1716 (app. of Gedney).

Marwood, William *Deputy Clerk of Signet* 1725–39.
Occ. as Deputy to Alexander from April 1725 to Nov. 1729 (SO 5/1–2), to Fry from April 1725 to Dec. 1739 (ibid.), to Weston from Nov. 1729 to Dec. 1739 (SO 5/2).

Maskelyne, Edmund *Clerk* (Townshend) Nov.–Dec. 1716; (Methuen) Dec. 1716–April 1717; (Addison) April 1717–March 1718; (Craggs) March 1718–Feb. 1721; (Carteret) March 1721–April 1724; (Newcastle) April 1724–March 1744.
Deputy Clerk of Signet 1735–March 1744.

App. as Clerk by Townshend notified 29 Nov. 1716 (SP 44/147); probably continued in office by Methuen; occ. as Clerk to Addison 1718 (Miège, *Present State* (1718), 362); presence in office as Clerk to Craggs notified 29 March 1718, 18 Dec. 1719 (SP 44/147); pd. as Clerk to Carteret from 29 Sept. 1723 to 3 April 1724 (MS Rawlinson C 367), to Newcastle from 4 April 1724 to 24 June 1733 (MSS Rawlinson C 367, 123); last occ. as Clerk to Newcastle 1743 (Chamberlayne, *Present State* (1743), pt. ii, 32). App. Deputy Clerk of Signet to Delafaye 30 June 1735 (Ind. 6762); last occ. Jan. 1744 (SO 5/2). D. March 1744 (Burke, *Landed Gentry* (1952), 892).

Maskelyne, Nevil *Clerk* (Bolingbroke) May 1713–Aug. 1714; (Townshend) Sept. 1714–c. Nov. 1716.

App. by Bolingbroke notified 18 May 1713 (SP 44/114); presence in office as Clerk to Townshend notified 30 Sept. 1714 (SP 44/116). Left office by 29 Nov. 1716 (app. of E. Maskelyne).

Massabeky, John *Interpreter of Oriental Languages* May 1734–c. July 1739.

App. notified 17 May 1734 (SP 44/128 p. 285). Left office by 9 July 1739 (SP 44/131 p. 138).

Massey, John *Office Keeper* (Tweeddale) Feb. 1742–Jan. 1746.

App. by Tweeddale probably Feb. 1742; first occ. 1743 (Chamberlayne, *Present State* (1743), pt. ii, 32). Left office Jan. 1746 on abolition of Scottish Department (Tweeddale MS Acc. 4862 Box 160/1 Bundle 4).

Matthews, Elizabeth *Necessary Woman* (Sandwich) c. 1765; (Grafton) July 1765–May 1766; (Richmond) May–July 1766; (Shelburne) July 1766–Oct. 1768; (Rochford) Oct. 1768–Dec. 1770; (Sandwich) Dec. 1770–Jan. 1771; (Halifax) Jan.–June 1771; (Suffolk) June 1771–Nov. 1775; (Weymouth) Nov. 1775–c. 1777.

Occ. as Necessary Woman to Sandwich 1765 (*Court and City Reg.* (1765), 110), to Grafton 1766 (ibid. (1766), 107); probably continued in office by Richmond; occ. as Necessary Woman to Shelburne from 1767 to 1768 (*Royal Kal.* (1767), 113; ibid. (1768), 117), to Rochford from 1769 to 1771 (sic) (ibid. (1769), 117; ibid. (1771), 115); probably remained in Northern Department Dec. 1770 on Rochford's transfer to Southern and continued in office under Sandwich and Halifax; occ. as Necessary Woman to Suffolk from 1772 to 1775 (ibid. (1772), 115; ibid. (1775), 107), to Weymouth from 1776 to 1777 (ibid. (1776), 109; ibid. (1777), 109).

Mauries, Francis *Clerk* (Dartmouth) c. 1711.

'Mr. Mauries'; probably identical with Francis Mauries (Dartmouth MS D 1778 I, ii no. 575a; *Letters of Denization and Acts of Naturalization for Aliens in England and Ireland 1701–1800*, ed. W. A. Shaw (Huguenot Soc. Publications, xxvii, 1923), 55). Occ. 1711 (Boyer, *Political State* (1711), 377).

Methuen, Paul *Secretary of State* (acting South) 21 June–Dec. 1716; (South) Dec. 1716–12 April 1717.

App. 21 June 1716 (*CTB*, xxx, 346). Left office 12 April 1717 (ibid. xxxi, 287).

Micklethwaite, Joseph *Chief Clerk* (Stanhope) Sept. 1714–April 1717.

App. by Stanhope probably Sept. 1714; heads list of his Clerks 1716 (Chamberlayne, *Present State* (1716), 528); kept accounts of his fees as Secretary of State (Stanhope MS 83 (12), Micklethwaite to Stanhope, 17 July to 6 Nov. 1716). Left office April 1717 on app. as Secretary to Stanhope as Chancellor of Exchequer (*Hist. Reg. Chron.* (1717), ii, 19).

Middleton, Charles (Middleton) 2nd Earl of *Secretary of State* (North) 24 Aug. 1684–Oct. 1688; (South) Oct.–Dec. 1688.

App. 24 Aug. 1684 (PC 2/70 p. 220). Left office Dec. 1688 (flight of James II).

Milburn, William *Office Keeper* (Holdernesse) April 1759–March 1761; (Bute) March 1761–May 1762; (Grenville) June–Oct. 1762; (Halifax) Oct. 1762–July 1765; (Seymour Conway) July 1765–Jan. 1768; (Weymouth) Jan. 1768–Dec. 1770; (Rochford) Dec. 1770–Nov. 1775; (Suffolk) Nov. 1775–March 1779; (Stormont) Oct. 1779–c. Feb. 1782.

App. by Holdernesse April 1759 (*Gent. Mag.* (1759), xxix, 195); occ. as Office Keeper to Holdernesse to 1761 (*Court and City Reg.* (1761), 106), to Bute 1762 (ibid. (1762), 106); probably continued in office by Grenville; occ. as Office Keeper to Halifax from 1763 to 1765 (ibid. (1763), 106; ibid. (1765), 110), to Seymour Conway from 1766 to 1768 (ibid. (1766), 107; *Royal Kal.* (1768), 118; Shelburne MS 134 p. 119), to Weymouth from 1769 to 1771 (sic) (*Royal Kal.* (1769), 117; ibid. (1771), 115); probably became Office Keeper to Rochford on his transfer to Southern Department Dec. 1770 and to Suffolk on Weymouth's app. as Secretary of State Nov. 1775; occ. as Office Keeper to Rochford from 1772 to 1775 (ibid. (1772), 115; ibid. (1775), 107), to Suffolk from 1776 to 1779 (ibid. (1776), 109; ibid. (1779), 109), to Stormont from 1780 to 1782 (ibid. (1780), 110; ibid. (1782), 110). D. by 1 Feb. 1782 (Prob 11/1087 f. 91).

Milnes, John *Clerk* (Craggs) Dec. 1719–Feb. 1721; (Carteret) March 1721–April 1724; (Newcastle) April 1724–Aug. 1725.

App. by Craggs notified 18 Dec. 1719 (SP 44/147); pd. as Clerk to Carteret from 29 Sept. 1723 to 3 April 1724 (MS Rawlinson C 367), to Newcastle from 4 April 1724 to 3 Aug. 1725 (ibid.).

Mitchell, Andrew *Under Secretary* (Tweeddale) Feb. 1742–Jan. 1746.

App. by Tweeddale notified 18 Feb. 1742 (SP 55/13 p. 1).

Mitton, William *Deputy Office Keeper* (Hillsborough) c. 1769–Aug. 1772; (Dartmouth) Aug. 1772–c. 1773.

Deputy to J. P. Muly; occ. as Deputy Office Keeper to Hillsborough from 1769 to 1772 (*Royal Kal.* (1769), 118; ibid. (1772), 116), to Dartmouth 1773 (ibid. (1773), 116).

Money, J. *Clerk* (Bedford) c. 1749.

Occ. 1749 (*Court and City Reg.* (1749), 107).

Money, William *Clerk* (Stormont) Aug. 1780–March 1782.

App. by Stormont notified 15 Aug. 1780 (FO 366/669 p. 31). Transferred to Foreign Office March 1782 (*1st Rept. on Fees*, 30).

Montgomery, John *Under Secretary* (Queensberry) Feb. 1709–July 1711.

App. by Queensberry probably Feb. 1709; occ. 1710 (Chamberlayne, *Present State* (1710), 515).

Montrose, James (Graham) 1st Duke of *Secretary of State* (Scotland) 24 Sept. 1714–5 Aug. 1715.

App. 24 Sept. 1714 (*CTB*, xxix, 335). Left office 5 Aug. 1715 (ibid. 860).

Moore, Francis *Deputy Writer of Gazette* c. 1791–31 Dec. 1796.

Occ. from 1791 to 1797 (sic) (*Royal Kal.* (1791), 104; ibid. (1797), 104). Res. 31 Dec. 1796 (*16th Rept. on Finance*, 319).

Moore, Henry *Clerk* (Newcastle) March 1725–Jan. 1731.

App. by Newcastle notified 6 March 1725 (SP 44/148); pd. from 25 Dec. 1724 to 8 Jan. 1731 (MSS Rawlinson C 367, 123).

Morainville, — *French Translator of Gazette* 1666–c. 7 Nov. 1678.

App. 1666 (A. Grey, *Debates of the House of Commons 1667–94* (London 1769), vi, 157); last occ. 7 Nov. 1678 (ibid.).

Morgann, Maurice *Assistant Under Secretary* (Shelburne) Oct. 1766–c. July 1768.

App. by Shelburne notified 8 Oct. 1766 (*CHOP 1766–9*, 84). Left office by 27 July 1768 (ibid. 434).

Morin (from 10 Nov. 1787 **Tirel Morin**), John *Clerk* (Seymour Conway) Oct. 1765–May 1766; (Richmond) May–July 1766; (Shelburne) July 1766–Oct. 1768; (Rochford) Oct. 1768–Nov. 1775; (Weymouth) Nov. 1775–c. April 1776. *Senior Clerk* (Weymouth) c. April 1776–Nov. 1779; (Hillsborough) Nov. 1779–March 1782.

Clerk of Signet 16 April 1781–19 March 1807.

App. as Clerk by Seymour Conway notified 11 Oct. 1765 (*CHOP 1760–5*, 607); presence in office notified as Clerk to Richmond 28 June 1766 (*CHOP 1766–9*, 54), to Shelburne 27 July 1768 (ibid. 434), to Rochford 4 Nov. 1768 (ibid. 435), to Weymouth 30 Nov. 1775 (*CHOP 1773–5*, 556). Probably app. Senior Clerk c. April 1776 in succession to J. Haynes; occ. as Senior Clerk to Weymouth from 1777 to 1779 (*Royal Kal.* (1777), 109; ibid. (1779), 109), to Hillsborough from 1780 to 1782 (ibid. (1780), 110; ibid. (1782), 110). Transferred to Home Office March 1782 (ibid. (1783), 110). Grant of clerkship of signet in reversion 13 Nov. 1767 (C 66/3715); succ. 16 April 1781 (d. of Copley). D. 19 March 1807 (*Gent. Mag.* (1807), lxxvii (1), 384).

Morin, Peter Michael *Clerk* (Newcastle) March 1741–March 1754; (Holdernesse) March 1754–c. April 1759. *Assistant Under Secretary* (Holdernesse) c. April 1759– March 1761. *Clerk* (Bute) March 1761–May 1762. *Assistant Under Secretary* (Grenville) June–Oct. 1762; (Halifax) Oct. 1762–July 1765; (Seymour Conway) July 1765–May 1766; (Richmond) May–July 1766; (Shelburne) July 1766–c. July 1768.

App. as Clerk by Newcastle notified 12 March 1741 (SP 44/148); occ. as Clerk to Newcastle to 1754 (*Court and City Reg.* (1754), 106), to Holdernesse from 1755 to 1760 (sic) (ibid. (1755), 106; ibid. (1760), 106). App. Assistant Under Secretary by Holdernesse jointly with Fraser probably c. April 1759 (*Grenville Papers*, ed. W. J. Smith (London 1852–3), i, 290–1); occ. as such 1761 (*Court and City Reg.* (1761), 106). Clerk to Bute from 1761 to 1762 (*Court and City Kal.* (1762), 111; *Notes and Queries*, cc (1955), 162, 445; ibid. cciv (1959), 95, 284). App. as Assistant Under Secretary notified by Grenville 12 July 1762 (*CHOP 1760–5*, 189), by Halifax 8 Nov. 1762 (ibid. 202), by Seymour Conway 23 July 1765 (ibid. 580), by Richmond 28 June 1766 (*CHOP 1766–9*, 54), by Shelburne 1 Aug. 1766 (ibid. 65). Left office by 27 July 1768 (ibid. 434).

Morley, Robert *Clerk* (Shrewsbury) c. 1689.

Occ. July 1689 (LS 13/231 p. 13).

Morrice, Nicholas *Clerk of Signet* 1678–20 Jan. 1708.

Grant in reversion 1 Feb. 1661 (C 66/2963); succ. 1678 (d. of Trumbull, sen.); admitted 29 March 1678 (*CSPD 1678*, 382–3). Surrendered office 20 Jan. 1708 (surrender recited in grant to Moyle).

Morrice, Sir William, kt. *Secretary of State* (North) 27 May 1660–c. 29 Sept. 1668.

App. 27 May 1660 (PC 2/54, pt. ii, 2). Left office by 29 Sept. 1668 (PC 2/61 p. 44).

Morrison, Robert *Clerk* (Holdernesse) c. 1757–March 1761; (Bute) March 1761–May 1762; (Grenville) June–Oct. 1762; (Halifax) Oct. 1762–July 1765; (Seymour Conway) July–c. Oct. 1765.

Occ. as Clerk to Holdernesse from 1757 to 1761 (*Court and City Reg.* (1757), 106; ibid. (1761), 106), to Bute 1762 (ibid. (1762), 106); presence in office notified as Clerk to Grenville 12 July 1762 (*CHOP 1760–5*, 189), to Halifax 8 Nov. 1762, 13 Sept. 1763, 30 April 1764 (ibid. 202, 302–3, 407); Clerk to Seymour Conway, left office by 11 Oct. 1765 (ibid. 607).

Mountsteven, John *Under Secretary* (Sunderland) Feb. 1679–Feb. 1681; Jan. 1683–Oct. 1688.

App. by Sunderland probably Feb. 1679; occ. from June or July 1679 to 12 Oct. 1680 (*CTB*, vi, 116; BM Add. MSS 28875 f. 135; 37990 f. 66); reapp. by Sunderland probably Jan. 1683; occ. from 28 June 1683 to 5 May 1688 (Hist. MSS Comm. *7th Rept.*, 364; BM Add. MS 28876 f. 109; Chamberlayne, *Present State* (1684), pt. ii, 7–8).

Moyle, Joseph *Clerk of Signet* 25 Aug. 1708–22 April 1736.

App. 25 Aug. 1708 (C 66/3465). Surrendered office 22 April 1736 (surrender recited in grant to Moyle, jun.).

Moyle (from March 1767 **Copley**), **Joseph** (cr. Bart. 28 Aug. 1778) *Deputy Clerk of Signet* 1735–6. *Clerk of Signet* 7 May 1736–16 April 1781.

Occ. as Deputy Clerk of Signet to Moyle, sen. from March 1735 to March 1736 (SO 5/2). App. Clerk of Signet 7 May 1736 (C 66/3595). D. 16 April 1781 (SO 5/4).

Muddiman, Henry *Writer of Gazette* Nov. 1665–Feb. 1666.

Wrote *Gazette* from Nov. 1665 to Feb. 1666 (J. G. Muddiman, *The King's Journalist* (London 1923), 187–8).

Muly, Elizabeth *Necessary Woman* (Hillsborough) c. 1769–Aug. 1772; (Dartmouth) Aug. 1772–Nov. 1775; (Germain) Nov. 1775–Feb. 1782; (Ellis) Feb.–March 1782.

Occ. as Necessary Woman to Hillsborough from 1769 to 1772 (*Royal Kal.* (1769), 118; ibid. (1772), 116), to Dartmouth from 1773 to 1775 (ibid. (1773), 116; ibid. (1775), 107), to Germain from 1776 to 1782 (ibid. (1776), 109; ibid. (1782), 110); continued in office by Ellis. Left office March 1782 on abolition of Colonial Department (T 1/579 Schedule 2).

Muly, John Philip *Office Keeper* (Hillsborough) c. 1769–Aug. 1772; (Dartmouth) Aug. 1772–Nov. 1775; (Germain) Nov. 1775–Feb. 1782.

Occ. as Office Keeper to Hillsborough from 1769 to 1772 (*Royal Kal.* (1769), 118; ibid. (1772), 116), to Dartmouth from 1773 to 1775 (ibid. (1773), 116; ibid. (1775), 107), to Germain from 1776 to 1782 (ibid. (1776), 109; ibid. (1782), 110). Left office by 12 Feb. 1782 (app. of Lackington).

Mynatt, William *Office Keeper* (Harley) c. 1706–Feb. 1708; (Boyle) Feb. 1708–Sept. 1710; (St. John/Bolingbroke) Sept. 1710–c. 1711.

Pd. as Office Keeper to Harley from 16 Nov. 1706 to 3 Sept. 1707 (BM Loan 29/162); occ. as Office Keeper to Harley 1707 (Chamberlayne, *Present State* (1707), 513–14), to Boyle from 1708 to 1710 (ibid. (1708), 586; ibid. (1710), 516), to St. John 1711 (Boyer, *Political State* (1711), 377).

Negri, Solomon *Interpreter of Oriental Languages* May 1723–c. May 1727.

App. notified 28 May 1723 (SP 44/123 p. 275). D. by 30 May 1727 (SP 44/125 p. 107).

Neubourg, George William *Decipherer* June 1753–1762.

Pd. from 24 June 1753 (T 53/45 p. 45). Left office 1762 (PRO 30/8/232, Bode Memorial May 1786).

Neubourg, Philip Ferdinand *Decipherer* June 1750–June 1753.

Pd. from 24 June 1750 to 24 June 1753 (T 53/43 p. 491; T 53/45 p. 45).

Newcastle, Thomas (Pelham Holles) 1st Duke of *Secretary of State* (South) 4 April 1724–Feb. 1748; (North) Feb. 1748–23 March 1754.

App. 4 April 1724 (T 53/31 p. 191). Left office 23 March 1754 (T 53/45 p. 87).

Newcomen, (?) Theophilus *Clerk* (Sunderland) c. 1710.

'Mr. Newcomen'; possibly identical with Theophilus Newcomen app. Clerk of Ingrossments, Alienation Office 3 May 1710 (*CTB*, xxiv, 270). Occ. as Clerk to Sunderland 1710 (Chamberlayne, *Present State* (1710), 515–16; SP 34/12 f. 165).

Nicholas, Sir Edward, kt. *Secretary of State* (South) May 1660–c. 15 Oct. 1662.

Took oath 27 Feb. 1659 (PC 2/54, pt. ii, 42); assumed functions at Restoration May 1660. Left office by 15 Oct. 1662 (PC 2/56 p. 174).

Nicholas, John (ktd. 23 April 1661) *Clerk of Signet* 1655–9 Jan. 1705.

Admitted 1655 (*CSPD Addenda 1660–85*, 471); retained office 1660 (*CSPD 1660–1*, 304). D. 9 Jan. 1705 (MI West Horsley, Surrey).

Noble, Joseph *Office Keeper* (Carteret) c. 1723–April 1724; (Newcastle) April 1724–March 1754; (Holdernesse) March 1754–7 April 1759.

Pd. as Office Keeper to Carteret from 25 March 1723 to 3 April 1724 (MS Rawlinson C 367), to Newcastle from 4 April 1724 to 24 June 1733 (MSS Rawlinson C 367, 123); occ. as Office Keeper to Newcastle to 1754 (*Court and City Reg.* (1754), 106), to Holdernesse from 1755 to 1759 (ibid. (1755), 106; ibid. (1759), 106). D. 7 April 1759 (*Gent. Mag.* (1759), xxix, 194).

Noble, Thomas *Clerk* (Newcastle) Sept. 1751–March 1754; (Holdernesse) March 1754–March 1761; (Bute) March–May 1761.

App. by Newcastle notified 20 Sept. 1751 (SP 44/148); occ. as Clerk to Newcastle to 1754 (*Court and City Reg.* (1754), 106), to Holdernesse from 1755 to 1761 (ibid. (1755), 106; ibid. (1761), 106). Res. May 1761 (*Notes and Queries*, cc (1955), 444).

Nottingham, Daniel (Finch) 2nd Earl of *Secretary of State* (North) 5 March 1689– June 1690; (Sole) June–Dec. 1690; (South) Dec. 1690–March 1692; (Sole) March 1692–March 1693; (South) March–6 Nov. 1693; 2 May 1702–22 April 1704.

App. 5 March 1689 (BM Add. MS 45731 f. 22). Left office 6 Nov. 1693 (Isham MS no. 1499). App. 2 May 1702 (PC 2/79 p. 110). Left office 22 April 1704 (*CTB*, xix, 245).

Nunes *see* **Cardozo Nunes**

Oakes, Richard *Under Secretary* (Suffolk) Oct. 1778–March 1779.

App. by Suffolk notified 28 Oct. 1778 (SP 44/141 p. 458).

Ombee (Umby), — *Necessary Woman* (Vernon) c. 1699–May 1702; (Nottingham) May 1702–April 1704; (Harley) May 1704–Feb. 1708; (Boyle) Feb. 1708–Sept. 1710; (St. John/Bolingbroke) Sept. 1710–Aug. 1714; (Townshend) Sept. 1714– Dec. 1716; (Methuen) Dec. 1716–April 1717; (Addison) April 1717–March 1718; (Craggs) March 1718–Feb. 1721; (Carteret) March 1721–Jan. 1724.

Necessary Woman to Vernon; possibly unnamed recipient of salary from Pope's death; pd. odd sum to 2 Sept. 1699 and then quarterly to 2 Sept. 1700 (BM Add. MS 40785 ff. 43, 49, 62); first named 14 Nov. 1700; pd. from 2 Sept. 1700 to 25 March 1702 (BM Add. MSS 40785 ff. 67, 71; 40786 f. 35); pd. 1 May 1702 for quarter to 24 June 1702 (BM Add. MS 40786 f. 37); probably remained continuously in office as above; pd. as Necessary Woman to Carteret from 29 Sept. 1723 to 30 Jan. 1724 (MS Rawlinson C 367).

Oudart, Nicholas *Secretary for Latin Tongue* 19 July 1666–c. 21 Dec. 1681.

App. 19 July 1666 (C 66/3085). Buried 21 Dec. 1681 (*Westminster Abbey Registers*, ed. J. L. Chester (London 1876), 204).

Palman, George Lewis *Clerk* (Germain) c. 1780–Feb. 1782; (Ellis) Feb.–March 1782.

Occ. as Clerk to Germain from 1780 to 1782 (*Royal Kal.* (1780), 110; ibid. (1782), 110), to Ellis March 1782 (T 1/579 Schedule 2). Transferred to Home Office March 1782 (*1st Rept. on Fees*, 24).

Patterson, William *Chief Clerk* (Tweeddale) March 1742–Jan. 1746.

App. by Tweeddale notified March 1742 (SP 55/13 p. 3). Left office Jan. 1746 on abolition of Scottish Department (Tweeddale MS Acc. 4862 Box 160/1 Bundle 4).

Pauncefort, Tracy *Clerk* (Harley) c. 1706–7.

Pd. from 16 Feb. 1706 to 3 Sept. 1707 (BM Loan 29/162); last occ. 1707 (Chamberlayne, *Present State* (1707), 513–14).

Paxton, Nathaniel *Chief Clerk* (Roxburghe) c. 1720–Aug. 1725.

In service of Roxburghe probably as Chief Clerk; occ. 10 Nov. 1720 (SP 55/9 ff. 137–9), 1723 (Miège, *Present State* (1723), pt. ii, 70); occ. as Chief Clerk 1726 (sic) (Chamberlayne, *Present State* (1726), pt. ii, 29).

Payzant, James *Clerk* (Trumbull) c. 1695–Dec. 1697; (Vernon) Dec. 1697–Nov. 1700; (Hedges) Nov. 1700–Dec. 1701; (Manchester) Jan.–May 1702; (Hedges) May 1702–Dec. 1706; (Sunderland) Dec. 1706–June 1710; (Dartmouth) June 1710–Aug. 1713; (Bromley) Aug. 1713–Sept. 1714; (Stanhope) Sept. 1714–April 1717; (Sunderland) April 1717–March 1718; (Stanhope) March 1718–Feb. 1721; (Townshend) Feb. 1721–May 1730; (Harrington) May 1730–Feb. 1742; (Carteret/ Granville) Feb. 1742–Nov. 1744; (Harrington) Nov. 1744–Oct. 1746; (Chesterfield) Oct. 1746–Feb. 1748; (Bedford) Feb. 1748–June 1751; (Holdernesse) June 1751– March 1754; (Robinson) March 1754–Nov. 1755; (Fox) Nov. 1755–Nov. 1756; (Pitt) Dec. 1756–23 July 1757.

Stated in 1757 to have served for seventy years (*Gent. Mag.* (1757), xxvii, 339); pd. as Clerk to Trumbull from 3 Nov. 1695 to 3 Feb. 1697 (Trumbull Add. MS 113), to Vernon from 2 June 1698 to 5 Nov. 1700 (BM Add. MS 40785 ff. 20, 66); occ. as Clerk to Hedges 1701 (Miège, *New State* (1701), pt. iii, 109), to Manchester 1701 (sic) (*Compleat History* (1701), 98), to Hedges from 1702 to 1707 (sic) (ibid. (1702), 69; Chamberlayne, *Present State* (1704), 530; ibid. (1707), 513), to Sunderland from 1708 to 1710 (Chamberlayne, *Present State* (1708), 585; ibid. (1710), 515–16; SP 34/12 f. 165), to Dartmouth 1711 (Boyer, *Political State* (1711), 377); probably continued in office by Bromley; occ. as Clerk to Stanhope from 1716 to 1717 (Chamberlayne, *Present State* (1716), 528; CTB, xxx, 312; ibid. xxxi, 138–9); pd. as Clerk to Sunderland from April 1717 to March 1718 (Sunderland MS D 1/36), to Stanhope from 29 Sept. 1718 to 29 Sept. 1720 (Stanhope MS 76); occ. as Clerk to Townshend from 1723 to 1729 (Miège, *Present State* (1723), 69; Chamberlayne, *Present State* (1729), pt. ii, 30), to Harrington from 1735 to 1741 (Chamberlayne,

Present State (1735), pt. ii, 43; ibid. (1741), pt. ii, 47), to Carteret 1743 (ibid. (1743), pt. ii, 32), to Harrington 1745 (ibid. (1745), pt. ii, 32); presence in office as Clerk to Chesterfield notified 21 Nov. 1746 (SP 44/129 p. 428); occ. as Clerk to Bedford from 1748 to 1751 (Chamberlayne, *Present State* (1748), pt. ii, 52; *Court and City Reg.* (1751), 108), to Holdernesse from 1752 to 1754 (*Court and City Reg.* (1752), 107; ibid. (1754), 106), to Robinson from 1755 to 1756 (sic) (Chamberlayne, *Present State* (1755), pt. ii, 53; *Court and City Reg.* (1756), 107); probably continued in office by Fox; presence in office as Clerk to Pitt notified 17 Dec. 1756 (SP 44/136 p. 399). D. 23 July 1757 (*Gent. Mag.* (1757), xxvii, 339).

Payzant, James *Clerk* (Holdernesse) Jan. 1752–March 1754; (Robinson) March 1754–Nov. 1755; (Fox) Nov. 1755–April 1756.

App. by Holdernesse notified 8 Jan. 1752 (SP 44/136 p. 191); occ. as Clerk to Holdernesse to 1754 (*Court and City Reg.* (1754), 106–7), to Robinson from 1755 to 1756 (sic) (Chamberlayne, *Present State* (1755), pt. ii, 53; *Court and City Reg.* (1756), 107). Removal from office by Fox notified 8 April 1756 (SP 44/136 p. 358).

Paz *see* **de Paz**

Peace, Charles *Clerk* (Germain) c. 1779–Feb. 1782; (Ellis) Feb.–March 1782.

Occ. as Clerk to Germain from 1779 to 1782 (*Royal Kal.* (1779), 109; ibid. (1782), 110); continued in office by Ellis. Left office March 1782 on abolition of Colonial Department (T 1/579 Schedule 2).

Pearson, — (?) *Office Keeper* (Dartmouth) c. 1711.

Possibly deputy to Smith; occ. 1711 (Boyer, *Political State* (1711), 377).

Pelham, Thomas (?) *Clerk* (Newcastle) Aug. 1726–June 1730.

App. by Newcastle notified 22 Aug. 1726 (SP 44/148); not a salaried Clerk (MS Rawlinson C 367). Probably left office June 1730 on app. as Secretary to Embassy to France (*Hist. Reg. Chron.* (1730), xv, 44; *Dip. Rep.*, 19).

Perrott, Charles *Writer of Gazette* Feb. 1666–c. 1672.

App. Feb. 1666 (*CSPD 1665–6*, 232; A. à Wood, *Athenae Oxonienses*, ed. P. Bliss (London 1817), iii, 1185); last occ. 28 Jan. 1672 (*CSPD 1671–2*, 107).

Phelps, Richard *Under Secretary* (Sandwich) Sept. 1763–July 1765; (Hillsborough) Jan.–June 1768; (Sandwich) Dec. 1770–Jan. 1771.

App. by Sandwich notified 9 Sept. 1763 (*CHOP 1760–5*, 302); received fees as Under Secretary to Hillsborough from 21 Jan. to 24 June 1768 (SP 45/32); app. by Sandwich notified 21 Dec. 1770 (*CHOP 1770–2*, 103).

Phipps, John *Deputy Office Keeper* (Harrington) March 1731–c. 1737.

Deputy to Sommer; received his fees from March 1731 (SP 45/26); occ. as Deputy Office Keeper to Harrington to 29 Oct. 1737 (T 52/40 p. 7).

Pin *see* **Le Pin**

Pitt, William *Secretary of State* (South) 6 Dec. 1756–5 Oct. 1761.

App. 6 Dec. 1756 (T 53/46 p. 117). Left office 5 Oct. 1761 (T 53/48 p. 200).

Plasket, Thomas Henry *Deputy Clerk of Signet* June 1837–1 Oct. 1850.

Occ. as Deputy to Bentinck from June 1837 to Oct. 1850 (SO 5/43). D. 1 Oct. 1850 (*Gent. Mag.* (1850), cxxvii, 561).

Pollock, William *Clerk* (Egremont) May–Aug. 1763; (Sandwich) Sept. 1763–July 1765; (Grafton) July 1765–May 1766; (Richmond) May–July 1766; (Shelburne) July 1766–Jan. 1768. *Chief Clerk* (Hillsborough) Jan. 1768–Aug. 1772; (Dartmouth) Aug. 1772–Nov. 1775; (Germain) Nov. 1775–Feb. 1782; (Ellis) Feb.–March 1782. *Deputy Clerk of Signet* 1785–17 Feb. 1816.

App. as Clerk by Egremont notified 20 May 1763 (*CHOP 1760–5*, 285); presence in office notified as Clerk to Sandwich 9 Sept. 1763, 30 April 1764 (ibid. 302, 408), to Grafton 23 July 1765 (ibid. 580), to Richmond 28 June 1766 (*CHOP 1766–9*, 54); occ. as Clerk to Shelburne from 1766 to 1768 (Shelburne MS 134 p. 119; *Royal Kal.* (1768), 117). App. Chief Clerk by Hillsborough Jan. 1768 (*1st Rept. on Fees*, 19); occ. as Chief Clerk to Hillsborough to 1772 (*Royal Kal.* (1772), 116), to Dartmouth from 1773 to 1775 (ibid. (1773), 116; ibid. (1775), 107), to Germain from 1776 to 1782 (ibid. (1776), 109; ibid. (1782), 110), to Ellis March 1782 (T 1/579 Schedule 2). App. Chief Clerk, Home Office May 1782 (*1st Rept. on Fees*, 19). Occ. as Deputy Clerk of Signet to Rivers from July 1785 to Aug. 1807 (SO 5/4, 20); app. Deputy to Bentinck 23 Dec. 1802 (Ind. 6769), to Gage 24 April 1807 (Ind. 6770); last occ. as Deputy 1816 (*Royal Kal.* (1816), 147). D. 17 Feb. 1816 (*Gent. Mag.* (1816), lxxxvi (1), 282).

Pope, — *Necessary Woman* (Trumbull) c. 1695–Dec. 1697; (Vernon) Dec. 1697 8 March/17 Aug. 1699.

Pd. as Necessary Woman to Trumbull from 3 May 1695 to 3 Feb. 1697 (Trumbull Add. MS 113), to Vernon from 2 March 1698 to 2 March 1699 (BM Add. MS 40785 ff. 13, 33). D. between 8 March and 17 Aug. 1699 (ibid. ff. 42, 43).

Poplett, Thomas *Clerk* (Germain) c. 1777–8.

Occ. from 1777 to 1778 (*Royal Kal.* (1777), 109; ibid. (1778), 109).

Porten, Stanier (ktd. 5 June 1772) *Under Secretary* (Shelburne) July–Oct. 1768; (Rochford) Oct. 1768–Nov. 1775; (Weymouth) Nov. 1775–Nov. 1779; (Hillsborough) Nov. 1779–March 1782.

Keeper of State Papers 3 May 1774–7 June 1789.

App. as Under Secretary notified by Shelburne 27 July 1768 (*CHOP 1766–9*, 434), by Rochford 4 Nov. 1768 (ibid. 435), by Weymouth 30 Nov. 1775 (*CHOP 1773–5*, 556); received fees as Under Secretary to Hillsborough from Nov. 1779 to 27 March 1782 (SP 45/34–5). App. Keeper of State Papers 3 May 1774 (C 66/3746). D. 7 June 1789 (T 53/59 p. 199).

Potenger, Richard *Under Secretary* (Holdernesse) June 1751–March 1761.

Received fees as Under Secretary to Holdernesse from June 1751 (SP 45/28); app. notified 31 July 1751 (SP 44/136 p. 180).

Potter, John *Under Secretary* (Chesterfield) Nov. 1746–Feb. 1748; (Bedford) Feb. 1748–29 May 1749.

App. by Chesterfield notified 21 Nov. 1746 (SP 44/129 p. 613); continued in office by Bedford (SP 45/28). D. 29 May 1749 (*Gent. Mag.* (1749), xix, 236).

Powlett, Thomas Norton *Clerk of Signet* 30 Oct. 1807–6 Dec. 1824.

App. 30 Oct. 1807 (C 66/4072). D. 6 Dec. 1824 (*Gent. Mag.* (1824), xciv (2), 645).

Pownall, John *Under Secretary* (Hillsborough) June 1768–Aug. 1772; (Dartmouth) Aug. 1772–Nov. 1775; (Germain) Nov. 1775–April 1776.

Received fees as Under Secretary from 24 June 1768 to 5 April 1776 (SP 45/32).

Pownall, John Lillingston *Clerk* (Hillsborough) c. 1769–Jan. 1770.

Occ. from 1769 to 1770 (*Royal Kal.* (1769), 118; ibid. (1770), 116). Probably left office Jan. 1770 on app. as Clerk, Board of Trade (*Journal of the Commissioners for Trade and Plantations 1768–75*, 164).

Preston, Richard (Graham) 1st Viscount *Secretary of State* (North) 29 Oct.–Dec. 1688.

App. 29 Oct. 1688 (PC 2/72 p. 783). Left office Dec. 1688 (flight of James II).

Prevereau, Daniel *Clerk* (Boyle) Feb. 1708–Sept. 1710; (St. John/Bolingbroke) Sept. 1710–Aug. 1714; (Townshend) Sept. 1714–Dec. 1716; (Methuen) Dec. 1716–April 1717; (Addison) April 1717–March 1718; (Craggs) March 1718–Dec. 1719. *Chief Clerk* (Craggs) Dec. 1719–Feb. 1721; (Carteret) March 1721–April 1724; (Newcastle) April 1724–1 April 1746.

Presence in office notified as Clerk to Boyle 23 Feb. 1708 (SP 44/107 p. 4), to St. John 23 Nov. 1710 (SP 44/109), to Townshend 30 Sept. 1714 (SP 44/116); occ. as Clerk to Addison 1718 (Miège, *Present State* (1718), 362); presence in office as Clerk to Craggs notified 29 March 1718 (SP 44/147). App. Chief Clerk by Craggs Dec. 1719 (*Hist. Reg. Chron.* (1719), iv, 42); occ. as Chief Clerk to Carteret from 30 May to 30 Dec. 1723 (T 52/32 p. 361; T 52/33 pp. 23, 51, 79, 275), to Newcastle from 1726 to 1746 (Chamberlayne, *Present State* (1726), pt. ii, 29; *Court and City Reg.* (1746), 99). D. 1 April 1746 (*Gent. Mag.* (1746), xvi, 222).

Price, — (?) *Office Keeper* (Nottingham) 1689.

Occ., probably as Office Keeper, July 1689 (LS 13/231 p. 14).

Price, John *Clerk* (Newcastle) July 1729–c. 1737.

App. by Newcastle notified 29 July 1729 (SP 44/148); pd. from April 1729 to 24 June 1733 (MSS Rawlinson C 367, 123); last occ. 29 Oct. 1737 (T 52/40 p. 7).

Pringle, Robert *Under Secretary* (Sunderland) Jan. 1709–June 1710; (Stanhope) Sept. 1714–April 1717.

App. by Sunderland Jan. 1709 (Luttrell, *Hist. Relation*, vi, 391—'John Pringle'); occ. almost certainly correctly as 'Robert Pringle' 1710 (Chamberlayne, *Present State* (1710), 515); app. by Stanhope notified 8 Oct. 1714 (SP 44/117 p. 5).

Prior, Matthew *Under Secretary* (Jersey) May 1699–June 1700.

App. by Jersey May 1699 (Luttrell, *Hist. Relation*, iv, 517).

Pulse, Philip *Clerk* (Newcastle) May 1748–c. 1751.

App. by Newcastle notified 26 May 1748 (SP 44/148); last occ. 1751 (*Court and City Reg.* (1751), 108).

Pulteney, John *Under Secretary* (Shrewsbury) Sept. 1689–June 1690; (Sydney) Dec. 1690–March 1692.

App. by Shrewsbury Sept. 1689 (Luttrell, *Hist. Relation*, i, 580), by Sydney Dec. 1690 (ibid. ii, 149; *CSPD 1690–1*, 195). The reports of his app. as Under Secretary by Trenchard March 1693 and by Shrewsbury March 1694 (Luttrell, *Hist. Relation*, iii, 61, 279) are inaccurate.

Queensberry, James (Douglas) 2nd Duke of *Secretary of State* (Scotland) 3 Feb. 1709–6 July 1711.

App. 3 Feb. 1709 (*CTB*, xxiii, 81). D. 6 July 1711.

Quin, William *Office Keeper* (Harrington) March 1732–Feb. 1742; (Carteret/Granville) Feb. 1742–Nov. 1744; (Harrington) Nov. 1744–c. 1746.

App. by Harrington March 1732 (*Gent. Mag.* (1732), ii, 680—'Winn'); received fees from April 1732 (SP 45/26); occ. as Office Keeper to Harrington to 1741 (Chamberlayne, *Present State* (1741), pt. ii, 47), to Carteret 1743 (ibid. (1743), pt. ii, 32), to Harrington from 1745 to 1746 (ibid. (1745), pt. ii, 32; *Court and City Reg.* (1746), 99).

Ramsden, Thomas *Clerk* (Newcastle) June 1730–1743. *Under Secretary* (Newcastle) 1743–April 1750.

Collector of State Papers 4 Jan. 1742–25 April 1791.

Secretary for Latin Tongue 20 April 1752–25 April 1791.

App. as Clerk by Newcastle notified 6 June 1730 (SP 44/148); last occ. as Clerk 1743 (Chamberlayne, *Present State* (1743), pt. ii, 31–2). App. Under Secretary by Newcastle probably 1743 (J. Haydn, *Book of Dignities*, 3rd ed. (London 1894), 225); first occ. as such 25 March 1743 (SP 44/148). Left office April 1750 (*Gent. Mag.* (1750), xx, 189—*but not dead*). App. Collector of State Papers 4 Jan. 1742 (C 66/3611), Secretary for Latin Tongue 20 April 1752 (C 66/3636, 3677). D. 25 April 1791 (T 53/60 p. 139).

Ramsey, Benjamin *Office Keeper* (Trumbull) May 1695–Dec. 1697; (Vernon) Dec. 1697–Nov. 1700; (Hedges) Nov. 1700–Dec. 1701; (Manchester) Jan.–May 1702; (Hedges) May 1702–Dec. 1706.

Pd. as Office Keeper to Trumbull from 3 May 1695 to 3 Feb. 1697 (Trumbull Add. MS 113), to Vernon from 2 March 1698 to 5 Nov. 1700 (BM Add. MS 40785 ff. 13, 66); occ. as Office Keeper to Hedges 1701 (Miège, *New State* (1701), pt. iii, 109), to Manchester 1701 (sic) (*Compleat History* (1701), 98), to Hedges from 1702 to 1707 (sic) (ibid. (1702), 69; Chamberlayne, *Present State* (1704), 530; ibid. (1707), 513). D. by 29 Oct. 1707 (*CTB*, xxviii, 452).

Randall, George *Clerk* (Shelburne) Sept. 1767–Oct. 1768; (Rochford) Oct. 1768–Nov. 1775; (Weymouth) Nov. 1775–Nov. 1779; (Hillsborough) Nov. 1779–March 1782.

App. by Shelburne notified 25 Sept. 1767 (*CHOP 1766–9*, 187); presence in office notified as Clerk to Shelburne 27 July 1768 (ibid. 434), to Rochford 4 Nov. 1768 (ibid. 435), to Weymouth 30 Nov. 1775 (*CHOP 1773–5*, 556); occ. as Clerk to Weymouth to 1779 (*Royal Kal.* (1779), 109), to Hillsborough from 1780 to 1782 (ibid. (1780), 110; ibid. (1782), 110). Transferred to Home Office March 1782 (*1st Rept. on Fees*, 22).

Raymond, Thomas *Keeper of State Papers* (?)–c. 31 Dec. 1661.

Grant in reversion 20 July 1640 (C 66/2873); had succ. by 31 Dec. 1661 when surrendered office (surrender recited in grant to J. Williamson).

Reeve *see* **Reid**

Reid (Reeve), George *Clerk* (Tweeddale) March 1742–Jan. 1746.

App. by Tweeddale notified March 1742 (SP 55/13 p. 3). Left office Jan. 1746 on abolition of Scottish Department (Tweeddale MS Acc. 4862 Box 160/1 Bundle 4).

Richards, John *Clerk* (Arlington) c. 1665–73. *Under Secretary* (Arlington) c. 1673– Sept. 1674.

Clerk to Arlington by Dec. 1665 when W. Godolphin ceased to be Under Secretary (*Letters to Sir Joseph Williamson 1673–4*, ed. W. D. Christie (Camden 2nd ser., viii, ix, 1874), i, 142). Under Secretary by 1673 (Evans, *Principal Secretary*, 192); last occ. 27 Feb. 1674 (*Letters to Williamson*, ii, 155).

Richardson, John *Deputy Clerk of Signet* c. 1722–14 Aug. 1724.

Occ. as Deputy to Alexander and Fry from Dec. 1722 to July 1724 (SO 5/1). D. 14 Aug. 1724 (*Hist. Reg. Chron.* (1724), ix, 38).

Richardson, John *Deputy Clerk of Signet* 1740–4.

Occ. as Deputy to Weston from Feb. 1740 to April 1744 (SO 5/2).

Richardson, Joseph *Clerk* (Sunderland) Oct. 1717–March 1718; (Stanhope) March 1718–Feb. 1721; (Townshend) Feb. 1721–May 1730; (Harrington) May 1730–Feb. 1742; (Carteret/Granville) Feb. 1742–Nov. 1744; (Harrington) Nov. 1744–March 1745. *Chief Clerk* (Harrington) March 1745–Oct. 1746; (Chesterfield) Oct. 1746– Feb. 1748; (Bedford) Feb. 1748–June 1751; (Holdernesse) June 1751–March 1754;

(Robinson) March 1754–Nov. 1755; (Fox) Nov. 1755–Nov. 1756; (Pitt) Dec. 1756–Oct. 1761; (Egremont) Oct. 1761–Aug. 1763; (Sandwich) Sept. 1763–July 1765; (Grafton) July 1765–10 May 1766.

App. as Clerk by Sunderland notified 12 Oct. 1717 (SP 44/120 p. 231); pd. as such to March 1718 (Sunderland MS D 1/36); pd. as Clerk to Stanhope from 29 Sept. 1718 to 29 Sept. 1720 (Stanhope MS 76); occ. as Clerk to Townshend from 31 May 1725 to 13 Sept. 1729 (T 52/33 p. 366; T 52/36 p. 403), to Harrington from 10 June 1730 to 20 Oct. 1741 (T 52/37 p. 122; T 52/41 p. 350), to Carteret from 17 Sept. 1742 to 15 Nov. 1743 (T 52/42 pp. 82, 324), to Harrington 1745 (Chamberlayne, *Present State* (1745), pt. ii, 32). App. Chief Clerk by Harrington March 1745 (*Gent. Mag.* (1745), xv, 165); presence in office as Chief Clerk to Chesterfield notified 21 Nov. 1746 (SP 44/129 p. 428); occ. as Chief Clerk to Bedford from 1748 to 1751 (Chamberlayne, *Present State* (1748), pt. ii, 52; *Court and City Reg.* (1751), 108), to Holdernesse from 1752 to 1754 (*Court and City Reg.* (1752), 107; ibid. (1754), 106), to Robinson from 1755 to 1756 (sic) (Chamberlayne, *Present State* (1755), pt. ii, 53; *Court and City Reg.* (1756), 107); probably continued in office by Fox; presence in office notified as Chief Clerk to Pitt 17 Dec. 1756 (SP 44/136 p. 399), to Egremont 13 Oct. 1761 (*CHOP 1760–5*, 70), to Sandwich 9 Sept. 1763, 30 April 1764 (ibid. 302, 408), to Grafton 23 July 1765 (ibid. 580). D. 10 May 1766 (*Gent. Mag.* (1766), xxxvi, 247).

Richardson, Thomas *Office Keeper of Signet Office* c. 1736–c. Sept. 1773.

Occ. from 1736 to 1772 (Chamberlayne, *Present State* (1736), pt. ii, 47; *Royal Kal.* (1772), 115). D. c. Sept. 1773 (SO 5/4).

Richmond, Charles (Lennox) 8th Duke of *Secretary of State* (South) 23 May–30 July 1766.

App. 23 May 1766 (T 53/50 p. 283). Left office 30 July 1766 (ibid.).

Rivers, James *Clerk* (Newcastle) March 1744–March 1754. *Under Secretary* (Robinson) March 1754–Nov. 1755; (Pitt) Dec. 1756–Oct. 1761; (Egremont) Oct. 1761–Aug. 1763; (Sandwich) Sept. 1763–July 1765.

Translator of Southern Languages Dec. 1755–c. 1765.

Clerk of Signet 22 Dec. 1762–29 Aug. 1807.

App. as Clerk by Newcastle notified 12 March 1744 (SP 44/148). App. Under Secretary by Robinson March 1754 (*Gent. Mag.* (1754), xxiv, 143); app. as Under Secretary notified by Pitt 17 Dec. 1756 (SP 44/136 p. 399), by Egremont 13 Oct. 1761 (*CHOP 1760–5*, 70), by Sandwich 9 Sept. 1763 (ibid. 302). App. as Translator of Southern Languages notified 12 Dec. 1755 (T 53/45 p. 461); last occ. as such 5 July 1765 (BM Add. MS 38339 f. 143) App. Clerk of Signet 22 Dec. 1762 (C 66/3688). D. 29 Aug. 1807 (*Gent. Mag.* (1807), lxxvii (2), 892).

Roberts, John Christopher *Clerk* (Egremont) Oct. 1761–Aug. 1763; (Sandwich) Sept. 1763–July 1765. *Assistant Under Secretary* (Seymour Conway) July 1765–May 1766; (Richmond) May–July 1766; (Shelburne) July–Oct. 1766.

Probably app. by Egremont; presence in office notified as Clerk to Egremont 13 Oct. 1761 (*CHOP 1760–5*, 70), to Sandwich 9 Sept. 1763, 30 April 1764 (ibid. 302, 408). App. as Assistant Under Secretary notified by Seymour Conway 23 July 1765 (ibid. 580), by Richmond 28 June 1766 (*CHOP 1766–9*, 54), by Shelburne 1 Aug. 1766 (ibid. 65). Left office by 8 Oct. 1766 (ibid. 84).

Roberts, Patricius *Clerk* (Vernon) c. 1698–Nov. 1700; (Hedges) Nov. 1700–Dec. 1701; (Manchester) Jan.–May 1702; (Hedges) May 1702–June 1706.

Pd. as Clerk to Vernon from 2 June 1698 to 5 Nov. 1700 (BM Add. MS 40785 ff. 20, 66); occ. as Clerk to Hedges 1701 (Miège, *New State* (1701), pt. iii, 109), to Manchester 1701 (sic) (*Compleat History* (1701), 98), to Hedges from 1702 to 1704 (ibid. (1702), 69; Chamberlayne, *Present State* (1704), 530). Removed from office June 1706 (Luttrell, *Hist. Relation*, vi, 54).

Robinson, James *Office Keeper* (Shrewsbury) c. 1689.

Occ., probably as Office Keeper, July 1689 (LS 13/231 p. 13).

Robinson, Sir Thomas, kt. *Secretary of State* (South) 24 March 1754–14 Nov. 1755.

App. 24 March 1754 (T 53/45 p. 87). Left office 14 Nov. 1755 (ibid. p. 468).

Rochford, William (Nassau de Zuylestein) 4th Earl of *Secretary of State* (North) 21 Oct. 1768–Dec. 1770; (South) Dec. 1770–10 Nov. 1775.

App. 21 Oct. 1768 (T 53/51 p. 228). Left office 10 Nov. 1775 (T 53/53 p. 143).

Rolleston, Henry *Deputy Writer of Gazette* c. 1804–29.

Occ. from 1804 to 1829 (*Royal Kal.* (1804), 133; ibid. (1829), 137).

Rolleston, Stephen *Deputy Writer of Gazette* 30 Jan. 1797–15 Jan. 1803. *Writer of Gazette* 15 Jan. 1803–19 Nov. 1828.

App. Deputy Writer of Gazette 30 Jan. 1797 (FO 366/413). App. Writer of Gazette 15 Jan. 1803 (C 66/4014). D. 19 Nov. 1828 (*Gent. Mag.* (1828), xcviii (2), 476).

Routledge, John *Office Keeper of Signet Office* c. 1773–82.

Occ. from 1773 to 1782 (*Royal Kal.* (1773), 115; ibid. (1782), 108).

Rowe, Nicholas *Under Secretary* (Queensberry) Feb. 1709–July 1711.

App. by Queensberry Feb. 1709 (Luttrell, *Hist. Relation*, vi, 404).

Rowley, William *Clerk* (Shrewsbury) c. 1697–Dec. 1698; (Jersey) May 1699–June 1700.

Question of app. by Shrewsbury mentioned 1 Sept. 1696 (Hist. MSS Comm. *Bath*, iii, 84); in his service Dec. 1697 (*Vernon Correspondence*, ed. G. P. R. James (London 1841), i, 437); pd. by Vernon during vacancy following Shrewsbury's res. from 25 Dec. 1698 to 25 March 1699 (BM Add. MS 40785 f. 34); occ. as Clerk to Jersey 22 May 1699 (Hist. MSS Comm. *Bath*, iii, 350). Occ. as Chief Clerk (sic) to Jersey jointly with Swinford 1700 (Chamberlayne, *Present State* (1700), 502). Apparently left office June 1700 on app. as Groom Porter (Hist. MSS Comm. *Buccleuch*, ii, 638, 639, 643, 652; C 66/3416).

Roxburghe, John (Kerr) 1st Duke of *Secretary of State* (Scotland) 13 Dec. 1716–25 Aug. 1725.

App. 13 Dec. 1716 (*CTB*, xxxi, 113). Left office 25 Aug. 1725 (T 53/32 p. 171).

Royer, Gideon *Embellisher of Letters* c. 1669–1703.

Occ. from 20 Jan. 1669 to 23 Aug. 1703 (*CSPD 1668–9*, 163; *CTB*, xviii, 378).

Royer, James *Clerk* (Newcastle) Nov. 1753–March 1754; (Holdernesse) March 1754–Dec. 1755.

Acted temporarily as Clerk during Newcastle's journey to Hanover from 31 March to 18 Nov. 1752 (T 52/46 pp. 44, 147); app. as Clerk to Newcastle notified 13 Nov. 1753 (SP 44/148); occ. as Clerk to Holdernesse 1755 (Chamberlayne, *Present State* (1755), pt. ii, 52–3). Probably left office Dec. 1755 on app. as Under Clerk, Treasury (T 29/32 p. 360).

St. Davids, Bishop of *see* **Willes**, Edward

St. John, Hon. Henry (cr. Viscount **Bolingbroke** 7 July 1712) *Secretary of State* (North) 21 Sept. 1710–Aug. 1713; (South) Aug. 1713–30 Aug. 1714.

App. 21 Sept. 1710 (*CTB*, xxiv, 485). Left office 30 Aug. 1714 (*Hist. Reg. Chron.* (1714–16), i, 39).

Salamé, Alexander Y.   *Interpreter of Oriental Languages* Jan. 1823–June 1835.

Pd. from 5 Jan. 1823 to 30 June 1835 (CO 701/2 p. 109; CO 701/3 p. 62).

Sanders, Henry William   *Office Keeper of Signet Office* 1832–7 Aug. 1851.

App. 1832 (*Rept. of Committee on Signet and Privy Seal Offices* (HC 1849, xxii), 6). Office abolished 7 Aug. 1851 (14 & 15 Vict., c 82, s 3).

Sandwich, John (Montagu) 4th Earl of   *Secretary of State* (North) 9 Sept. 1763–11 July 1765; 19 Dec. 1770–22 Jan. 1771.

App. 9 Sept. 1763 (T 53/49 p. 226). Left office 11 July 1765 (T 53/50 p. 12). App. 19 Dec. 1770 (T 53/52 p. 117). Left office 22 Jan. 1771 (ibid.).

Sandys, William   *Clerk* (Newcastle) Aug. 1727–April 1729.

App. by Newcastle notified 7 Aug. 1727 (SP 44/148); pd. to 24 April 1729 (MS Rawlinson C 367). App. Sept. 1729 Secretary to Earl of Kinnoull, Ambassador to Turkey (*Hist. Reg. Chron.* (1729), xiv, 53; *Dip. Rep.*, 53).

Sawer, William   *Clerk* (Hillsborough) Feb. 1768–Aug. 1772; (Dartmouth) Aug. 1772–Nov. 1775; (Germain) Nov. 1775–1776. *Senior Clerk* (Germain) 1776–Feb. 1782; (Ellis) Feb.–March 1782.

App. 'Secretary' (Clerk) by Hillsborough Feb. 1768 (*Gent. Mag.* (1768), xxxviii, 95); occ. as Clerk to Hillsborough to 1772 (*Royal Kal.* (1772), 116), to Dartmouth from 1773 to 1775 (ibid. (1773), 116; ibid. (1775), 107), to Germain 1776 (ibid. (1776), 109). Probably app. Senior Clerk c. Jan. 1776 in succession to Serle; occ. as Senior Clerk to Germain from 1777 to 1782 (ibid. (1777), 109; ibid. (1782), 110); continued in office by Ellis. Left office March 1782 on abolition of Colonial Department (T 1/579 Schedule 2).

Scholing, —   *Decipherer* May 1743–1748.

Pd. from 21 May 1743 (T 53/41 p. 466). D. 1748 (T 53/43 p. 491).

Schweinfurt *see* **Swinford**

Scott, —   *Writer of Gazette* c. 1711.

Occ. 1711 (Boyer, *Political State* (1711), 377).

Scott, Henry Dundas   *Deputy Clerk of Signet* Oct. 1850–7 Aug. 1851.

Occ. as Deputy to Bentinck from Oct. 1850 to Aug. 1851 (SO 5/43). Office abolished 7 Aug. 1851 (14 & 15 Vict., c 82, s 3).

Scott, Thomas   *Clerk* (Queensberry) c. 1710. *Under Secretary* (Roxburghe) Dec. 1716–Aug. 1725.

Occ. as Clerk to Queensberry 1710 (Chamberlayne, *Present State* (1710), 515). App. Under Secretary by Roxburghe probably Dec. 1716; occ. from 22 Jan. 1717 to 1726 (sic) (SP 55/8 p. 10; SP 55/9 p. 209; Chamberlayne, *Present State* (1718), pt. ii, 31; ibid. (1726), pt. ii, 29).

Sedgwick, —   *Office Keeper* (Nottingham) c. 1689.

Occ., probably as Office Keeper, July 1689 (LS 13/231 p. 14).

Sedgwick, Edward   *Under Secretary* (Halifax) Sept. 1763–July 1765; Jan.–June 1771.

App. by Halifax notified 13 Sept. 1763 (*CHOP 1760–5*, 302–3), 22 Jan. 1771 (*CHOP 1770–2*, 193).

Serle, Ambrose   *Senior Clerk* (Hillsborough) 1768–Aug. 1772; (Dartmouth) Aug. 1772–Nov. 1775; (Germain) Nov. 1775–Jan. 1776.

App. by Hillsborough probably 1768; occ. as Senior Clerk to Hillsborough from

1769 to 1772 (*Royal Kal.* (1769), 118; ibid. (1772), 116), to Dartmouth from 1773 to 1775 (ibid. (1773), 116; ibid. (1775), 107), to Germain 1776 (ibid. (1776), 109). Left office Jan. 1776 on app. as Solicitor and Clerk of Reports, Board of Trade (*Journal of the Commissioners for Trade and Plantations 1776–82*, 2).

Seymour Conway, Hon. Henry   *Secretary of State* (South) 10 July 1765–May 1766; (North) May 1766–c. 20 Jan. 1768.

App. 10 July 1765 (T 53/50 p. 13). Left office by 20 Jan. 1768 (app. of Weymouth).

Shadwell, Richard   *Clerk* (Newcastle) Oct. 1745–March 1754; (Holdernesse) March 1754–March 1761; (Bute) March 1761–May 1762; (Grenville) June–Oct. 1762; (Halifax) Oct. 1762–Sept. 1763. *Senior Clerk* (Halifax) Sept. 1763–July 1765; (Seymour Conway) July 1765–Jan. 1768; (Weymouth) Jan. 1768–Dec. 1770; (Sandwich) Dec. 1770–Jan. 1771; (Halifax) Jan.–June 1771; (Suffolk) June 1771–Oct. 1772. *Chief Clerk* (Suffolk) Oct. 1772–Nov. 1775; (Weymouth) Nov. 1775–Nov. 1779; (Hillsborough) Nov. 1779–March 1782.
Deputy Clerk of Signet April 1769–1 June 1785.

App. as Clerk by Newcastle notified 24 Oct. 1745 (SP 44/148); occ. as Clerk to Newcastle to 1754 (*Court and City Reg.* (1754), 106), to Holdernesse from 1755 to 1761 (Chamberlayne, *Present State* (1755), pt. ii, 52–3; *Court and City Reg.* (1761), 106), to Bute 1762 (*Court and City Reg.* (1762), 106); presence in office notified as Clerk to Grenville 12 July 1762 (*CHOP 1760–5*, 189), to Halifax 8 Nov. 1762 (ibid. 202). Presence in office notified as Senior Clerk to Halifax 13 Sept. 1763, 30 April 1764 (ibid. 302–3, 407), to Seymour Conway 15 Aug. 1766 (*CHOP 1766–9*, 67), to Weymouth 20 Jan. 1768 (ibid. 293), to Sandwich 21 Dec. 1770 (*CHOP 1770–2*, 103), to Halifax 22 Jan., 20 March 1771 (ibid. 193, 225), to Suffolk 12 June 1771 (ibid. 265). Presence in office notified as Chief Clerk to Suffolk 2 Oct. 1772 (ibid. 556), to Weymouth 30 Nov. 1775 (*CHOP 1773–5*, 556); occ. as Chief Clerk to Weymouth to 1779 (*Royal Kal.* (1779), 109), to Hillsborough from 1780 to 1782 (ibid. (1780), 110; ibid. (1782), 110). Transferred to Home Office March 1782 (SP 45/35). App. Deputy Clerk of Signet to Rivers April 1769 (Ind. 6766); last occ. Jan. 1785 (SO 5/4). D. 1 June 1785 (*Gent. Mag.* (1785), lv (1), 490).

Shadwell, Thomas   *Clerk* (Shelburne) Sept. 1767–Oct. 1768; (Rochford) Oct. 1768–c. 1772.

App. by Shelburne notified 25 Sept. 1767 (*CHOP 1766–9*, 187); presence in office notified as Clerk to Shelburne 27 July 1768 (ibid. 434), to Rochford 4 Nov. 1768 (ibid. 435); last occ. 1772 (*Royal Kal.* (1772), 115). Probably left office c. 1771 on app. as Secretary to Lord Grantham, Ambassador to Spain (*Dip. Rep.*, 137).

Shaftoe (*later* **Delaval**), George   *Clerk* (Craggs) Dec. 1719–Feb. 1721; (Carteret) March 1721–c. 1724.

App. by Craggs notified 18 Dec. 1719 (SP 44/147); last occ. as Clerk to Carteret 4 Feb. 1724 (ibid.).

Shaw, John   *Office Keeper* (Stormont) c. 1782.

Probably app. c. Feb. 1782 in succession to Milburn. Transferred to Foreign Office March 1782 (*Royal Kal.* (1783), 110; *1st Rept. on Fees*, 32).

Shelburne, William (Petty) 2nd Earl of   *Secretary of State* (South) 30 July 1766–21 Oct. 1768.

App. 30 July 1766 (T 53/50 p. 311). Left office 21 Oct. 1768 (T 53/51 p. 102).

Shelley, Thomas   *Clerk* (Holdernesse) March 1752–March 1754; (Robinson) March

1754–Nov. 1755; (Fox) Nov. 1755–Nov. 1756; (Pitt) Dec. 1756–24 Aug. 1758.

App. by Holdernesse notified 31 March 1752 (SP 44/136 p. 208); occ. as Clerk to Holdernesse to 1754 (*Court and City Reg.* (1754), 106–7), to Robinson from 1755 to 1756 (sic) (Chamberlayne, *Present State* (1755), pt. ii, 53; *Court and City Reg.* (1756), 107); probably continued in office by Fox; presence in office as Clerk to Pitt notified 17 Dec. 1756 (SP 44/136 p. 399). D. 24 Aug. 1758 (*Gent. Mag.* (1758), xxviii, 377).

Shepherd, John   *Clerk* (Stanhope) July 1715–April 1717; (Sunderland) April–Dec. 1717.

App. by Stanhope notified 15 July 1715 (SP 44/117 p. 202); pd. as Clerk to Sunderland from 12 April to Dec. 1717 (Sunderland MS D 1/36). D. Dec. 1717 (ibid.).

Shirley (from c. 1759 **Barrington**), Priscilla   *Necessary Woman* (Bedford) c. 1751; (Holdernesse) June 1751–March 1754; (Robinson) March 1754–Nov. 1755; (Fox) Nov. 1755–Nov. 1756; (Pitt) Dec. 1756–Oct. 1761; (Egremont) Oct. 1761–c. 1763.

Occ. as Necessary Woman to Bedford 1751 (*Court and City Reg.* (1751), 109), to Holdernesse from 1752 to 1754 (ibid. (1752), 107–8; ibid. (1754), 106–7), to Robinson 1755 (Chamberlayne, *Present State* (1755), pt. ii, 53; *Court and City Reg.* (1756), 107–8); probably continued in office by Fox; occ. as Necessary Woman to Pitt from 1757 to 1761 (*Court and City Reg.* (1757), 106–7; ibid. (1761), 106); pd. as Necessary Woman to Egremont from 10 Oct. 1761 to 5 July 1763 (PRO 30/47/37/1–7).

Shorter, Thomas   *Office Keeper* (Shrewsbury) c. 1689; c. 1697–Dec. 1698; (Jersey) May 1699–June 1700; (Vernon) Nov. 1700–May 1702; (Nottingham) May 1702–April 1704; (Harley) May 1704–Feb. 1708; (Boyle) Feb. 1708–Sept. 1710; (St. John/Bolingbroke) Sept. 1710–Aug. 1714; (Townshend) Sept. 1714–Dec. 1716; (Methuen) Dec. 1716–April 1717; (Addison) April 1717–3 Feb. 1718.

Stated in 1705 to have served for twenty years (Hist. MSS Comm. *Portland*, viii, 190); in service of Shrewsbury, probably as Office Keeper, July 1689 (LS 13/231 p. 13); occ. as Office Keeper to Shrewsbury 5 Aug. 1697 (BM Add. MS 35107 f. 43); pd. by Vernon during vacancy following Shrewsbury's res. from 25 Dec. 1698 to 25 March 1699 (BM Add. MS 40785 f. 34); probably continued in office by Jersey May 1699; in his service 1700 (Chamberlayne, *Present State* (1700), 502); pd. by Vernon during vacancy following Jersey's res. from 24 June to 24 Sept. 1700 (BM Add. MS 40785 f. 65); transferred to Vernon's service Nov. 1700; pd. from 29 Sept. 1700 to 25 March 1702 and on 1 May 1702 for quarter to 24 June 1702 (BM Add. MSS 40785 f. 71; 40786 ff. 35, 37); occ. as Office Keeper to Nottingham from 1702 to 1704 (*Compleat History* (1702), 69; Chamberlayne, *Present State* (1704), 529–30); pd. as Office Keeper to Harley from 16 Feb. 1706 to 3 Sept. 1707 (BM Loan 29/162); occ. as Office Keeper to Boyle from 1708 to 1710 Chamberlayne, *Present State* (1708), 586; ibid. (1710), 516), to St. John 1711 (Boyer, *Political State* (1711), 377), to Townshend 1716 (Chamberlayne, *Present State* (1716), 527–8—'James Shorter'); probably continued in office by Methuen; occ. as Office Keeper to Addison 1718 (ibid. (1718), pt. ii, 31). D. 3 Feb. 1718 (*Hist. Reg. Chron.* (1718), iii, 6).

Shrewsbury, Charles (Talbot) 12th Earl of (cr. Duke of **Shrewsbury** 30 April 1694)   *Secretary of State* (South) 19 Feb. 1689–3 June 1690; (North) 2 March 1694–April 1695; (South) April 1695–14 Dec. 1698.

App. 19 Feb. 1689 (PC 2/73 p. 10). Left office 3 June 1690 (BM Add. MS 34095 ff. 22–3). App. 2 March 1694 (Luttrell, *Hist. Relation*, iii, 278). Left office 14 Dec. 1698 (ibid. iv, 461).

Shuckburgh, Samuel *Clerk* (Pitt) Sept. 1758–Aug. 1761.

App. by Pitt notified 21 Sept. 1758 (SP 44/136 p. 508). Dismissal notified 21 Aug. 1761 (*CHOP 1760–5*, 62).

Smart, Elizabeth *Necessary Woman* (Sunderland) April 1717–March 1718; (Stanhope) March 1718–Feb. 1721; (Townshend) Feb. 1721–May 1730; (Harrington) May 1730–Feb. 1742; (Carteret/Granville) Feb. 1742–c. 1743.

Pd. as Necessary Woman to Sunderland from April 1717 to March 1718 (Sunderland MS D 1/36), to Stanhope from 29 Sept. 1718 to 29 Sept. 1720 (Stanhope MS 76); occ. as Necessary Woman to Townshend from 1728 to 1729 (Chamberlayne, *Present State* (1728), pt. ii, 30; ibid. (1729), pt. ii, 30), to Harrington from 1735 to 1741 (ibid. (1735), pt. ii, 43; ibid. (1741), pt. ii, 47), to Carteret 1743 (ibid. (1743), pt. ii, 32).

Smith, Thomas *Office Keeper* (Trumbull) c. 1695–Dec. 1697; (Vernon) Dec. 1697–Nov. 1700; (Hedges) Nov. 1700–Dec. 1701; (Manchester) Jan.–May 1702; (Hedges) May 1702–Dec. 1706; (Sunderland) Dec. 1706–June 1710; (Dartmouth) June 1710–Aug. 1713; (Bromley) Aug. 1713–Sept. 1714; (Stanhope) Sept. 1714–April 1717; (Sunderland) April 1717–March 1718; (Stanhope) March 1718–Feb. 1721; (Townshend) Feb. 1721–c. Dec. 1729.

Pd. as Office Keeper to Trumbull from 3 Nov. 1695 to 3 Feb. 1697 (Trumbull Add. MS 113), to Vernon from 2 March 1698 to 5 Nov. 1700 (BM Add. MS 40785 ff. 13, 66); occ. as Office Keeper to Hedges 1701 (Miège, *New State* (1701), pt. iii, 109), to Manchester 1701 (sic) (*Compleat History* (1701), 98), to Hedges from 1702 to 1707 (sic) (ibid. (1702), 69; Chamberlayne, *Present State* (1704), 530; ibid. (1707), 513), to Sunderland from 1708 to 1710 (Chamberlayne, *Present State* (1708), 585; ibid. (1710), 515–16; SP 34/12 f. 65); probably continued in office by Dartmouth and Bromley; occ. as Office Keeper to Stanhope 1716 (Chamberlayne, *Present State* (1716), 528); pd. as Office Keeper to Sunderland from April 1717 to March 1718 (Sunderland MS D 1/36), to Stanhope from 29 Sept. 1718 to 29 Sept. 1720 (Stanhope MS 76); occ. as Office Keeper to Townshend from 1723 to 1729 (Chamberlayne, *Present State* (1723), 483; ibid. (1729), pt. ii, 30). D. c. Dec. 1729 (SP 45/26; Prob 11/635 f. 19).

Sneyd, Francis *Clerk* (Bedford) Feb. 1748–c. Dec. 1750.

App. by Bedford notified 27 Feb. 1748 (SP 44/129 p. 449). Left office by 4 Dec. 1750 (SP 44/136 p. 113).

Sneyd, Jeremiah *Clerk* (Bedford) Dec. 1750–June 1751; (Holdernesse) June 1751–March 1754; (Robinson) March 1754–Nov. 1755; (Fox) Nov. 1755–Nov. 1756; (Pitt) Dec. 1756–Oct. 1761; (Egremont) Oct. 1761–Aug. 1763; (Sandwich) Sept. 1763–July 1765; (Grafton) July 1765–May 1766; (Richmond) May–July 1766; (Shelburne) July 1766–Oct. 1768; (Rochford) Oct. 1768–April 1769. *Chief Clerk* (Rochford) April 1769–Nov. 1775; (Suffolk) Nov. 1775–March 1779; (Stormont) Oct. 1779–March 1782.

App. as Clerk by Bedford notified 4 Dec. 1750 (SP 44/136 p. 113); occ. as Clerk to Bedford to 1751 (*Court and City Reg.* (1751), 108—'Francis Sneyd'), to Holdernesse from 1752 to 1754 (ibid. (1752), 107–8; ibid. (1754), 106), to Robinson from 1755 to 1756 (sic) (Chamberlayne, *Present State* (1755), pt. ii, 53; *Court and City*

Reg. (1756), 107); probably continued in office by Fox; presence in office notified as Clerk to Pitt 17 Dec. 1756 (SP 44/136 p. 399), to Egremont 13 Oct. 1761 (*CHOP 1760–5*, 70), to Sandwich 9 Sept. 1763, 30 April 1764 (ibid. 302, 408), to Grafton 23 July 1765 (ibid. 580), to Richmond 28 June 1766 (*CHOP 1766–9*, 54), to Shelburne 27 July 1768 (ibid. 434), to Rochford 4 Nov. 1768 (ibid. 435). App. Chief Clerk by Rochford in succession to G. Brown probably April 1769; occ. as Chief Clerk to Rochford from 1770 to 1775 (*Royal Kal.* (1770), 115; ibid. (1775), 107); became Chief Clerk to Suffolk Nov. 1775, exchanging places with R. Shadwell (*CHOP 1773–5*, 556; SP 45/33); occ. as such from 1776 to 1779 (*Royal Kal.* (1776), 109; ibid. (1779), 109); presence in office as Chief Clerk to Stormont notified 9 Nov. 1779 (FO 366/669 p. 16). Transferred to Foreign Office March 1782 (*1st Rept. on Fees*, 27).

Sommer, John   *Office Keeper* (Townshend) Jan.–May 1730; (Harrington) May 1730–Feb. 1742; (Carteret/Granville) Feb. 1742–Nov. 1744; (Harrington) Nov. 1744–Oct. 1746; (Chesterfield) Oct. 1746–Feb. 1748; (Bedford) Feb. 1748–June 1751; (Holdernesse) June 1751–March 1754; (Robinson) March 1754–Nov. 1755; (Fox) Nov. 1755–Nov. 1756; (Pitt) Dec. 1756–Oct. 1761; (Egremont) Oct. 1761– Aug. 1763; (Sandwich) Sept. 1763–July 1765; (Grafton) July 1765–May 1766; (Richmond) May–July 1766; (Shelburne) July 1766–Oct. 1768; (Rochford) Oct. 1768–Dec. 1770; (Sandwich) Dec. 1770–Jan. 1771; (Halifax) Jan.–June 1771; (Suffolk) June 1771–Nov. 1775; (Weymouth) Nov. 1775–c. May 1777.

App. by Townshend (Thomson, *Secretaries of State*, 180); received fees as Office Keeper to Townshend Jan. 1730 (SP 45/26); continued in office by Harrington; fees received by deputies, Brooke and Phipps from Feb. 1730 to Dec. 1733 (ibid.); occ. as Office Keeper to Harrington from 7 May 1740 to 20 Oct. 1741 (T 52/41 pp. 24, 350), to Carteret from 17 Sept. 1742 to 15 Nov. 1743 (T 52/42 pp. 82, 324), to Harrington from 1 May 1745 to 1746 (T 52/43 p. 134; *Court and City Reg.* (1746), 99); probably continued in office by Chesterfield; occ. as Office Keeper to Bedford from 1748 to 1751 (Chamberlayne, *Present State* (1748), pt. ii, 52; *Court and City Reg.* (1751), 108–9), to Holdernesse from 1752 to 1754 (*Court and City Reg.* (1752), 107–8; ibid. (1754), 106–7), to Robinson from 1755 to 1756 (sic) (Chamberlayne, *Present State* (1755), pt. ii, 53; *Court and City Reg.* (1756), 107–8); probably continued in office by Fox; occ. as Office Keeper to Pitt from 1757 to 1761 (*Court and City Reg.* (1757), 106–7; ibid. (1761), 106); pd. as Office Keeper to Egremont from 10 Oct. 1761 to 5 July 1763 (PRO 30/47/37/1–7); occ. as Office Keeper to Sandwich from 1764 to 1765 (*Court and City Reg.* (1764), 106; ibid. (1765), 110), to Grafton 1766 (ibid. (1766), 107); probably continued in office by Richmond; occ. as Office Keeper to Shelburne from 1766 to 1768 (Shelburne MS 134 p. 119; *Royal Kal.* (1768), 117), to Rochford from 1769 to 1771 (sic) (*Royal Kal.* (1769), 117; ibid. (1771), 115); probably remained in Northern Department Dec. 1770 on Rochford's transfer to Southern and continued in office under Sandwich and Halifax; received fees as Office Keeper to Suffolk from Jan. 1772 to Nov. 1775 (SP 45/33), to Weymouth from Nov. 1775 to May 1777 (SP 45/33–4).

Southcott, Mary   *Necessary Woman* (Holdernesse) c. 1759–March 1761; (Bute) March 1761–May 1762; (Grenville) June–Oct. 1762; (Halifax) Oct. 1762–July 1765; (Seymour Conway) July 1765–Jan. 1768; (Weymouth) Jan. 1768–Dec. 1770; (Rochford) Dec. 1770–Nov. 1775; (Suffolk) Nov. 1775–March 1779; (Stormont) Oct. 1779–March 1782.

Occ. as Necessary Woman to Holdernesse from 1759 to 1761 (*Court and City Reg.* (1759), 106; ibid. (1761), 106), to Bute 1762 (ibid. (1762), 106); probably continued in office by Grenville; occ. as Necessary Woman to Halifax from 1763 to 1765 (ibid. (1763), 106; ibid. (1765), 110), to Seymour Conway from 1766 to 1768 (ibid. (1766), 107; *Royal Kal.* (1768), 118; Shelburne MS 134 p. 119), to Weymouth from 1769 to 1771 (sic) (*Royal Kal.* (1769), 117; ibid. (1771), 115); probably became Necessary Woman to Rochford on his transfer to Southern Department Dec. 1770 and to Suffolk on Weymouth's app. Nov. 1775; occ. as Necessary Woman to Rochford from 1772 to 1775 (ibid. (1772), 115; ibid. (1775), 107), to Suffolk from 1776 to 1779 (ibid. (1776), 109; ibid. (1779), 109), to Stormont from 1780 to 1782 (ibid. (1780), 110; ibid. (1782), 110). Transferred to Foreign Office March 1782 (ibid. (1783), 110).

Southern, Samuel   *Clerk* (Nottingham) c. 1702–4.

Occ. from 1702 to 1704 (*Compleat History* (1702), 69; Chamberlayne, *Present State* (1704), 530).

Stamma, Filippo   *Interpreter of Oriental Languages* July 1739–c. Sept. 1755.

App. notified 9 July 1739 (SP 44/131 p. 138). Left office by 26 Sept. 1755 (SP 44/136 p. 328).

Stanhope, Charles   *Under Secretary* (J. Stanhope) Oct. 1714–April 1717.

App. by J. Stanhope notified 8 Oct. 1714 (SP 44/117 p. 5).

Stanhope, James (cr. Viscount **Stanhope** 3 July 1717; Earl **Stanhope** 14 April 1718) *Secretary of State* (South) 22 Sept. 1714–Dec. 1716; (North) Dec. 1716–15 April 1717; 19 March 1718–5 Feb. 1721.

App. 22 Sept. 1714 (*CTB*, xxix, 335). Left office 15 April 1717 (ibid. xxxi, 287). App. 19 March 1718 (ibid. xxxii, 270). D. 5 Feb. 1721.

Stanhope, Lovell   *Law Clerk* 4 Aug. 1747–2 Oct. 1774.

Under Secretary (Halifax) May 1764–July 1765; (Grafton) July 1765; (Halifax) Jan.–March 1771.

App. Law Clerk 4 Aug. 1747 (C 66/3622, 3677). Res. 2 Oct. 1774 (*CHOP 1773–5*, 246). App. as Under Secretary notified by Halifax 10 May 1764 (*CHOP 1760–5*, 410), by Grafton 19 July 1765 (ibid. 578). Left office by 23 July 1765 (ibid. 579). App. as Under Secretary by Halifax notified 22 Jan. 1771 (*CHOP 1770–2*, 193). Left office by 20 March 1771 (ibid. 225).

Stanhope, Hon. Thomas   *Under Secretary* (Harrington) May 1739–Nov. 1741.

App. by Harrington notified 28 May 1739 (SP 44/129 p. 137). Left office by 24 Nov. 1741 (ibid. p. 275).

Stanyan, Abraham   (?) *Chief Clerk* (Trenchard) March 1693–April 1695; (Trumbull) May 1695–July 1697; (Vernon) May 1698–March 1699. *Under Secretary* (Manchester) Jan.–May 1702.

Question of app. as Clerk mentioned 26 Dec. 1690 (Hist. MSS Comm. *Downshire*, i, 367). Possibly app. Chief Clerk by Trenchard March 1693; heads list of his Clerks 1694 (Chamberlayne, *Present State* (1694), 243); probably continued in office by Trumbull; in his service 13 April 1697 (Hist. MSS Comm. *Bath*, iii, 109); the fact that he was not one of Trumbull's salaried Clerks (Trumbull Add. MS 113) suggests that he was Chief Clerk during his secretaryship. Left office July 1697 on app. as Secretary to Embassy at Venice (*CSPD 1697*, 380). Occ. as Chief Clerk to Vernon 1700 (sic) (Chamberlayne, *Present State* (1700), 502–3); received the fees of Vernon's office, probably as his Chief Clerk, from 31 May 1698 to 30 March 1699

(BM Add. MS 40785 ff. 12, 33). Left office on app. as Secretary to Embassy to France (*CSPD 1699–1700*, 240). App. Under Secretary by Manchester Jan. 1702 (Luttrell, *Hist. Relation*, v, 127).

Stanyan, Temple   *Clerk* (Boyle) Feb. 1708–Feb. 1709. *Chief Clerk* (Queensberry) Feb. 1709–July 1711; (?) (Mar) Sept. 1713–Sept. 1714; (Montrose) Sept. 1714–Aug. 1715. *Under Secretary* (Townshend) Oct. 1715–Dec. 1716; (Methuen) Dec. 1716–April 1717; (Addison) April 1717–March 1718; (Craggs) March 1718–Feb. 1721; (Carteret) March 1721–April 1724; (Newcastle) April 1724–June 1729.

Presence in office as Clerk to Boyle notified 23 Feb. 1708 (SP 44/107 p. 4). App. Chief Clerk by Queensberry Feb. 1709 (*Post Boy* no. 2144); possibly continued in office by Mar; occ. in service of Montrose, probably as Chief Clerk, from 5 Nov. 1714 to 20 July 1715 (SP 55/4 pp. 5, 70). App. Under Secretary by Townshend Oct. 1715 (*Hist. Reg. Chron.* (1714–16), i, 70); probably continued in office by Methuen; app. Under Secretary by Addison April 1717 (ibid. (1717), ii, 20); app. as Under Secretary by Craggs notified 29 March 1718 (SP 44/147); occ. as Under Secretary to Carteret from 20 April 1721 to 29 April 1723 (ibid.; SP 44/123 p. 252), to Newcastle from 17 July 1724 to 5 May 1729 (SP 44/148). Res. June 1729 (BM Add. MS 32687 f. 346).

Stapleton, Augustus Granville   *Clerk of Signet* 8 May 1826–30 July 1831.

App. 8 May 1826 (C 66/4304, 4376). Grant determined 30 July 1831 (C 66/4391).

Stawell, Hon. Edward   *Under Secretary* (Bromley) Aug. 1713–c. 1714.

App. by Bromley Aug. 1713 (*Post Boy* no. 2852). Probably left office by 13 Feb. 1714 (app. of Holt).

Steele, Richard   *Writer of Gazette* May 1707–Oct. 1710.

App. May 1707 (*Reliquiae Hearnianae*, ed. P. Bliss (London 1869), i, 128). Dis. Oct. 1710 (Luttrell, *Hist. Relation*, vi, 643).

Stepney, Joseph   *Clerk* (Newcastle) April 1724–March 1754; (Holdernesse) March 1754–March 1761; (Bute) March–23 April 1761.

App. by Newcastle notified 29 April 1724 (SP 44/147); occ. as Clerk to Newcastle to 1754 (*Court and City Reg.* (1754), 106), to Holdernesse from 1755 to 1761 (Chamberlayne, *Present State* (1755), pt. ii, 52–3; *Court and City Reg.* (1761), 106), to Bute March 1761 (*Notes and Queries*, cc (1955), 117). D. 23 April 1761 (ibid. 310).

Stewart, Thomas   *Clerk* (Shelburne) Sept. 1767–Oct. 1768; (Rochford) Oct. 1768–c. Oct. 1771.

App. by Shelburne notified 25 Sept. 1767 (*CHOP 1766–9*, 187); presence in office notified as Clerk to Shelburne 27 July 1768 (ibid. 434), to Rochford 4 Nov. 1768 (ibid. 435). D. shortly after 1 Oct. 1771 (*CHOP 1770–2*, 304).

Stone, Andrew   *Under Secretary* (Newcastle) July 1734–April 1751.

Collector of State Papers 18 May 1739–26 June 1741. *Keeper of State Papers* 5 May 1741–16 Dec. 1773.

App. Under Secretary by Newcastle July 1734 (*Gent. Mag.* (1734), iv, 392); app. notified 26 Sept. 1734 (SP 44/128 p. 415). Left office April 1751 on app. as Tutor to Prince of Wales (*Gent. Mag.* (1751), xx, 188). App. Collector of State Papers 18 May 1739 (C 66/3600). Grant determined 26 June 1741 (app. of Weston and Couraud). App. Keeper of State Papers 5 May 1741 (C 66/3604, 3685). D. 16 Dec. 1773 (T 53/53 p. 223).

Stonehewer, Richard   *Interpreter of Oriental Languages* Sept. 1755–c. June 1763. *Under Secretary* (Grafton) July 1765–May 1766; (Richmond) May–July 1766.

App. as Interpreter of Oriental Languages notified 26 Sept. 1755 (SP 44/136 p. 328; *CHOP 1760–5*, 30). Left office by 15 June 1763 (*CHOP 1760–5*, 289). App. as Under Secretary notified by Grafton 23 July 1765 (ibid. 579), by Richmond 28 June 1766 (*CHOP 1766–9*, 54).

Stormont, David (Murray) 7th Viscount *Secretary of State* (North) 27 Oct. 1779–27 March 1782.

App. 27 Oct. 1779 (T 53/54 p. 437). Left office 27 March 1782 (T 53/55 p. 213).

Strahan, William *Under Secretary* (Mar) Sept. 1713–Sept. 1714.

App. by Mar Sept. 1713 (*Post Boy* no. 2863).

Suffolk, Henry (Howard) 12th Earl of *Secretary of State* (North) 12 June 1771–6 March 1779.

App. 12 June 1771 (T 53/52 p. 278). D. 6 March 1779.

Sunderland, Charles (Spencer) 3rd Earl of *Secretary of State* (South) 3 Dec. 1706–14 June 1710; (North) 12 April 1717–15 March 1718.

App. 3 Dec. 1706 (*CTB*, xxi, 157). Left office 14 June 1710 (ibid. xxiv, 367). App. 12 April 1717 (ibid. xxxi, 274). Left office 15 March 1718 (ibid.).

Sunderland, Robert (Spencer) 2nd Earl of *Secretary of State* (North) 10 Feb. 1679–April 1680; (South) April 1680–c. 2 Feb. 1681; (North) 28 Jan. 1683–April 1684; (South) April 1684–28 Oct. 1688.

App. 10 Feb. 1679 (PC 2/67 p. 87). Left office by 2 Feb. 1681 (app. of Conway). App. 28 Jan. 1683 (Hist. MSS Comm. *7th Rept.*, 362). Left office 28 Oct. 1688 (BM Add. MS 45731 f. 38).

Sutton, Richard *Under Secretary* (Shelburne) Aug. 1766–Oct. 1768; (Rochford) Oct. 1768–Oct. 1772.

App. notified by Shelburne 1 Aug. 1766 (*CHOP 1766–9*, 65), by Rochford 4 Nov. 1768 (ibid. 435). Res. 1 Oct. 1772 (*CHOP 1770–2*, 556).

Swaddell, John *Clerk* (Bennet/Arlington) Aug. 1663–c. 1673.

App. Clerk in Bennet's office by Williamson Aug. 1663 (*CSPD 1663–4*, 251); last occ. 1 Aug. 1673 (*Letters to Sir Joseph Williamson 1673–4*, ed. W. D. Christie (Camden. 2nd ser., viii, ix, 1874), i, 142).

Swinford (Schweinfurt), John *Clerk* (Trumbull) 1695. *Chief Clerk* (Jersey) May 1699–June 1700; (Hedges) Nov. 1700–Dec. 1701; May 1702–Dec. 1706.

Served as Clerk to Trumbull 1695 (BM Add. MS 28887 f. 189). Left office July 1695 on app. to service of Villiers (Jersey), Envoy to United Provinces (ibid. f. 172). Occ. as Chief Clerk to Jersey 1700 (Chamberlayne, *Present State* (1700), 502–3); probably app. as such May 1699 (Hist. MSS Comm. *Bath*, iii, 350). Pd. as Clerk by Vernon during vacancy following Jersey's res. from 24 June to 29 Sept. 1700 (BM Add. MS 40785 f. 66). App. Chief Clerk by Hedges probably Nov. 1700; occ. as such 1701 (Miège, *New State* (1701), pt. iii, 109); was keeping accounts of fees in Hedges' office 31 May 1701 (BM Add. MS 40784 f. 36); not continued in office by Manchester Jan. 1702 (*Compleat History* (1701), 98); reapp. by Hedges probably May 1702; heads list of his Clerks from 1702 to 1707 (sic) (ibid. (1702), 69; Chamberlayne, *Present State* (1704), 530; ibid. (1707), 513). Not continued in office by Sunderland Dec. 1706 (*The Letters of Joseph Addison*, ed. W. Graham (Oxford 1941), 63).

Sydney, Henry (Sydney) 1st Viscount *Secretary of State* (North) 26 Dec. 1690–c. 5 March 1692.

App. 26 Dec. 1690 (PC 2/74 p. 89). Left office c. 5 March 1692 (Luttrell, *Hist. Relation*, ii, 378).

Taylor, Bridges *Deputy Clerk of Signet* April 1841–Oct. 1846.

Occ. as Deputy to Sir Brook Taylor from April 1841 to Oct. 1846 (SO 5/43).

Taylor, Brook (ktd. 1822) *Clerk of Signet* 24 Jan. 1801–15 Oct. 1846.

App. 24 Jan. 1801 (C 66/3984). D. 15 Oct. 1846 (*Gent. Mag.* (1847), cxx, 82).

Taylor, William *Clerk* (Bute) c. 1762; (Grenville) June–Oct. 1762; (Halifax) Oct. 1762–July 1765; (Seymour Conway) July 1765–Jan. 1768; (Weymouth) Jan. 1768–Dec. 1770; (Sandwich) Dec. 1770–Jan. 1771; (Halifax) Jan.–June 1771; (Suffolk) June 1771–Jan. 1774.

Occ. as Clerk to Bute 1762 (*Court and City Reg.* (1762), 106); presence in office notified as Clerk to Grenville 12 July 1762 (*CHOP 1760–5*, 189), to Halifax 8 Nov. 1762, 13 Sept. 1763, 30 April 1764 (ibid. 202, 302–3, 407), to Seymour Conway 15 Aug. 1766 (*CHOP 1766–9*, 67), to Weymouth 20 Jan. 1768 (ibid. 293), to Sandwich 21 Dec. 1770 (*CHOP 1770–2*, 103), to Halifax 22 Jan., 20 March 1771 (ibid. 193, 225), to Suffolk 12 June 1771, 2 Oct. 1772 (ibid. 265, 556). Dis. 27 Jan. 1774 (*CHOP 1773–5*, 301).

Tempest, Roland *Private Secretary* (Preston) Nov.–Dec. 1688.

App. by Preston Nov. 1688 (*Ellis Corr.*, ii, 287).

Tench, John *Deputy Clerk of Signet* c. 1682–1701.

Occ. from 1682 to 1701 (Chamberlayne, *Present State* (1682), pt. i, 194; Miège, *New State* (1701), pt. iii, 109).

Thomas, William *Clerk* (Harley) 1706–c. 1707.

Probably app. by Harley 1706; pd. from 1706 to 3 Sept. 1707 (BM Loan 29/162); last occ. 1707 (Chamberlayne, *Present State* (1707), 513–14).

Thompson, Benjamin *Under Secretary* (Germain) Oct. 1780–Oct. 1781.

Pd. from 10 Oct. 1780 to 4 Oct. 1781 (SP 45/32). Res. 4 Oct. 1781 (ibid.).

Thynne, Henry Frederick *Under Secretary* (Coventry) July 1672–April 1680.

App. by Coventry July 1672 (Coventry MS 119 ff. 1–2, 3).

Tickell, Richard *Clerk* (Addison) Jan.–March 1718; (Craggs) March 1718–Feb. 1721; (Carteret) March 1721–April 1724; (Newcastle) April–Oct. 1724.

App. by Addison notified 24 Jan. 1718 (SP 44/147); presence in office as Clerk to Craggs notified 29 March 1718, 18 Dec. 1719 (ibid.); pd. as Clerk to Carteret from 29 Sept. 1723 to 3 April 1724 (MS Rawlinson C 367), to Newcastle from 4 April to 7 Oct. 1724 (ibid.). Probably left office Oct. 1724 on app. as Secretary at War, Ireland (*Hist. Reg. Chron.* (1724), ix, 44).

Tickell, Thomas *Under Secretary* (Addison) April 1717–March 1718; (Craggs) March 1718–Feb. 1721; (Carteret) March 1721–April 1724.

App. by Addison April 1717 (*Hist. Reg. Chron.* (1717), ii, 20); app. by Craggs notified 29 March 1718 (SP 44/147); occ. as Under Secretary to Carteret from 31 March 1721 to April 1724 (ibid.; *Hist. Reg. Chron.* (1724), ix, 20).

Tigh, Edmund *Clerk* (Carteret) Oct. 1722–April 1724; (Newcastle) April 1724.

App. by Carteret notified 13 Oct. 1722 (SP 44/147); pd. as Clerk to Carteret from 29 Sept. 1723 to 3 April 1724 (MS Rawlinson C 367), to Newcastle from 4 to 17 April 1724 (ibid.). Left office by 29 April 1724 on app. as Secretary to Edward Finch, Minister Plenipotentiary to Imperial Diet (SP 44/147; *Dip. Rep.*, 41).

Tilson, George *Clerk* (Jersey) (?)–June 1700; (Vernon) Nov. 1700–May 1702; (Nottingham) May 1702–1703. *Under Secretary* (Boyle) Feb. 1708–Sept. 1710; (St.

John/Bolingbroke) Sept. 1710–Aug. 1714; (Townshend) Sept. 1714–Dec. 1716; (Methuen) Dec. 1716–April 1717; (Sunderland) April 1717–March 1718; (Stanhope) March 1718–Feb. 1721; (Townshend) Feb. 1721–May 1730; (Harrington) May 1730–17 Nov. 1738.

Collector of State Papers 20 Jan. 1725–17 Nov. 1738.

Clerk to Jersey June 1700; pd. by Vernon during vacancy following Jersey's res. from 24 June to 24 Sept. 1700 (BM Add. MS 40785 f. 65); transferred to Vernon's service Nov. 1700; pd. from 29 Sept. 1700 to 25 March 1702 and on 1 May for quarter to 24 June 1702 (BM Add. MSS 40785 f. 70; 40786 ff. 35, 37); occ. as Clerk to Nottingham 1702 (*Compleat History* (1702), 69). Left office 1703 on app. as Secretary to Lord Raby, Envoy to Prussia (*CTB*, xxi, 261; *Dip. Rep.*, 104). App. Under Secretary by Boyle Feb. 1708 (Luttrell, *Hist. Relation*, vi, 267), by St. John Sept. 1710 (ibid. 635), by Townshend Sept. 1714 (*Hist. Reg. Chron.* (1714–16), i, 5), by Methuen Dec. 1716 (Hist. MSS Comm. *Polwarth*, i, 169), by Sunderland April 1717 (*Hist. Reg. Chron.* (1717), ii, 20); occ. as Under Secretary to Stanhope from 3 May 1718 to 21 April 1719 (SP 44/120 pp. 328, 463), to Townshend from 28 Feb. 1721 (SP 44/122 p. 11); received fees as Under Secretary to Townshend to May 1730 (SP 45/26), to Harrington from June 1730 (ibid.). App. Collector of State Papers 20 Jan. 1725 (C 66/3557). D. 17 Nov. 1738 (date of death recited in grant of office of Collector of State Papers to Weston and Stone 18 May 1739).

Tirel Morin *see* **Morin**

Tomlin, George   *Embellisher of Letters* c. 1662–7.

Occ. from 15 Oct. 1662 to 21 Dec. 1667 (*CSPD 1661–2*, 518; *CSPD 1667–8*, 101).

Tooke, Charles   *Clerk* (Nottingham) c. 1704.

Occ. 1704 (Chamberlayne, *Present State* (1704), 530).

Topham, John   *Methodiser of State Papers* 30 April 1781–7 March 1800.

App. 30 April 1781 (T 52/69 pp. 374–5; T 52/78 pp. 55–7). Office abolished 7 March 1800 (T 52/85 pp. 473–4).

Townshend, Charles (Townshend) 2nd Viscount   *Secretary of State* (North) 17 Sept. 1714–12 Dec. 1716; 6 Feb. 1721–16 May 1730.

App. 17 Sept. 1714 (*CTB*, xxix, 335). Left office 12 Dec. 1716 (ibid. xxx, 591). App. 6 Feb. 1721 (T 53/29 pp. 3–4). Left office 16 May 1730 (*CTBP 1729–30*, 606).

Townshend, Hon. Thomas   *Under Secretary* (Viscount Townshend) April 1724–Sept. 1729.

App. by Viscount Townshend April 1724 (*Hist. Reg. Chron.* (1724), ix, 20—'William Townshend'). Left office Sept. 1729 (ibid. (1729), xiii, 53; SP 45/26).

Trenchard, Sir John, kt.   *Secretary of State* (North) 23 March–Nov. 1693; (Sole) Nov. 1693–March 1694; (South) March 1694–27 April 1695.

App. 23 March 1693 (PC 2/75 p. 115). D. 27 April 1695 (J. Hutchins, *The History and Antiquities of the County of Dorset*, 3rd ed. (1861–70), i, 182).

Trevor, Sir John, kt.   *Secretary of State* (North) 29 Sept. 1668–28 May 1672.

App. 29 Sept. 1668 (PC 2/61 p. 44). D. 28 May 1672 (G. Lipscomb, *The History and Antiquities of the County of Buckingham* (London 1847), ii, 297).

Trevor, Hon. Robert   *Clerk* (Townshend) Nov. 1729–May 1730; (Harrington) May 1730–c. 1733.

App. by Townshend notified 28 Nov. 1729 (SP 44/122 p. 377); occ. as Clerk to Harrington from 10 June 1730 to 27 Sept. 1732 (T 52/37 pp. 122, 469) and 1735 (sic) (Chamberlayne, *Present State* (1735), pt. ii, 43). Probably left office 1733 on app. as Secretary to Horatio Walpole, Envoy to United Provinces (*Dip. Rep.*, 163–4).

Trumbull, William   *Clerk of Signet* 1660–78.

Grant in reversion 11 Nov. 1635 (C 66/2693); probably entered office Aug. 1660 (*CSPD 1660–1*, 245). D. by 29 March 1678 (*CSPD 1678*, 382–3).

Trumbull, William (ktd. 21 Nov. 1684)   *Clerk of Signet* 15 Jan. 1683–13 Feb. 1716. *Secretary of State* (North) 3 May 1695–1 Dec. 1697.

Grant of clerkship of signet in reversion 13 June 1664 (C 66/3061); succ. 15 Jan. 1683 (d. of Warwick); admitted 16 Jan. 1683 (*CSPD Jan.–June 1683*, 16). Surrendered office 13 Feb. 1716 (surrender recited in grant to Alexander). App. Secretary of State 3 May 1695 (PC 2/76 p. 129). Left office 1 Dec. 1697 (Trumbull Add. MS 125 f. 20).

Tucker, John   *Clerk* (?) 1685; (Shrewsbury) Feb. 1689–June 1690. (?) *Chief Clerk* (Sydney) Dec. 1690–March 1692. *Under Secretary* (Trenchard) July 1694–April 1695; (Trumbull) May 1695–Dec. 1697; (Hedges) Nov. 1700–Dec. 1701; May 1702–Dec. 1706.

Keeper of State Papers 16 July 1702–18 Nov. 1714.

Probably serving as a Clerk in one of the offices 30 Nov. 1685 (Hist. MSS Comm. *Downshire*, i, 64); occ. as Clerk to Shrewsbury July 1689 (LS 13/231 p. 13). App. Clerk, possibly Chief Clerk, by Sydney Dec. 1690 (*CSPD 1690–1*, 195). App. Under Secretary by Trenchard probably July 1694 in succession to Bridgeman; serving as such April 1695 on d. of Trenchard (Luttrell, *Hist. Relation*, iii, 468); app. Under Secretary by Trumbull May 1695 (ibid.), by Hedges Nov. 1700 (ibid. iv, 705), May 1702 (ibid. v, 169). App. Keeper of State Papers 16 July 1702 (C 66/3432). Grant determined 18 Nov. 1714 (app. of H. Howard).

Tully, Richard   *Interpreter of Oriental Languages* Jan. 1794–July 1802.

Pd. from 5 Jan. 1794 to 5 July 1802 (HO 82/3). D. c. 5 July 1802 (ibid.).

Turfery, Elizabeth   *Necessary Woman* (Harrington) c. 1745–Oct. 1746; (Chesterfield) Oct. 1746–Feb. 1748; (Bedford) 1748.

Occ. as Necessary Woman to Harrington 1745 (Chamberlayne, *Present State* (1745), pt. ii, 32); probably continued in office by Chesterfield; occ. as Necessary Woman to Bedford 1748 (ibid. (1748), pt. ii, 52). D. by 8 Dec. 1748 (Prob 11/766 f. 382).

Turner, John   *Office Keeper* (Shrewsbury) c. 1697–Dec. 1698; (Jersey) May 1699–June 1700; (Vernon) Nov. 1700–May 1702.

Occ. as Office Keeper to Shrewsbury 5 Aug. 1697 (BM Add. MS 35107 f. 43); pd. by Vernon during vacancy following Shrewsbury's res. from 25 Dec. 1698 to 25 March 1699 (BM Add. MS 40785 f. 34); probably continued in office by Jersey May 1699; in his service 1700 (Chamberlayne, *Present State* (1700), 502); pd. by Vernon during vacancy following Jersey's res. from 24 June to 24 Sept. 1700 (BM Add. MS 40785 f. 65); transferred to Vernon's service Nov. 1700; pd. from 29 Sept. 1700 to 25 March 1702 and on 1 May 1702 for quarter to 24 June 1702 (BM Add. MSS 40785 f. 71; 40786 ff. 35, 37). Not continued in office by Nottingham May 1702 (*Compleat History* (1702), 69).

Turner, (?) John   *Office Keeper* (Queensberry) c. 1710; (Roxburghe) Dec. 1716–Aug. 1725.

Occ. as Office Keeper to Queensberry 1710 (Chamberlayne, *Present State* (1710), 515—'Mr. Turner'); app. by Roxburghe probably Dec. 1716; occ. 1718, 1723 (ibid. (1718), pt. ii, 31; ibid. (1723), 484—'F. Turner'), 1726 (sic) (ibid. (1726), pt. ii, 29—'John Turner').

Turner, Richard   *Office Keeper* (Newcastle) Jan. 1752–March 1754; (Holdernesse) March 1754–March 1761; (Bute) March 1761–May 1762; (Grenville) June–Oct. 1762; (Halifax) Oct. 1762–July 1765; (Seymour Conway) July 1765–Jan. 1768; (Weymouth) Jan. 1768–Dec. 1770; (Rochford) Dec. 1770–Nov. 1775; (Suffolk) Nov. 1775–March 1779; (Stormont) Oct. 1779–March 1782.

His deputy, Ancell, received his fees as Office Keeper to Newcastle from Jan. 1752 (SP 45/27); occ. as Office Keeper to Newcastle to 1754 (*Court and City Reg.* (1754), 106), to Holdernesse from 1755 to 1761 (Chamberlayne, *Present State* (1755), pt. ii, 52–3; *Court and City Reg.* (1761), 106), to Bute 1762 (*Court and City Reg.* (1762), 106); probably continued in office by Grenville; occ. as Office Keeper to Halifax from 1763 to 1765 (ibid. (1763), 106; ibid. (1765), 110), to Seymour Conway from 1766 to 1768 (ibid. (1766), 107; *Royal Kal.* (1768), 118), to Weymouth from 1769 to 1771 (sic) (*Royal Kal.* (1769), 117; ibid. (1771), 115); probably became Office Keeper to Rochford on his transfer to Southern Department Dec. 1770 and to Suffolk on Weymouth's app. as Secretary of State Nov. 1775; occ. as Office Keeper to Rochford from 1772 to 1775 (ibid. (1772), 115; ibid. (1775), 107), to Suffolk from 1776 to 1779 (ibid. (1776), 109; ibid. (1779), 109), to Stormont from 1780 to 1782 (ibid. (1780), 110; ibid. (1782), 110). Transferred to Foreign Office March 1782 (*1st Rept. on Fees*, 32).

Tweeddale, John (Hay) 4th Marquess of   *Secretary of State* (Scotland) 25 Feb. 1742–4 Jan. 1746.

App. 25 Feb. 1742 (T 53/41 p. 41). Left office 4 Jan. 1746 (T 53/42 p. 195).

Umby *see* **Ombee**

Vanbrugh, Kendrick   *Clerk* (Vernon) c. 1698–Nov. 1700; (Hedges) Nov. 1700–Dec. 1701; (Manchester) Jan.–May 1702; (Hedges) c. 1702.

Pd. as Clerk to Vernon from 2 June 1698 to 5 Nov. 1700 (BM Add. MS 40785 ff. 20, 66); occ. as Clerk to Hedges 1701 (Miège, *New State* (1701), pt. iii, 109), to Manchester 1701 (sic) (*Compleat History* (1701), 98), to Hedges 1702 (ibid. (1702), 69—'Henry Vanbrug').

Venables, Thomas   *Deputy Clerk of Signet* 1816–25 June 1837.

Deputy to Bentinck and Gage; probably app. 1816 in succession to Pollock; occ. from 1817 to June 1837 (*Royal Kal.* (1817), 147; SO 5/43). D. 25 June 1837 (Burke, *Landed Gentry* (1952), 2597).

Vernon, James   *Under Secretary* (Shrewsbury) Feb. 1689–June 1690; (Trenchard) March 1693–March 1694; (Shrewsbury) March 1694–Dec. 1697. *Secretary of State* (North) 2 Dec. 1697–Dec. 1698; (Sole) Dec. 1698–May 1699; (North) May 1699–June 1700; (Sole) June–Nov. 1700; (South) Nov. 1700–Jan. 1702; (North) Jan.–1 May 1702.

App. Under Secretary by Shrewsbury probably Feb. 1689; occ. as such July 1689 (LS 13/231 p. 13); app. Under Secretary by Trenchard March 1693 (BM Add. MS 34096 f. 322; Luttrell, *Hist. Relation*, iii, 66), by Shrewsbury March 1694 (Luttrell, *Hist. Relation*, iii, 279; *CSPD 1695*, 243). App. Secretary of State 2 Dec. 1697 (*CSPD 1697*, 497–8). Left office 1 May 1702 (*CTB*, xviii, 228).

Vernon, James   (?) *Chief Clerk* (Shrewsbury) Nov. 1697–(?).

'Young Mr. Vernon'; probably identical with the younger James Vernon. App. Clerk, possibly Chief Clerk, by Shrewsbury in succession to Bernard Nov. 1697 (Luttrell, *Hist. Relation*, iv, 301); no further occ.

Vic *see* **de Vic**

Vrigny *see* de Lacombe de Vrigny

Wace, Francis *Clerk* (Harrington) April 1745–Oct. 1746; (Chesterfield) Oct. 1746–Feb. 1748; (Bedford) Feb. 1748–June 1751; (Holdernesse) June 1751–March 1761; (Bute) March 1761–May 1762; (Grenville) June–Oct. 1762; (Halifax) Oct. 1762–Sept. 1763. *Senior Clerk* (Halifax) Sept. 1763–July 1765; (Seymour Conway) July 1765–Jan. 1768; (Weymouth) Jan. 1768–Dec. 1770; (Sandwich) Dec. 1770–Jan. 1771; (Halifax) Jan.–June 1771; (Suffolk) June 1771–March 1779; (Stormont) Oct. 1779–c. 27 July 1780.

Deputy Writer of Gazette c. 1770–c. 27 July 1780.

Acted temporarily as Clerk during Harrington's journey to Hanover from 6 May to 20 Oct. 1741 (T 52/41 p. 350); app. as Clerk by Harrington notified 3 April 1745 (SP 44/129 p. 382); presence in office as Clerk to Chesterfield notified 21 Nov. 1746 (ibid. p. 428); occ. as Clerk to Bedford from 1748 to 1751 (Chamberlayne, *Present State* (1748), pt. ii, 52; *Court and City Reg.* (1751), 108), to Holdernesse from 1752 to 1761 (*Court and City Reg.* (1752), 107–8; ibid. (1761), 106), to Bute 1762 (ibid. (1762), 106); presence in office notified as Clerk to Grenville 12 July 1762 (*CHOP 1760 5*, 189), to Halifax 8 Nov. 1762 (ibid. 202). Presence in office notified as Senior Clerk to Halifax 13 Sept. 1763, 30 April 1764 (ibid. 302–3, 407), to Seymour Conway 15 Aug. 1766 (*CHOP 1766–9*, 67), to Weymouth 20 Jan. 1768 (ibid. 293), to Sandwich 21 Dec. 1770 (*CHOP 1770–2*, 103), to Halifax 22 Jan., 20 March 1771 (ibid. 193, 225), to Suffolk 12 June 1771, 2 Oct. 1772 (ibid. 265, 556), to Stormont 9 Nov. 1779 (FO 366/669 p. 16). Occ. as Deputy Writer of Gazette from 1770 to 1780 (*Royal Kal.* (1770), 116; ibid. (1780), 110). D. by 27 July 1780 (FO 366/669 p. 27; LC 3/67 p. 119; Prob 6/156).

Wace, John *Clerk* (Dartmouth) April 1711–Aug. 1713; (Bromley) Aug. 1713–Sept. 1714; (Stanhope) Sept. 1714–April 1717. *Chief Clerk* (Sunderland) April 1717–March 1718; (Stanhope) March 1718–Feb. 1721; (Townshend) Feb. 1721–May 1730; (Harrington) May 1730–Feb. 1742; (Carteret/Granville) Feb. 1742–Nov. 1744; (Harrington) Nov. 1744–19 March 1745.

Deputy Keeper of State Papers c. 1718–19 March 1745.

App. as Clerk by Dartmouth notified 26 April 1711 (SP 44/110 p. 8); probably continued in office by Bromley; occ. as Clerk to Stanhope 1716 (Chamberlayne, *Present State* (1716), 528). App. Chief Clerk by Sunderland April 1717 (*Hist. Reg. Chron.* (1717), ii, 20); occ. as Chief Clerk to Stanhope from 6 May to 14 Nov. 1719 (*acting Under Secretary*) (T 52/29 p. 403; T 52/30 p. 16), to Townshend from 30 May 1723 to 13 Sept. 1729 (T 52/32 p. 361; T 52/36 p. 403), to Harrington from 10 June 1730 to 20 Oct. 1741 (T 52/37 p. 122; T 52/41 p. 350), to Carteret 1743 (Chamberlayne, *Present State* (1743), pt. ii, 32), to Harrington 1745 (ibid. (1745), pt. ii, 32). Occ. as Deputy Keeper of State Papers from 1718 to 1745 (Miège, *Present State* (1718), pt. i, 362; Chamberlayne, *Present State* (1745), pt. ii, 32). D. 19 March 1745 (*Gent. Mag.* (1745), xv, 164).

Waite, Thomas *Law Clerk* 10 Feb. 1743–4 Aug. 1747.

App. 10 Feb. 1743 (C 66/3612). Grant determined 4 Aug. 1747 (app. of L. Stanhope). App. Secretary to Lords Justices, Ireland June 1747 (*Gent. Mag.* (1747), xvii, 297).

Wallace, James *Clerk* (Chesterfield) Feb. 1747–Feb. 1748; (Newcastle) Feb. 1748–June 1751. *Under Secretary* (Newcastle) June 1751–March 1754; (Holdernesse) March 1754–c. April 1759.

Translator of German Language Sept. 1748–March 1772.

App. as Clerk by Chesterfield notified 27 Feb. 1748 (SP 44/129 p. 431); occ. as Clerk to Newcastle from 10 May 1748 to 4 Nov. 1750 (T 52/44 p. 372; T 52/46 p. 324). App. Under Secretary by Newcastle June 1751 in succession to Amyand; received fees from July 1751 to March 1754 (SP 45/27); app. Under Secretary by Holdernesse March 1754 (*Gent. Mag.* (1754), xxiv, 143); last occ. as such 1759 (*Court and City Reg.* (1759), 106). Probably left office c. April 1759 (*Grenville Papers*, ed. W. J. Smith (London 1852–3), i, 290–1; *Notes and Queries*, cxcix (1954), 62). App. Translator of German Language Sept. 1748 (*Bedford Correspondence*, ed. Lord J. Russell (London 1842–6), i, 526; T 53/43 p. 377). D. March 1772 (*Correspondence of George III*, ed. Sir J. Fortescue (London 1927–8), iii, 38; Prob 6/148).

Wallis, John   *Decipherer* April 1701–28 Oct. 1703.

App. April 1701 (*CTB*, xvi, 243). D. 28 Oct. 1703 (MI St. Mary's Oxford).

Walpole, Horatio   *Under Secretary* (Boyle) Feb. 1708–Sept. 1710; Townshend) Sept. 1714–Oct. 1715.

App. by Boyle Feb. 1708 (Luttrell, *Hist. Relation*, vi, 267), by Townshend Sept. 1714 (*Hist. Reg. Chron.* (1714–16), i, 5). Left office Oct. 1715 on app. as Secretary to Treasury (ibid. 70).

Walpole, Robert   *Secretary of State* (acting for Northern and Southern Departments) 29 May–31 Dec. 1723.

App. 29 May 1723 (T 53/30 p. 407). Left office 31 Dec. 1723 (T 53/31 p. 19).

Walsh, Frederick Thomas   *Clerk* (Germain) c. 1782; (Ellis) Feb.–March 1782.

Occ. as Clerk to Germain 1782 (*Royal Kal.* (1782), 110); continued in office by Ellis. Left office March 1782 on abolition of Colonial Department (T 1/579 Schedule 2).

Ward, Alexander   *Office Keeper* (Carteret) c. 1723–April 1724; (Newcastle) April 1724–c. March 1750.

Pd. as Office Keeper to Carteret from 29 Sept. 1723 to 3 April 1724 (MS Rawlinson C 367), to Newcastle from 4 April 1724 to 24 June 1733 (MSS Rawlinson C 367, 123); received fees to March 1750 (SP 45/27). D. by 13 June 1750 (Prob 11/780 f. 217).

Warre, Richard   *Under Secretary* (Williamson) (?) Sept. 1676–Feb. 1679; (Preston) Nov.–Dec. 1688; (Nottingham) March 1689–Nov. 1693; May 1702–April 1704; (Harley) May 1704–Feb. 1708; (Dartmouth) June 1710–Aug. 1713.

The occ. of 'Mr. Warre' in association with Bridgeman 5 Sept. 1678 (*CSPD 1678*, 393) probably indicates that he was Under Secretary at that date; possibly app. by Williamson Sept. 1676 in succession to Brisbane; app. Under Secretary by Preston Nov. 1688 (*Ellis Corr.*, ii, 287), by Nottingham March 1689 (BM Add. MS 45731 f. 122), May 1702 (*Post Man* no. 964; Luttrell, *Hist. Relation*, v, 169), by Harley May 1704 (Luttrell, *Hist. Relation*, v, 426), by Dartmouth June 1710 (ibid. vi, 595).

Warwick, Sir Philip, kt.   *Clerk of Signet* Nov. 1638–15 Jan. 1683.

Grant in reversion 23 Aug. 1632 (C 66/2612); admitted 13 Nov. 1638 (*CSPD 1638–9*, 103). D. 15 Jan. 1683 (*Gent. Mag.* (1790), lx (2), 781).

Watkins, Fleetwood   *Clerk* (Jersey) c. 1700.

Occ. 1700 (Chamberlayne, *Present State* (1700), 502).

Welby, Adlard   *Clerk* (Trenchard) c. 1694. *Chief Clerk* (Vernon) Dec. 1697–May 1698. *Clerk* (Vernon) May 1698–March 1699. *Chief Clerk* (Vernon) March 1699–May 1702.

Occ. as Clerk to Trenchard 1694 (Chamberlayne, *Present State* (1694), 243). His signature (BM Add. MS 40784 f. 75) indicates that he was the person responsible for keeping Vernon's accounts as Secretary of State; kept accounts of fees from 1697 to 1698 (BM Add. MS 40783) and from 1699 to 1702 (BM Add. MS 40784) and of receipts and expenditure from 1697 to 1702 (BM Add. MSS 40785, 40786). Received fees of Vernon's office, probably as his Chief Clerk, from 8 Dec. 1697 to 31 May 1698 when this function devolved upon A. Stanyan (BM Add. MS 40785 ff. 1, 12). Received salary as one of Vernon's junior Clerks from 2 June 1698 to 2 June 1699 (ibid. ff. 30, 38). Again received fees of Vernon's office, probably as Chief Clerk in succession to A. Stanyan, from 30 March 1699 to 1 May 1702 (BM Add. MSS 40785 f. 34; 40786 f. 36). Occ. as Chief Clerk to Vernon 1701 (Miège, *New State* (1701), pt. iii, 109).

West, Gilbert   *Clerk* (Townshend) Sept. 1726–May 1730; (Harrington) May 1730–c. 1735.

App. by Townshend notified 16 Sept. 1726 (SP 44/122 p. 307); occ. as Clerk to Townshend to 13 Sept. 1729 (T 52/36 p. 403), to Harrington from 10 June 1730 to 1735 (T 52/37 p. 122; Chamberlayne, *Present State* (1735), pt. ii, 43).

Weston, —   *Clerk* (Dartmouth) c. 1711.

Occ. 1711 (Boyer, *Political State* (1711), 377).

Weston, Edward   *Under Secretary* (Townshend) Sept. 1729–May 1730; (Harrington) May 1730–Feb. 1742; (Carteret/Granville) Feb. 1742–Nov. 1744; (Harrington) Nov. 1744–Oct. 1746; (Bute) March 1761–May 1762; (Grenville) June–Oct. 1762; (Halifax) Oct. 1762–May 1764.

Clerk of Signet 13 Nov. 1729–15 July 1770.

Collector of State Papers 18 May 1739–4 Jan. 1742.

Writer of Gazette 22 Nov. 1741–15 July 1770.

App. Under Secretary by Townshend Sept. 1729 (*Hist. Reg. Chron.* (1729), xiv, 53); received fees as Under Secretary to Townshend to May 1730 and to Harrington from June 1730 (SP 45/26); occ. as Under Secretary to Harrington to 20 Oct. 1741 (T 52/41 p. 350), to Carteret 1743 (Chamberlayne, *Present State* (1743), pt. ii, 32), to Harrington from 1 May to 31 Aug. 1745 (T 52/43 pp. 134, 213). Left office Oct. 1746 on app. as Chief Secretary to Lord Lieutenant, Ireland (SP 44/129 p. 428). App. Under Secretary by Bute March 1761 (*Gent. Mag.* (1761), xxxi, 189); app. as Under Secretary notified by Grenville 12 July 1762 (*CHOP 1760–5*, 189), by Halifax 8 Nov. 1762 (ibid. 202). Left office between 30 April and 10 May 1764 (ibid. 407, 410). App. Clerk of Signet 13 Nov. 1729 (C 66/3578); held office until d. App. Collector of State Papers 18 May 1739 (C 66/3600, 3606). Left office by 4 Jan. 1742 (app. of Couraud and Ramsden). App. Writer of Gazette 22 Nov. 1741 (C 66/3611); held office until d. D. 15 July 1770 (SO 5/3).

Weston, Francis   *Clerk* (Grenville) July–Oct. 1762; (Halifax) Oct. 1762–c. 1763.

App. by Grenville notified 16 July 1762 (*CHOP 1760–5*, 190); presence in office as Clerk to Halifax notified 8 Nov. 1762 (ibid. 202); last occ. 1763 (*Court and City Reg.* (1763), 106).

Weston, Henry   *Clerk* (Shrewsbury) (?)–Dec. 1698; (Jersey) May 1699–June 1700; (Vernon) Nov. 1700–May 1702.

Clerk to Shrewsbury Dec. 1698; pd. by Vernon during vacancy following Shrewsbury's res. from 25 Dec. 1698 to 25 March 1699 (BM Add. MS 40785 f. 34); occ. as Clerk to Jersey 1700 (Chamberlayne, *Present State* (1700), 502); pd. by Vernon during vacancy following Jersey's res. from 24 June to 24 Sept. 1700 (BM

Add. MS 40785 f. 66); transferred to Vernon's service Nov. 1700; pd. from 29 Sept. 1700 to 25 March 1702 and on 1 May 1702 for quarter to 24 June 1702 (BM Add. MSS 40785 f. 70; 40786 ff. 35, 37). Not continued in office by Nottingham May 1702 (*Compleat History* (1702), 69).

Weymouth, Thomas (Thynne) 3rd Viscount *Secretary of State* (North) 20 Jan.-Oct. 1768; (South) Oct. 1768–19 Dec. 1770; 10 Nov. 1775–March 1779; (Sole) March–25 Nov. 1779.

App. 20 Jan. 1768 (T 53/50 p. 496). Left office 19 Dec. 1770 (T 53/52 p. 54). App. 10 Nov. 1775 (T 53/53 p. 350). Left office 25 Nov. 1779 (T 53/54 p. 194).

Whately, Thomas *Under Secretary* (Suffolk) June 1771–26 May 1772.

App. by Suffolk notified 12 June 1771 (*CHOP 1770–2*, 265). D. 26 May 1772 (*Gent. Mag.* (1772), xlii, 247).

White, John *Office Keeper* (Chesterfield) c. 1746–8; (Bedford) Feb. 1748–June 1751; (Holdernesse) June 1751–March 1754; (Robinson) March 1754–Nov. 1755; (Fox) Nov. 1755–Nov. 1756; (Pitt) Dec. 1756–Oct. 1761; (Egremont) Oct. 1761–Aug. 1763; (Sandwich) Sept. 1763–July 1765; (Grafton) July 1765–May 1766; (Richmond) May–July 1766; (Shelburne) July 1766–c. 1768.

App. by Chesterfield c. 1746–8 (Thomson, *Secretaries of State*, 180); occ. as Office Keeper to Bedford from 1748 to 1751 (Chamberlayne, *Present State* (1748), pt. ii, 52; *Court and City Reg.* (1751), 108–9), to Holdernesse from 1752 to 1754 (*Court and City Reg.* (1752), 107–8; ibid. (1754), 106–7), to Robinson from 1755 to 1756 (sic) (Chamberlayne, *Present State* (1755), pt. ii, 53; *Court and City Reg.* (1756), 107–8); probably continued in office by Fox; occ. as Office Keeper to Pitt from 1757 to 1761 (*Court and City Reg.* (1757), 106–7; ibid. (1761), 106); pd. as Office Keeper to Egremont from 10 Oct. 1761 to 5 July 1763 (PRO 30/47/37/1–7); occ. as Office Keeper to Sandwich from 1764 to 1765 (*Court and City Reg.* (1764), 106; ibid. (1765), 110), to Grafton 1766 (ibid. (1766), 107); probably continued in office by Richmond; occ. as Office Keeper to Shelburne from 1766 to 1768 (Shelburne MS 134 p. 119; *Royal Kal.* (1768), 117).

Whittaker, — *Clerk* (Sunderland) c. 1708–10.

Occ. from 1708 to 1710 (Chamberlayne, *Present State* (1708), 585; ibid. (1710), 515–16; SP 34/12 f. 165).

Whittaker, Charles *Under Secretary* (Nicholas) May 1660–Oct. 1662.

App. by Nicholas probably May 1660; occ. from 2 June 1660 to 18 Aug. 1662 (*CSPD 1660–1*, 36; *CSPD 1661–2*, 463).

Widdows, — *Clerk* (Middleton) c. 1684.

Occ. as 'Writing Clerk' 1684 (Evans, *Principal Secretary*, 193).

Wiggs, John *Clerk* (Newcastle) April 1724–Dec. 1726.

App. by Newcastle notified 29 April 1724 (SP 44/147); pd. from 4 April 1724 to 25 Dec. 1726 (MS Rawlinson C 367).

Wilkinson, Montagu *Clerk of Signet* 15 July 1770–June 1797.

Grant in reversion 27 April 1767 (C 66/3712); succ. 15 July 1770 (d. of E. Weston). D. June 1797 (*Gent. Mag.* (1797), lxvii (2), 616).

Willes, Edward (app. Bishop of **St. Davids** 1742; of **Bath and Wells** 1743) *Decipherer* June 1716–24 Nov. 1773.

App. June 1716 (*CTB*, xxx, 252); remained in office until d. (*Correspondence of George III*, ed. Sir J. Fortescue (London 1927–8), iii, 38). D. 24 Nov. 1773 (*Gent. Mag.* (1773), xliii, 582).

Willes, Edward   *Decipherer* c. 1741–c. 1804.
    App. c. 1741 (*1st Rept. on Fees*, 35); last occ. 7 Jan. 1804 (BM Add. MS 38358 f. 24).

Willes, Edward   *Decipherer* (?)–25 Sept. 1793.
    Res. 25 Sept. 1793 (BM Add. MS 45519 f. 66).

Willes, Francis (ktd. 11 Aug. 1784)   *Decipherer* c. 1763–c. 1807.
    Under Secretary (Rochford) Oct. 1772–Nov. 1775.
    Began service as unpaid Decipherer c. 1758 (BM Add. MS 45519 ff. 58–9); first occ. in receipt of salary 5 April 1763 (L. B. Namier, *The Structure of Politics at the Accession of George III*, 2nd ed. (London 1960), 193); last occ. as Decipherer 2 Sept. 1807 (BM Add. MS 45519 f. 110). App. as Under Secretary by Rochford notified 4 Oct. 1772 (*CHOP 1770–2*, 557).

Willes, Francis   *Decipherer* c. 1801–1 Oct. 1844.
    First occ. 24 May 1801 (BM Add. MS 38357 f. 64). Office abolished 1 Oct. 1844 (ibid. 45520 ff. 53–4).

Willes, William   *Decipherer* Sept. 1744–c. 1761.
    Pd. from 29 Sept. 1744 (T 53/41 p. 466); last occ. 6 Jan. 1761 (PRO 30/8/83, pt. i, Todd to Newcastle, 6 Jan. 1761).

Willes, William   *Decipherer* Oct. 1793–(?).
    Entered office 10 Oct. 1793 (BM Add. MS 45519 f. 66); no further occ.

Williams *see* **Hanbury Williams**

Williams Wynn, Henry Watkin   *Deputy Clerk of Signet* Feb. 1801–c. 1803.
    App. Deputy to Taylor Feb. 1801 (Ind. 6769); last occ. 1803 (*Royal Kal.* (1803), 133).

Williamson, Joseph (ktd. 24 Jan. 1672)   *Under Secretary* (Nicholas) July 1660–Oct. 1662; (Bennet/Arlington) Oct. 1662–Sept. 1674. *Secretary of State* 11 Sept. 1674– c. 10 Feb. 1679.
    Keeper of State Papers 31 Dec. 1661–3 Oct. 1701.
    App. Under Secretary by Nicholas July 1660 (*CSPD 1660–1*, 145); occ. from 30 July 1660 to 12 Oct. 1662 (ibid. 135; *CSPD 1661–2*, 513); continued in office by Bennet; occ. from 15 Oct. 1662 to 9 Sept. 1674 (*CSPD 1661–2*, 518; *CSPD 1673–5*, 347). App. Secretary of State 11 Sept. 1674 (PC 2/64 p. 272). Left office by 10 Feb. 1679 (app. of Sunderland). App. Keeper of State Papers 31 Dec. 1661 (C 66/2980). D. 3 Oct. 1701 (*Westminster Abbey Registers*, ed. J. L. Chester (London 1876), 249).

Williamson, Robert   *Deputy Clerk of Signet* c. 1682–9.
    Occ. from 1682 to July 1689 (Chamberlayne, *Present State* (1682), pt. i, 194; LS 13/231 p. 14).

Wilmot, Eardley   *Clerk* (Dartmouth) c. 1775; (Germain) Nov. 1775–Feb. 1782; (Ellis) Feb.–March 1782.
    Clerk of Signet June 1797–2 Jan. 1801.
    Occ. as Clerk to Dartmouth 1775 (*Royal Kal.* (1775), 107), to Germain from 1776 to 1782 (ibid. (1776), 109; ibid. (1782), 110), to Ellis March 1782 (T 1/579 Schedule 2). Transferred to Home Office March 1782 (*1st Rept. on Fees*, 23). Grant of clerk-ship of signet in reversion 15 July 1783 (C 66/3799); succ. June 1797 (d. of Wilkinson). D. 2 Jan. 1801 (*Gent. Mag.* (1801), lxxi (1), 90).

Windebanke, Sir Thomas, 1st Bart.   *Clerk of Signet* c. 1645–74.
    Grant in reversion 25 April 1633 (C 66/2631); succ. between 5 Aug. 1641 (grant of reversion to Bere) and 17 Dec. 1645 (W. H. Black, *Docquets of Letters Patent*

1642–6 (London 1837), 411); failed to make good his claim to execute office at Restoration; following trial at law Bere authorised by order in council to continue to perform duties 3 Sept. 1662 (PC 2/56 p. 123). Ceased to be formally in possession of office between 12 June 1674 (grant of reversion to Gauntlet) and 2 May 1678 (grant of reversion to W. Cooke).

Wood, Robert   *Under Secretary* (Pitt) Dec. 1756–Oct. 1761; (Egremont) Oct. 1761–Aug. 1763; (Weymouth) Jan. 1768–Dec. 1770.

App. notified by Pitt 17 Dec. 1756 (SP 44/136 p. 399), by Egremont 13 Oct. 1761 (*CHOP 1760–5*, 70), by Weymouth 20 Jan. 1768 (*CHOP 1766–9*, 293).

Woodeson, George   *Deputy Clerk of Signet* c. 1682–6 July 1716.

Clerk (Trumbull) 1695–Feb. 1696.

Occ. as Deputy Clerk of Signet from 1682 to d. (Chamberlayne, *Present State* (1682), pt. i, 194; Trumbull Add. MS 90). D. 6 July 1716 (*Hist. Reg. Chron.* (1714–1716), i, 64). Pd. as Clerk to Trumbull from 3 Nov. 1695 to 3 Feb. 1696 (Trumbull Add. MS 113).

Woodward, George   *Clerk* (Sunderland) Dec. 1717–March 1718; (Stanhope) March 1718–Feb. 1721; (Townshend) Feb. 1721–c. Nov. 1726.

App. by Sunderland; pd. as Clerk to Sunderland from Dec. 1717 to March 1718 (Sunderland MS D 1/36), to Stanhope from 29 Sept. 1718 to 29 Sept. 1720 (Stanhope MS 76); occ. as Clerk to Townshend from 1723 to 9 Jan. 1726 (Miège, *Present State* (1723), 69; T 52/33 p. 366; T 52/34 pp. 14, 82). Probably left office Nov. 1726 on app. as Secretary to Embassy to Empire (*Dip. Rep.*, 35).

Wright, James   *Clerk* (Holdernesse) c. 1755–March 1761; (Bute) March 1761–May 1762; (Grenville) June–Oct. 1762; (Halifax) Oct. 1762–July 1765; (Seymour Conway) July 1765–Jan. 1768; (Weymouth) Jan. 1768–Dec. 1770; (Sandwich) Dec. 1770–Jan. 1771; (Halifax) Jan.–June 1771; (Suffolk) June 1771–Oct. 1772. *Senior Clerk* (Suffolk) Oct. 1772–c. 1779.

First occ. as Clerk to Holdernesse 21 April 1755 (T 52/47 pp. 101–2); app. as such notified 9 May 1757 (SP 44/148); occ. as Clerk to Holdernesse to 1761 (*Court and City Reg.* (1761), 106), to Bute 1762 (ibid. (1762), 106); presence in office notified as Clerk to Grenville 12 July 1762 (*CHOP 1760–5*, 189), to Halifax 8 Nov. 1762, 13 Sept. 1763, 30 April 1764 (ibid. 202, 302–3, 407), to Seymour Conway 15 Aug. 1766 (*CHOP 1766–9*, 67), to Weymouth 20 Jan. 1768 (ibid. 293), to Sandwich 21 Dec. 1770 (*CHOP 1770–2*, 103), to Halifax 22 Jan., 20 March 1771 (ibid. 193, 225), to Suffolk 12 June 1771, 2 Oct. 1772 (ibid. 265, 556). Probably app. Senior Clerk Oct. 1772 in succession to R. Shadwell; occ. as Senior Clerk to Suffolk from 1773 to 1779 (*Royal Kal.* (1773), 115; ibid. (1779), 109). Left office by 9 Nov. 1779 (FO 366/669 p. 16).

Wright, William   *Office Keeper* (Shrewsbury) c. 1689.

Occ., probably as Office Keeper, July 1689 (LS 13/231 p. 13).

Wynn *see* **Williams Wynn**

Wynne, Owen   *Under Secretary* (Jenkins) April 1680–April 1684; (Godolphin) April–Aug. 1684; (Middleton) Aug. 1684–Dec. 1688; (Shrewsbury) Feb.–Sept. 1689.

App. Under Secretary by Jenkins probably April 1680; occ. as such from 24 May 1681 to 2 March 1684 (*CSPD 1680–1*, 292; *CSPD 1683–4*, 303); continued in office by Godolphin (Evans, *Principal Secretary*, 192), by Middleton (ibid.; *Ellis Corr.*, ii, 287), by Shrewsbury (LS 13/231 p. 13). Dis. Sept. 1689 (Luttrell, *Hist. Relation*, i, 579–80).

Yard, Robert   *Clerk* (Arlington) c. 1668–Sept. 1674; (Williamson) Sept. 1674–Feb. 1679; (Sunderland) Feb. 1679–Feb. 1681; (Conway) Feb. 1681–Jan. 1683; (Sunderland) Jan. 1683–Oct. 1688; (?) (Middleton or Preston) Oct.–Dec. 1688. (?) *Chief Clerk* (Shrewsbury) Feb. 1689–June 1690; (Nottingham) June 1690–Nov. 1693. *Under Secretary* (Shrewsbury) March 1694–Dec. 1698; (Jersey) May 1699–June 1700; (Vernon) Nov. 1700–May 1702.

   Writer of Gazette c. 1673–May 1702.

   Clerk in Arlington's office attached to Williamson; later Clerk to Williamson as Secretary of State; occ. from 29 Feb. 1668 to 12 Feb. 1679 (*CSPD 1667–8*, 255; *CSPD 1679–80*, 81); probably continued in office by Sunderland; occ. as Clerk to Conway from 17 Jan. to 9 June 1682 (BM Add. MS 37983 ff. 24, 210); probably continued in office by Sunderland; his newsletters from 23 Nov. 1685 to 4 Jan. 1686 (Hist. MSS Comm. *Downshire*, i, 56, 93) were probably written as Clerk to Sunderland; possibly continued in office by Middleton or Preston. App. Clerk, possibly Chief Clerk, by Shrewsbury Feb. 1689; heads list of his Clerks July 1689 (LS 13/231 p. 13); probably became Chief Clerk to Nottingham on Shrewsbury's res. June 1690; heads list of his Clerks 1694 (sic) (Chamberlayne, *Present State* (1694), 243); his newsletters from 7 Nov. 1690 to 30 May 1693 (Hist. MSS Comm. *Downshire*, i, 363, 367; *CSPD 1691–2*, 194, 492; BM Add. MS 34096 ff. 44, 395) were probably written while in Nottingham's service. App. Under Secretary by Shrewsbury March 1694 (*CSPD 1695*, 243), by Jersey May 1699 (Luttrell, *Hist. Relation*, iv, 517), by Vernon Nov. 1700 (ibid. 705). The report of his app. as Under Secretary by Nottingham May 1702 (ibid. vi, 169) is inaccurate. App. Writer of Gazette by 13 June 1673 (*Letters to Sir Joseph Williamson 1673–4*, ed. W. D. Christie (Camden 2nd ser., viii, ix, 1874), i, 30); last occ. 24 April 1702 (*CTB*, xvii, 196). Probably left office May 1702 at same time as he ceased to be Under Secretary.

Zolman, Philip Henry   *Translator of German Language* July 1735–Aug. 1748.

   App. July 1735 (*CTBP 1735–8*, 37). D. Aug. 1748 (T 53/42 p. 377).